CYCLES OF CHILD MALTREATMENT

WILEY SERIES

in

CHILD CARE AND PROTECTION

Series Editors

Kevin D. Browne
School of Psychology
The University of Birmingham, UK

Margaret A. Lynch
Newcomen Centre
Guy's Hospital, London, UK

The Child Care and Protection Series aims to further the understanding of health, psychosocial and cultural factors that influence the development of the child, early interactions and the formation of relationships in and outside the family. This international series will cover the psychological as well as the physical welfare of the child and will consider protection from all forms of maltreatment.

The series is intended to become essential reading for all professionals concerned with the welfare and protection of children and their families. All books in the series will have a practice orientation with referenced information from theory and research. The style will be informal, graphically illustrated with tables and figures and appropriate to a multidisciplinary audience.

Published
Dorota Iwaniec — The Emotionally Abused and Neglected Child: Identification, Assessment, and Intervention

Ann Buchanan — Cycles of Child Maltreatment: Facts, Fallacies and Interventions

Forthcoming
Jacqui Saradjian — Women who Sexually Abuse Children: From Research to Practice

Leonard Dalgleish — Risk and Decision in Child Protection

Michelle Aldridge — Interviewing Children: A Guide to Child Care and Forensic Practitioners

Potential authors are invited to submit further information to either of the series editors or to Comfort Jegede, Publishing Editor, John Wiley & Sons Ltd, Baffins Lane, Chichester, West Sussex PO19 1UD, UK. Proposals should include a short statement of the target readership, scope and features of the book proposal and short notes on two or three of the nearest books in the field.

CYCLES OF CHILD MALTREATMENT

Facts, Fallacies and Interventions

Ann Buchanan
University of Oxford, UK

JOHN WILEY & SONS
Chichester · New York · Brisbane · Toronto · Singapore

Copyright © 1996 by John Wiley & Sons Ltd,
Baffins Lane, Chichester,
West Sussex PO19 1UD, England

National   01243 779777
International   (+44) 1243 779777
e-mail (for orders and customer service enquiries):
cs-books@wiley.co.uk
Visit our Home Page on http://www.wiley.co.uk
            or http://www.wiley.com

Other Wiley Editorial Offices

John Wiley & Sons, Inc., 605 Third Avenue,
New York, NY 10158-0012, USA

Jacaranda Wiley Ltd, 33 Park Road, Milton,
Queensland 4064, Australia

John Wiley & Sons (Canada) Ltd, 22 Worcester Road,
Rexdale, Ontario M9W 1L1, Canada

John Wiley & Sons (Asia) Pte Ltd, 2 Clementi Loop #02-01,
Jin Xing Distripark, Singapore 0512

Library of Congress Cataloging-in-Publication Data

Buchanan, Ann.
    Cycles of child maltreatment : facts, fallacies, and interventions
/ Ann Buchanan.
        p.   cm. — (Wiley series in child care and protection)
    Includes bibliographical references.
    ISBN 0-471-96174-4 (cloth). — ISBN 0-471-95889-1 (pbk.)
    1. Child abuse.   2. Child abuse—Prevention.   3. Abused children—
Family relationships.   4. Intergenerational relations.   I. Title.
II. Series.
HV6626.5.B83   1996
362.7'6—dc20   96–18899
                                                           CIP

British Library Cataloguing in Publication Data

A catalogue record for this book is available from the British Library

ISBN 0-471-96174-4 (cloth)
      0-471-95889-1 (paper)

Typeset in 10/12pt Palatino by Dorwyn Ltd, Rowlands Castle, Hants
Printed and bound in Great Britain by Biddles Ltd, Guildford
This book is printed on acid-free paper responsibly manufactured from sustainable
forestation, for which at least two trees are planted for each one used for paper
production.

CONTENTS

LIST OF FIGURES

LIST OF TABLES

ABOUT THE AUTHOR

Ann Buchanan—*Department of Applied Social Studies and Social Research, University of Oxford, Barnett House, Wellington Square, Oxford OX1 2ER, UK*

Ann Buchanan is currently lecturer in Applied Social Studies and a Fellow of St Hilda's College at the University of Oxford, where she has responsibilities for both teaching and researching on issues relating to children and families.

At the start of her career she spent one year working as a Mothering Aide for Henry Kempe at the NSPCC. She then worked on the Intergenerational Studies in Wiltshire as a research assistant before entering social work and spending ten years in a children and families' team in an inner-urban area. She obtained her doctorate in 1990 and entered academic life in 1991. She has published widely.

It is Ann Buchanan's ability to relate research findings from a range of disciplines to the realities of day to day policy-making and practice which gives this book its particular relevance.

SERIES PREFACE

The **Wiley Series in Child Care and Protection** is a new series of books primarily written for policy makers and professionals in research and practice concerned with the care, welfare and protection of children and their families.

The aim of the series is to publish books on child care and protection covering both the psychological and physical welfare of the child, including legal and social policy aspects. The series was prompted by the need to recognise that work in child protection is best viewed within the wider concepts of child care and social welfare. After three decades of remarkable growth in child protection work, which has led to widespread public awareness and professional understanding of child maltreatment, it has become increasingly recognised that child protection is enhanced by the improvements in the welfare of families and the promotion of positive parenting and child care. Indeed, child care, family welfare and effective child protection are interlinked and cannot be separated.

For example, the inability of maltreating parents to adaptively interact with their children is seen by many professionals as being representative of a general lack of interpersonal skills. Abusive and neglective parents often share a common pattern of social isolation, poor work history and few friendships with others outside the home. This isolation means that parents unable to cope are usually unwilling, or unable, to seek help by themselves from outside agencies who could provide assistance or emotional support. If such parents do interact with others they are most likely to choose those with similar problems to themselves, thereby gaining no experience of alternative parenting styles or positive coping strategies and continuing to be ineffective in promoting the optimal development of their children. Hence, child protection is multi-faceted, involving many different aspects of child care and the social welfare of families.

Books in the series will be from a wide range of disciplines and each book will be encouraged to link research and practice to inform, in an easily accessible way, professionals, policy makers and the public in general. In this way it is hoped to further the knowledge and understanding of health, psychosocial and cultural factors that influence the development of the child, early interactions and the formation of relationships in and outside the family.

In this, the second book in the series, Ann Buchanan systematically sets about disentangling and dissecting the interacting cycles of maltreatment that can result in the abuse of successive generations of children. In so doing she demonstrates the multidimensional backdrop against which the abuse of individual children occurs. While the evidence is assembled with academic rigour, the book clearly benefits from the author's years as a practising social worker. Both researchers and practitioners will have pertinent issues raised for them. Jaded professionals will find looking at abuse from the wide perspective offered by this book both refreshing and thought-provoking, while the serious newcomer will find it a fascinating introduction to a complex topic.

Despite the depressing implications of accepting the concept of inter-generational cycles of child abuse, this is a positive book presenting the understanding of such cycles as a starting point for intervention. Practical interventions are illustrated with accounts of successes from both the industrialised and developing worlds and also with case study material.

The original inspiration behind this book was Dr J. E. Oliver and the editors wish to join the author in expressing their thanks and respect.

Margaret A. Lynch
Kevin D. Browne

ACKNOWLEDGEMENTS

The original idea for this book was that of Dr J. E Oliver, FRCPsych. For over 30 years, Jack, as a consultant psychiatrist in both child psychiatry and mental handicap, worked tirelessly as a clinician with families where children had been maltreated and/or had been admitted to one of the two hospitals for the mentally handicapped under his supervision. He was not a theoretician working apart from the realities of the world. Daily, he saw the tragedies of children who had been abused and worked with families as well as other professionals to try and prevent further maltreatment.

Jack, however, was more than a clinician. Faced by the climate of disbelief in the early 1970s that children could be severely battered, he meticulously documented their injuries, and traced their histories back to those of their parents, grandparents, great-grandparents. In this he was helped by the extensive records in the area maintained by the NSPCC. Jack also linked together other records from social services, health and hospital. Over his career, he published more than 50 papers from these studies.

In 1969 and 1970, I was working with the NSPCC in London as part of a team of mothering aides set up and supervised by the late Professor Henry Kempe and his wife Ruth during his sabbatical year in England. On coming to Wiltshire, I joined Jack Oliver as a research assistant on his studies. Perhaps the most interesting paper from that time was 'Abuse and neglect as a cause of mental retardation' (Buchanan & Oliver, 1977). I then moved on to work as a practising social worker for ten years before entering academic life.

In 1992, Jack, who at this time was just about to retire, approached me and asked if I could help him bring a book together on intergenerational child maltreatment. Jack's main interest was on the intrafamilial patterns but he recognised that within the cycle of child maltreatment, psychological and biological factors were only part of the story. He felt there was a need for a book which linked together the extrafamilial factors—socio-political and cultural, with the intrafamilial.

So, the idea for this book was Jack's. Sadly, Jack found that in retirement, his botanical interests became more pressing, but he kindly gave the author his blessing to bring the book to fruition. In doing so, he handed over his vast collection of international papers. These papers have formed the core of this book.

In acknowledging the many who have contributed, I would, therefore, firstly like to record my thanks to Jack Oliver, not only for teaching me much about patterns and realities of child maltreatment, but for being involved in the early stages of planning this book and for giving me the opportunity to bring it all together.

Secondly, I would like to thank the late Professor Kempe and his wife, for what they taught me while working under their supervision at the NSPCC all those years ago.

Thirdly, I would like to record my thanks to Wendy Hudlass and Wiley for having the confidence that such a book was possible. In particular I would like to acknowledge the help of Martin Herbert, Margaret Lynch, David Gough and Kevin Browne for their constructive comments on earlier drafts of the manuscript.

Fourthly, I would like to thank my colleagues at the University of Oxford and international visitors to the Department, not only for broadening my horizons and making suggestions, but also for giving me the time, in my first year as a Lecturer in Applied Social Sciences, to complete this work.

Finally, I would like to acknowledge what families and children taught me about living in poverty and the difficulties of parenting while I worked as a social worker. As the research evidence was brought together for this book, it was helpful to remember the real world out there; a world where solutions can only be a compromise between what we know and do not know, what is desirable, and what is possible.

Oxford, January, 1996

I

BACKGROUND TO THE DEBATE

1

INTRODUCTION

State parties shall take all appropriate legislative, administrative, social and educational measures to protect the child from all forms of physical or mental violence, injury or abuse, neglect or negligent treatment, maltreatment or exploitation including sexual abuse, while in the care of parent(s), legal guardian(s) or any other person who has care of the child. (United Nations Convention on the Rights of the Child Article 19, 1989)

It has been said that the Children's Rights Movement is a social movement with no clear beginning and no obvious end in sight, and that it started as long ago as 450 BC (Radbill, 1968) with measures to protect children, and that it came of age with the UN Convention on the Rights of the Child (UN, 1989). Yet despite the Convention and in particular the sustained international effort during the last 30 years to afford effective protection to children, large numbers of children continue to suffer. But what is worse, when these children themselves become parents, some of them are unable to protect their offspring from, or actually inflict, the suffering they themselves endured.

This book is about continuing intergenerational cycles of child maltreatment and the controversies that surround the theories. Although it is recognised that violence to children cannot be separated from issues relating to the whole complex of family violence, sibling abuse, violence between partners and elder abuse, the focus here is more specifically on the factors that may lead to cycles of child maltreatment in its broadest sense. With this remit, there is only a limited focus on cycles of sexual abuse. Again, although it is recognised that many of the mechanisms of transmission may be the same, there are also other factors which may be very different and within the confines of this book it has not been possible to explore these.

By taking a broad international perspective, this book brings together the more important findings from research, and suggests that in intergenerational child maltreatment, there may be not just one cycle, but at least four separate cycles operating both outside the family (extrafamilial) and within the family (intrafamilial). It is the thesis of this book, that if the overall levels of child maltreatment are to be reduced, it is necessary to unwind the separate cycles that link together in sometimes imperceptible unison, and focus interventions at the different strands that together form the pathological whole.

Children are both the bricks and the mortar of our future societies. Cycles of child maltreatment, therefore, concern us all. It is an international, a national, a local and an individual concern. Among those especially involved are those, in whatever capacity, with a responsibility for ensuring that each child, each group of children, is both protected from harm and that their overall welfare is promoted. Those involved will be found in international organisations, academia (for example, sociologists, social policy analysts, anthropologists, economists) amongst politicians and policy-makers, the medical profession, judiciary and the police, local politicians, legal officers, educationalists, health professionals, psychologists, social workers and their managers, and voluntary agencies. A central aim of this book has been to bring together a wide range of research from the different disciplines and organisations involved and make this accessible to those, who by working together, have a role in promoting the welfare of children in this generation and the next.

WHY IS A FOCUS ON INTERGENERATIONAL CHILD MALTREATMENT IMPORTANT?

The immediate consequences of child maltreatment are the injuries experienced by the victim. Daily the media remind us that the death of a child is another tragic outcome. These children do not go on to repeat a cycle of abuse, but other surviving children are disabled or damaged in ways that impair their future lives (Buchanan & Oliver, 1977) and they in turn may impair the lives of their offspring. The mechanisms involved are complex and far from certain. Abused children have frequently been noted to have numerous cognitive, emotional and social difficulties (Starr, 1987) which may lead to more aggressive behaviour. There is considerable evidence that violence and abuse extend beyond the home into society as a whole. Widom (1989) and others (Schmitt & Kempe, 1975; Carr, 1977; Loeber & Stouthamer-Loeber, 1986) note that abused and neglected children are more likely than non-abused children to be arrested for delinquency, adult criminality and violent criminal behaviour. The legacy of abuse may have consequences not only on the lives of the abused, but on the lives of their offspring, and the future well-being of society as a whole.

It is important that those of us who are entrusted by our professions to promote the welfare of children and their families understand the debate that surrounds the concept of intergenerational transmission, are aware of the possible mechanisms involved in transmission, and have information about possible interventions to break the cycles. From this understanding, we may find better ways to limit its consequences in practice.

WHAT THIS BOOK IS ABOUT AND WHAT IT IS NOT ABOUT

This book is not about inevitable cycles of intergenerational abuse, from which there is no escape. There are considerable controversies about the existence of such cycles (Egeland, 1993; Kaufman & Zigler, 1993). There is substantive evidence that within the family most victims of maltreatment do not go on to abuse their children (for example, Kaufman & Zigler, 1993; Egeland,1993).

This book supports the views of the writer who wrote to the *Radio Times*:

> I deeply resent the assumption that abused children become abusing adults. I am nearly 50 and was abused . . . I spent many years blaming myself . . . contrary to the apparent consensus among the experts, I have a heightened awareness of how much my three children need to be protected and educated. I would like to have someone to talk to about my life, but with the present climate of opinion, would I dare to admit that I had been abused? No way. I have had enough guilt for one lifetime. (*Radio Times*, 1991: anonymous letter)

Reports show how the uncritical acceptance of the intergenerational hypothesis has caused grave injustices. Kaufman and Zigler (1993) give the example of a woman in her 70s who was badly abused as a child, who was advised by her mental health professional never to have children because it would be inevitable that she would repeat the cycle of abuse. In addition, reports show how a history of abuse in a parent has led to biased responses by mental health workers and influenced the outcome of court decisions (Kaufman & Zigler, 1993). These practices have rightly been criticised.

But although most families do not repeat the patterns of their childhood, there is evidence that, for whatever reason, substantial numbers do. Kaufman and Zigler (1987) in reviewing studies that examined what has become known as 'the cycle of violence hypothesis' show how rates vary from 18% to 70% or higher. They estimate that the true rate of intergenerational transmission is around 30%. This figure is also supported by Oliver (1993) in his review of the literature.

The debate, however, is still open. Kaufman and Zigler (1993) conclude that because the rate has been overestimated in the past, it is time for the intergenerational 'myth' to be set aside. Others, however, feel this view is insupportable (Egeland, 1993; Gelles & Cornell, 1990). Although the 30% figure is considerably less than some earlier estimates, the rate is considerably more than the 2% and 4% rate of abuse found in the general population, and therefore a history of abuse is a major risk factor for abusing the next generation.

The book is in four parts. In Part I, the challenge is to face up to these controversies. Does the intergenerational transmission of child maltreatment apply to a few clearly pathological families, while being relatively unimportant for the majority? Why are there such divergent estimates on the rates? If transmission is numerically important, what percentage of the general population of maltreated parents become maltreating parents? Chapter 2 focuses on this important debate.

In Part II, the possible mechanisms of transmission are explored. Chapters 3 and 4 break into the central hypothesis in exploring factors outside the family which may place some parents at greater risk. Chapter 3 discusses socio-political mechanisms which can lay down the conditions where child maltreatment is more likely, while Chapter 4 considers factors within the culture of societies which may directly or indirectly support these intergenerational patterns. Chapters 5 and 6 highlight psychological and biological factors which may be operating within families.

The third part of the book explores possible interventions within the cycles. Chapter 7 outlines a possible set of principles which should govern interventions and the three main levels of preventive strategy. Chapter 8 considers interventions in the socio-political cycle, while Chapter 9 focuses on possible interventions in the cultural cycle. Finally, Chapter 10 brings the psychological and biological cycles together in suggesting intrafamilial interventions.

The fourth part of the book, Chapter 11, returns to practice. Examples are given of strategies employed in different countries with differing levels of development and their achievements. These have been undertaken, by different organisations, different groups, different individuals, with differing levels of responsibilities. They are given to illustrate that we all can have a role to play in breaking cycles of child maltreatment. Finally a four-generational case study is described to remind us that cycles of maltreatment are about real children and real families, and how such families pose real difficulties and dilemmas when professionals try to intervene to break the patterns.

DEFINITIONS OF CHILD MALTREATMENT USED IN THIS BOOK

The issue of definition in child maltreatment has dogged researchers and practitioners in the field of family violence for the last 30 years (Zigler, 1977; Giovannoni & Becarra, 1979; Kahn & Kamerman, 1980; Ross & Zigler, 1980; Rosenthal & Louis, 1981; Duquette, 1982; Gelles, 1982; Biller & Solomon, 1986; Hutchison, 1994; Department of Health, 1995).

One of the problems in defining child maltreatment stems from the fact that different groups and professions devise and use definitions for different purposes. Ross and Zigler (1980) have suggested that no single definition has succeeded in fulfilling all the functions. Cartwright (1973) has demonstrated that the way a social problem is defined leads to the strategies that will resolve the problem. As we will see in the next chapter, a range of socio-political factors and theories of causality influences how a social problem is defined. Legal regulations then create frameworks to respond to the agreed definition of the social problem.

The next issue, 'who shall define?', is essentially a political question, but this is also related to theoretical considerations. Two views have been put forward. Firstly, there is the view that the definition should be made by professionals and secondly, there is the view that the definition of child maltreatment is a matter of social definition involving a cross-section of the community (Hutchison, 1994).

In defining child maltreatment, there is also the question of whether this should focus on *caregiver variables*, that is a focus on *parental pathology and intention* (abuse, neglect, emotional abuse, sexual abuse) or *harm to the child* variables such as outlined by the criteria of 'significant harm' in the 1989 Children Act in England and Wales. Hutchison (1994) concludes: 'Many legal scholars attempt to resolve the issue . . . by arguing that harm to the child must be tied to behaviors of the caregiver(s)' (Hutchison, 1994, p. 19). It is interesting that the Child Abuse Prevention and Treatment Act in 1974 in the USA defined child abuse and neglect as:

> The physical and mental injury, sexual abuse, negligent treatment, or maltreatment of a child under the age of eighteen by a person who is responsible for the child's welfare *under circumstances which indicate that the child's health or welfare is harmed or threatened thereby.* (Child Abuse Prevention and Treatment Act 1974, USA)

This definition focuses on outcomes for children, but it is limited in that the responsibility for the maltreatment is laid at the door of the 'person who is responsible for the child's welfare'.

A further debate is whether child maltreatment should be defined 'narrowly', focusing on abuse, neglect, emotional abuse and sexual abuse, or broadly. A *narrow* focus makes it easier to guide judicial and social work areas (Besharov, 1985; Wild, 1975), and limits the error in diagnosing incidents and the cost of screening (Gelles, 1979; Besharov, 1985; Stein, 1984). A *broad* definition focuses attention on the role of extrafamilial factors, socio-political and cultural mechanisms, as well as intrafamilial factors, both psychological and biological, in the aetiology of child maltreatment.

As the focus here is on the four cycles leading to patterns of intergenerational child maltreatment, a broad definition has been chosen to emphasise this wider perspective. The following conceptual definition proposed by Gil (1981) comes nearest to meeting the requirements of this book. This definition would also cover sexual abuse but here, our focus is limited to physical maltreatment and neglect.

> Abuse of children is human-originated acts of commission or omission and human-created or tolerated conditions that inhibit or preclude unfolding and development of inherent potential of children. (Gil, 1981, p. 295)

It is recognised that in order to know what human acts 'inhibit or preclude unfolding and development of inherent potential of children', there is a need to consider *outcomes* for children. This will be a recurring theme in many of the following chapters.

THE FOUR CYCLES

This book takes as its central theme that four major cycles directly or indirectly lead to intergenerational child maltreatment. These cycles are socio-political factors leading to cycles of child maltreatment, recurring cultural patterns, and psychological and biological factors. The first two are extrafamilial with society as the focus, whereas the last two are predominantly intrafamilial and personal.

Socio-political Factors in Intergenerational Cycles of Child Maltreatment

Rutter and others have demonstrated that parents need 'permitting circumstances' (DHSS, 1974) in order to rear their young. What is considered 'permitting' is, like poverty, a relative term and varies between societies. Direct government politics and policies can however have dramatic effects on parental attitudes to child-rearing. Policies that lead to political conflict have led to thousands of children being traumatised (Richman, 1993). There is also now considerable evidence that where mothers are forced to have children because of lack of access to birth control or abortion, especially when they have previously had these rights, the children are more likely to be maltreated/abandoned and the affects can be intergenerational (Dytrych, 1992; Radulian, 1992). Socio-political factors which lead to certain ethnic or gender groups being dis-criminated against also lead to intergenerational patterns of child abuse. It is estimated that in Asia Minor there are 1 million fewer girls than would be expected by population estimates, because they are perceived to be of lesser worth than boys (UNICEF, 1991).

Intergenerational transmission of child maltreatment is closely related to political ideologies. For example, the extent which social problems are recognised: 'Family life could not be a problem in Communist Poland because the millennial official ideology dictated that the regime had abol-ished all social pathologies' (Dingwall, 1994, p. 54). Prevailing political ideologies also influence: how social problems are identified, defined and regulated (Parton, 1985); the extent to which family rights versus child's rights are balanced (Maclean & Kurczewski, 1994); the effects on child protection of the politics of 'individualism' versus 'collectivism' (Cooper, Hetherington, Baistow, Pitts & Spriggs, 1995).

Some researchers would say that any child who is living in poverty is being abused (Gil, 1970). There is considerable evidence that disadvan-tageous social factors lower the threshold at which parents can parent effectively and these patterns can affect parenting over two or more gen-erations. It is easy to think of situations in the developing world where children are neglected or abandoned, but this is also a phenomenon in the relative prosperity of the developed world (Durning, 1992).

The paradox is that many parents, despite severe social disadvantage, provide adequate care for their young, and it would be a gross injustice to them to suggest otherwise. However, it is the growing recognition that there is a relationship between social adversity and the quality of care parents are able to give their young which has moved the focus away from child abuse *per se* towards policies which support families and pre-vent child maltreatment (National Research Council USA, 1993; Depart-ment of Health, *Messages from Research*, 1995). Evidence that many, although not all, of the long-term negative outcomes from physical, emotional and sexual abuse may also be accounted for by the matrix of childhood disadvantaged from which they so often emerge, is adding fuel to the fire (Mullen, Martin, Anderson, Romans & Herbison, 1996).

Cultural Factors in the Cycle of Child Maltreatment

Throughout history there has been a wide range of culturally condoned child maltreatment, leading to a tendency for each surviving generation to repeat the suffering that they endured as children. It is easy to find practices in other societies which to Western ethnocentric eyes appear barbaric, but it is important to understand both the meaning and the purposes of the practices and the specific circumstances in which such practices have arisen (Finkelhor & Korbin, 1988). Western professionals, for example, may condemn the unnecessary suffering and dangers of female circumcision, yet male circumcision which is widely accepted can also cause unnecessary suffering and dangers (Bruce-Chwatt, 1985).

Clues to the mechanisms behind some forms of intergenerational violence can be found in examining cross-cultural studies. Levinson (1989) shows how factors within a society can influence whether that society is more or less violent. Whiting and Edwards (1988) demonstrate that parenting styles which are more or less aggressive can evolve from different living conditions.

Intergenerational child maltreatment may also relate to the extent that physical chastisement is accepted by societies. (Newson & Newson, 1965; Newell, 1989; Leach, 1993). When we consider the high rates of physical chastisement in both the developing and the developed world, it is tempting to believe that physical chastisement is a necessary part of child-rearing. Some societies, however, do not need to beat children in order to rear them effectively (Levinson, 1989; Haeuser 1992). The dilemma is, where does chastisement end and abuse begin?

Objective decisions may need to be made but who is to make these decisions and how can they be objective?

The Cycle of Psychological Maltreatment

This third cycle has longer recognition. When a history of abuse in the parents was first associated with abuse in their offspring, paediatricians and psychiatrists looked towards the pathology within the family to explain the phenomenon. The psychiatric model originally focused on the abuser's personality and characteristics as the chief determinant of violence and abuse.

The theories relating to learnt behaviour and the concept that 'violence begets violence' originated from psychologists. The idea is that children brought up in a family where there are high levels of violence will learn that violence is an acceptable way of solving any problems. They will also learn the moral justifications for their behaviour. Linked into this is the theory of exchange control. That is 'people hit and abuse each other because they can' (Gelles, 1983). This suggests that the 'rewards' from using violence are greater than the deterrents. This links into the violence begets violence theory because children learn from their parents that violence pays.

The classic studies by Harlow on primates have also demonstrated that monkeys reared in isolation, with non-responding feeding machines, are very likely to become rejecting, neglectful or abusing parents (Harlow, 1961).

Another area is the concept of 'learned helplessness' (Seligman, 1975). This is the theory which suggests that young people can learn to become helpless because every effort they take to change things results in failure. In Seligman's experiments, animals became apathetic when faced with continual failure to escape from the maze. Similarly learned helplessness and the consequent low esteem can lead to intergenerational patterns of child maltreatment. Young people grow up believing they are 'helpless' to change the patterns of their violent lives when they in turn become parents (Rutter, Quinton & Liddle, 1983).

In Chapter 5, theories on attachment behaviour which can explain patterns of intergenerational psychological maltreatment are also considered (Crittenden & Ainsworth, 1989).

The Biological Cycle of Maltreatment

There is recognition now in the 1990s, that ignoring this biological dimension is being as one-sided as those who underrated the social influences in the 1890s. Chapter 6 considers some of the latest research which is finding biological explanations for particular types of behaviour which could be associated with intergenerational patterns of maltreatment (Loehlin, 1992). The tentative nature of some of these findings is recognised.

In addition this chapter considers the role of the rare hereditary diseases which afflict certain families, in particular the rare hereditary dementias which strike afflicted families during the process of child-rearing (Oliver & Dewhurst, 1969) and the larger range of psychiatric disorders with some hereditary component: for example, types of depression and psychosis. Finally, conditions responsible for maternal ill-health over two or more generations, such as anaemias or iodine deficiency, are considered.

Interventions in the Cycles

Cataloguing the mechanisms operating in the four cycles can present a rather depressing picture of a world where no hope dawns. Research, however, has moved on, and there is now a range of strategies, focused on specific mechanisms within the cycles, that can be used to effect change in patterns of intergenerational child maltreatment. Some of these strategies are outlined in the last five chapters. Within the remit of this book, it has only been possible to indicate a few of the many approaches which have proved effective, but it is hoped that those outlined will stimulate ideas for practice.

Separating biological factors, or indeed any of the separate cycles, from other factors is, of course, artificial. In the final chapters a development of Belsky's (1980) 'ecological model' is used to explain the complex interrelationships between the cycles, and the possible interventions within them.

THE HISTORY OF TRANSMITTED CHARACTERISTICS

There is an ancient history of transmitted characteristics and behaviours from one generation to the next, as the following biblical injunction concerning worshipping false gods illustrates: 'For I the Lord thy God am a jealous God, visiting the iniquity of the fathers upon the children unto the third and fourth generation of them that hate me' (Exodus 20.5). The same theme continues in the Old Testament book of Numbers (14.18), and Isaiah (14:20–21 and 30) where the prophet claims that 'The seed of evildoers shall never be renowned' (Numbers 14.18). These gloomy warnings in the Bible give clues how the observed transmission of characteristics was explained. It was an intrafamilial explanation, be it biological such as hereditary defects, or psychological in the form of the observed transmission of learned behaviour. These ancient codes were important to limit hereditary defects and instil tribal cohesion, but they suggest that the fathers were aware that what they were committing was an iniquity and that there was an element of choice in choosing so to do. However, what was considered 'evil' was culturally defined.

Throughout the ages, generations of children have been maltreated (Aries, 1962; Radbill, 1968). Historically, cruelties inflicted on children have been condoned because of higher perceived needs. Infanticide, for example, was acceptable where it was perceived there was some imperfection which might threaten the stability of the group (Levinson, 1989). Paradoxically the recognition that parents might be responsible for transmitting undesirable behavioural characteristics to their children has led to generations of children being maltreated. In many societies, it has been almost mandatory as a child-rearing method that children should be physically chastised. In colonial America, fathers were implored to 'beat the devil out of their children' (Hampton, Gullotta, Adams, Potter & Weissberg, 1993). The implication was that unbeaten children would corrupt society by their resultant uncontrolled behaviour.

There is also an early recognition that factors in society generally as well as factors within families, could lead to an intergenerational pattern of child maltreatment. Children in Mesopotamia 6000 years ago were allocated a patron goddess and child protection laws were legislated as long ago as 450 BC (Radbill, 1968). The Greeks and Romans established orphan homes and some accounts also mention the existence of foster care.

During the Renaissance children came to be seen as a dependent class needing the protection of, and protection from, society. In the enlightenment of the eighteenth century the dire conditions of poor children demanded increased attention and services. For example, the London Foundling Hospital not only gave paediatric care but was a centre campaigning to control the availability of gin which was seen as the root cause of many problems that affected families and children (Robin, 1982). History suggests there is nothing new in implicating factors both within the family and without the family to explain intergenerational patterns of child maltreatment.

From early times, however, until the start of this century, the predominant model of developmental influences was predeterminism—the concept that all human developmental change was biologically and maturationally determined (Hunt, 1961). In 1885, Sir Francis Galton, influenced by his cousin Darwin's studies on the 'Origin of Species', undertook systematic research applying some of the principles to humans. Galton was one of the earlier scientists to recognise the influence of both biological and environmental factors. A central interest was the role agencies within the environment played in fashioning the development of human beings. He is more often remembered for his controversial eugenic theories. In founding the 'Eugenics Movement' the stated purpose of which was to draw attention to factors which could improve or impair the qualities of future generations physically or mentally, Galton's studies led to considerable scientific activity.

Inspired by this work, a spate of studies arose which focused on the 'bad gene' to explain multi-problem families such as the Jukes (Dugdale, 1877, 1910), and other families where mental handicap and other social problems moved from generation to generation (Davenport, 1911; Goddard, 1912, 1914; Androp, 1935). These works were family studies, sometimes spanning three to six generations, dealing in each generation with learning disabilities, families who experienced multiple social problems and, where there was a pattern of poor child care, disease and institutionalisation.

Dugdale's studies (1877, 1910) were not entirely focused on biological factors to explain the observed intergenerational patterns. He made allowance for important sociological factors, the micro-culture in which the Jukes lived, and the need for parental education in childcare.

The tragic consequences of this embryonic and only partly understood research are now history. In 1936, two years after Adolf Hitler had manoeuvred himself into a position of absolute power, 56 000 people were sterilised in Germany. Members of the medical profession were criticised for sanctioning the beginnings of an increasingly horrendous negative eugenic programme (Trevor-Roper, 1985; Meyer-Lindenberg, 1991), shortly to become in Nazi Germany a ruthless system of Race Purity. There were critics *at the time*, such as the psychiatric geneticist Eliot Slater (1936) who was to become editor of the *British Journal of Psychiatry*. In addition to the moral condemnation, Slater also highlighted medical, legal and bureaucratic irrationalities in the German programme. After the war such was the revulsion at what had occurred that for half a century any consideration of biological factors in child maltreatment was largely omitted from most of the scientific literature.

In 1946 Caffey tried to recreate interest in the plight of children. Caffey's important paper highlighted children who had both chronic subdural haematoma and multiple long bone fractures. In 1951, there was a further reminder of the suffering of children. Eustace Chesser in England (1951), reported that from NSPCC figures alone, 1 child in 16 was ill-treated. This was a substantial proportion of the general population. Caffey and Chesser were ignored. It was another ten years before scientists were prepared to 'rediscover' child abuse and intergenerational factors which might have bearing on the problem.

It is tempting to omit this history, but it is important in helping to understand of some of the strong feelings generated in this area. It is also important to remind us of the dire consequences which can result from ill-formulated and ill-understood research.

THE DIFFICULTIES AND DILEMMAS IN THIS AREA

It was not until 1961 that child abuse was 'rediscovered'. The watershed came that year with Kempe's presentation to the American Academy of

Paediatricians. This paper, which was published in 1962 (Kempe, Silverman, Steele, Droegemueller & Silver, 1962), dramatically described the 'battered child syndrome'. Kempe was a dedicated paediatrician and a determined and effective publicist who forced public, press and professionals not to avert their gaze. Keen to disassociate themselves from the earlier research, they emphasised that children were maltreated by apparently normal and respectable families. One major effect of the Denver research by Kempe, and his colleagues, Steele and Pollock (1968), was that professionals sought evidence of ill-treatment in the antecedent generation to explain the cruelties by the next generation. They found it. Much of this early writing reported that abusing parents were themselves abused, which led to the belief in the transmission of abuse or the 'Intergenerational hypothesis'. Widom (1989) notes that it is currently the 'premier' hypothesis in the field of abuse and neglect. Of all the theories for child maltreatment this has been the most enduring, partly because, as Egeland says, it makes intuitive sense and has popular appeal (Egeland, 1993).

But with knowledge have come the controversies. The media look for 'simple truths' where there are no simple truths. The whole area of intergenerational violence is fraught with difficulties for researchers, and knowledge is still in an early state of development (Egeland, 1993; Kaufman & Zigler, 1993). The dilemma is that family violence and intergenerational patterns of child maltreatment are a political concern. The experts are very powerful because they define what social policies should be designed and what interventions will be used. It is the contention of this book that the arguments should be opened out so that those who seek to promote the well-being of children and families can judge for themselves what value to place on the research. It is only by joining in partnership with those who work with families day by day that better ways will be found of breaking cycles of child maltreatment. If we are to protect children better, it is in the spirit of the UN Convention of the Rights of the Child, that we pool our knowledge and resources.

2

CYCLES OF CHILD MALTREATMENT: FACTS AND FALLACIES

Too much controversy in the family of family violence experts has, at times, led to professional family dysfunction, with enemies rather than colleagues, opposition rather than cooperation, sabotage rather than assistance, silence rather than communication. (Loseke & Gelles, 1993, p. xv)

INTRODUCTION

Some of the most bitter debates in the field of family violence research have centred around what has become known as the 'Intergenerational Hypothesis'. The purpose of this chapter is not to fuel the debate, but to outline the different arguments as objectively as possible, so that those who daily grapple with the complexities of protecting children can make sense of the central messages.

Researchers in this field, despite the controversies, do share considerable common ground. They are united in their task to limit the tragic consequences of family violence and they are united in agreeing that an intergenerational pattern of child maltreatment exists. Where they disagree is over what they feel is the cause of the phenomenon, what they feel is its extent, and from this what credence should be placed upon it by practitioners.

Central to the disagreements are differing conceptual frameworks of the problem. Theoretical perspectives might seem esoteric and only of interest to those who are, first and foremost, involved in academic study, but an understanding of these conceptual frameworks, and where a particular researcher stands in relation to them, is crucially important.

Theoretical frameworks define where we should look if we want to make sense of violence, and hence where we should intervene if we want to stop it. (Loseke & Gelles, 1993, p. x)

If the researcher believes primarily that individual psychopathology is the cause, efforts will be made to find intrafamilial pathological features and to treat these. If it is believed that it is the structure and inequalities in society that result in intergenerational maltreatment, efforts will be made to identify the socio-political factors and to effect changes. It may be that the researcher believes that cultural factors endemic in particular societies condone continuing patterns of abusive parenting, or it may be that the researcher believes in a biological basis to violent behaviour. Each of these differing perspectives, by their very definition of the problem, comes to very different conclusions, and consequently advocates very different solutions. But are such adversarial approaches necessary? Common sense suggests that each approach is only part of the jigsaw, and that if we are to understand the whole, we need to put the pieces of the jigsaw together. In putting the pieces together, some parts may not fit and judgements may have to be made whether in fact they belong or whether with new knowledge new parts may make the whole picture clearer.

The actual size of the phenomenon is also important. Does intergenerational maltreatment occur in 90% of families or 18%? It is common in the popular press to see assertions that 99% of all abused children become abusive parents (Kaufman & Zigler, 1993). These views direct not only the resources that are allocated to resolving and helping those families 'at risk', but also decisions made with current abusing families.

In this chapter, the starting point will be an overview of how we came to be, research-wise, where we are today. The main theoretical frameworks which have bearing on intergenerational patterns of abusive parenting will then be discussed. This will be followed by a summary of the different types of research and, in order to evaluate their worth, some of the methodological difficulties inherent in each type of study. Finally we will look to the evidence from all the main studies to see the facts and fallacies inherent in the 'Intergenerational Hypothesis'.

Recent Scientific History

With the 'rediscovery' of child abuse by Kempe in the 1960s and the recognition that there was a pattern of intergenerational transmission, researchers, many of whom were psychiatrists, using the traditional medical model, looked for pathology in families to explain the phenomenon and to indicate those that might be at risk. One of the most influential of the early studies was that of Steele and Pollock (1968), who found in a sample of 60 child-abusing parents that abusing parents recreated the pattern of their rearing with their own children 'without exception'.

However, this finding was a little ambiguous, as Kaufman and Zigler (1989) pointed out, because Steele and Pollock also reported that some parents 'never laid a hand on them [their children]'.

Other work, such as that in Wiltshire in the UK (Oliver & Taylor 1971; Oliver & Cox 1973; Oliver, Cox, Taylor & Baldwin, 1974; Oliver & Buchanan, 1979), demonstrated that a number of families continued an intergenerational pattern of chronic and very severe child maltreatment over many generations. Statutory authorities, in many cases, were unaware of the extent of abuse and even of child deaths, and the full picture only emerged through extensive record linkage. These families continued the pattern despite substantial support and intervention.

In the UK in 1972, Sir Keith Joseph, Secretary of State at the Department of Health and Social Services, made a speech concerning 'The Cycle of Deprivation'. Why, despite affluence, were there still many people who remained at an irreducible level of deprivation? This challenge triggered a whole series of studies on deprivation and disadvantage in Britain (SSRC/DHSS, 1976–1983). It is important to note that the focus of the research was not specifically on child maltreatment. These studies high-lighted that although intrafamilial factors had a role on perpetuating disadvantage, it was not possible to isolate these from external issues such as poverty, bad housing, or large-scale health and education prob-lems (Rutter & Madge, 1976; Coffield, Robinson & Sarsby, 1980; Blaxter, 1982; Blaxter & Paterson, 1981; Brown & Madge, 1982; Mortimore & Blackstone, 1982; Murie, 1982; Essen & Wedge, 1983). Also, although there were intergenerational patterns, there were 'discontinuities' as well as 'continuities'.

The importance of extrafamilial factors was echoed in the USA. Family sociologists such as Gil (1970), Gelles (1973) and Straus, Gelles & Stein-metz (1980) strongly emphasised the role of social factors and advocated a social system approach to family violence.

Another important influence at this time was the work of the feminists. Erin Pizzey, working in a refuge for battered wives, wrote her first book *Scream Quietly or the Neighbours Will Hear* in 1974. In the USA, Martin (1976) published *Battered Wives*. Research focused on the patriarchal forces in society which led to patterns of women abuse. There was a justifiable need to change the structure of society. 'We were constantly amazed at the courage of these women to survive a seemingly endless nightmare of physical and emotional abuse' (Jaffe, Wolfe & Wilson, 1990, p. 11).

The women, however, were not the only ones to be abused. Dobash and Dobash (1979, 1992) and Jaffe, Wolfe and Wilson (1990) have all demonstrated that even if the children were not maltreated, some children suffered permanent psychological scars from their traumatic life experiences.

Meanwhile in the USA, the term coined by researchers, 'The Intergenerational Hypothesis' was having a major effect on legal judgments. There were strong reactions against the injustice of this approach (Kaufman & Zigler, 1987, 1989). The pendulum moved away from the intergenerational hypothesis, and some US commentators went further than their UK counterparts in avoiding any hint of recognition of biological or personal propensities in favour of broad social issues, to explain patterns of child abuse (Cicchetti & Aber, 1980).

Despite the changing research fashions in the USA and UK important studies continued on psychological and personal processes, with very strong intergenerational implications. Bowlby (1953, 1979, 1984) took the most tenable of psychoanalytical insights, and integrated these with work from the fields of zoology and psychology. Studies on primates (Harlow & Suomi, 1971) and human attachment became more focused, with research in the USA in particular (Main & Goldwyn, 1984; Crittenden & Ainsworth, 1989). In Oxford too, for instance, 'bonding failure' was emphasised (Ounsted, Oppenheimer & Lindsay, 1974), giving parallels with the animal studies by the Nobel prizewinners Nikolaas Tinbergen and Konrad Lorenz on 'imprinting'. The generalisations from this approach have been criticised as being over-simplified (Richards, 1974; Sluckin, Herbert & Sluckin, 1983).

From the late 1970s there was a growing international literature on child maltreatment. A pattern emerged of nations first denying the existence of child maltreatment only to discover it. But these discoveries forced a re-examination of commonly held definitions of, and causal explanations for, child abuse and neglect.

Cultural mores could lead to patterns of abusive parenting being passed from generation to generation, but cross-cultural variability in child-rearing beliefs and behaviours made it clear that there was no universal standard of optimal child care or of child abuse. Central to this debate was the work of Korbin (1980, 1987, 1991), Finkelhor and Korbin (1988) and Levinson (1989). Recent campaigns have also focused on the role of cultural factors in the physical chastisement of children. Organisations such as EPOCH and APPROACH have been set up to challenge accepted child-rearing practices (Newell, 1989).

An important influence more recently, with the discoveries in the field of DNA, has been the resurgence of biological factors to explain vulnerability to certain types of behaviour (Loehlin, 1992). Although these do not relate directly to patterns of child maltreatment, they throw light on factors which could influence intergenerational transmission. How far increasing knowledge of DNA will contribute to the field of family violence is a hotly debated area. At an important conference in London in 1993 Plomin summarised the current view:

> Papers in this conference underline the important contribution of genetics to many areas of developmental psychopathology. However we should not lose sight of the fact that these same genetic data provide the best available evidence for the importance of nongenetic factors. Rarely does genetic influence account for more than half of the variance of behavioural dimensions and disorders. (Plomin, 1994b)

Plomin's work illustrates the limitations of a single focus in some of the early models to explain child maltreatment and family violence. Often these models only included factors from single domains or ecological levels. The psychiatric and the sociological models were unidirectional and hence did not allow for the important interactions between causal factors which were seen, for example, in the British studies on deprivation and disadvantage. These problems were overcome by a number of researchers who developed multi-domain, multi-factor interactional models (Garbarino, 1977; Bronfenbrenner, 1977, 1979; Belsky, 1980). In Oxford, in the 1970s, Margaret Lynch and her colleagues were already linking psycho-social factors leading to child abuse in their 'critical path' approaches (Lynch, 1976).

In the following section a brief outline is given of the main models which have been used to explain intergenerational continuities. They are grouped into those implicating extrafamilial factors; those implicating intrafamilial factors, and those which link factors within and without the family to explain the phenomenon.

MODELS FOCUSING ON FACTORS OUTSIDE THE FAMILY

Socio-economic Models

Gil's work in the USA (Gil, 1970) highlighted the fact that children reported to social services came overwhelmingly from the lower socio-economic classes. Gil argued that society itself set the preconditions for child abuse by condoning structural inequalities. Because some families were unable to escape from extreme poverty and deprivation, society should share the blame when a child was abused. Individual pathology could not be blamed. This view implies that child abuse cannot be left to the individual professional.

Children's Rights

Linked into this, is the children's rights' perspective. With the signing of the Convention on the Rights of the Child (UN, 1989), there has been a growing realisation that if children were independent beings with their own political rights rather than the property of their parents, this would limit the extent of abuse (Eekelaar, 1986, 1992; Newell, 1992).

Under the United Nations Convention of the Rights of the Child, there are 41 articles outlining the child's rights. In the preamble to the Convention it notes that children need special care and protection because of their very vulnerability. It recognises that the family has the primary responsibility for their care and protection, but there is a need for legal protection in addition.

Among the rights outlined are the following. Decisions should always be made in the child's best interest (Article 3). The state has a duty to ensure the child's survival (Article 6), to protect the child's identity and to re-unify him or her with their family if separated (Articles 7, 10). The child has the right to express opinions on matters affecting him or her and the right to appropriate information (Articles 12, 17). The state has an obligation to protect children from abuse and neglect, to provide accommodation if they cannot live safely with their families (Articles 19, 20) and to give special care to handicapped children (Article 23). The child has a right to health services, social security, education, the right to leisure, protection from child labour, drug abuse, sexual exploitation, sale, trafficking and abduction and other forms of exploitation including torture (Articles 24–37). In addition, states have an obligation in armed conflicts to protect children, to help refugees and not to recruit children into the armed forces, as well as to assist in rehabilitating them (Articles 38, 22, 39). When a child is charged with an offence, there should be respect of human rights, access to legal procedures and avoidance wherever possible of institutional placements.

As we investigate the cycles of child maltreatment in the following chapters, it is useful to question the extent to which these children's rights have been achieved.

Newell would argue (1991) that in the advanced economy of the UK, there is still a long way to go before the rights outlined by the Convention have been fully implemented. Indeed the Convention was not ratified in the UK until 1991.

Newell (1989) would also argue that whereas adults are prosecuted for inflicting physical harm on others, hundreds of parents daily physically chastise their children without fear of recrimination. He feels that it is society's acceptance that children can be beaten by their parents, that leads to a failure to inhibit continuing patterns of child maltreatment. His solution is parental education, to teach alternative methods of discipline, and legal measures to limit all physical chastisement.

The Feminist Approach

Linked into the idea of structural inequalities in society is the position of women. As society is essentially patriarchal, the prevailing beliefs about all aspects of social organisation are framed from a male point of view. By ignoring issues of gender, this leads to a blinkered approach. In highlighting the unequal treatment of *The Girl Child*, UNICEF has been important (1991).

In addition to the inequalities of female children, there are concerns about the effects of domestic violence on women. Domestic violence is not just an individual problem, but a social and political one (Dobash & Dobash, 1992; Hanmer & Maynard, 1987). Yllo (1993) demonstrates that feminist analysis has made an enormous contribution to the understanding of family violence. Social expectations regarding masculinity and femininity give shape to women's relationships. Dobash and Dobash (1979) illustrate that male violence can be seen as a means of controlling women in general. Yllo (1993) would add that psychological explanations for when men batter such as a man's low self-esteem, poor impulse control, traumatic childhood, and so on, have served to relieve the batterers from their responsibility for criminally assaulting their partners. Because women suffer, so do their children.

The feminist perspective offers two solutions. Firstly, change should be initiated at a societal level to change gender-related structural inequalities. Secondly, at an individual level, in particular with child sexual abuse, investigation and treatment of abusing parents should be more gender-sensitive and empower mothers to play a more influential role in setting up of self-help groups as an alternative to 'professional treatment' (Kitzinger, 1989).

The opening of centres for women who experience violence from males has highlighted the fact that many of these women were sexually abused in their own childhoods (Rush, 1981). Stark and Flitcraft (1985) demonstrate that if intergenerational patterns of maltreatment are to be broken these women must be supported, rather than condemned as child abusers:

> Children whose mothers are battered are more than twice as likely to be physically abused than children whose mothers are not abused. Those who are concerned about child abuse would do well to look toward advocacy and protection of battered mothers as the best available means to prevent current child abuse as well as child abuse in the future. (Stark & Flitcraft, 1985, p. 147)

Resource Theory

Resource theory rests on the notion that levels of violence and child maltreatment in family relationships depend to some extent on the value of resources each person brings to the relationship. The more resources a person can muster—social, personal and economic—the less he or she will need to use violence (Goode, 1971). As in most societies men control more resources than women, this contradicts some of the feminist theories. However, this model has been developed in what has become called Status Inconsistency Theory. This suggests that violence is more likely to occur when an individual's power or status is inconsistent (high in one social setting, low in another). From an intergenerational context it is important, because it helps to explain why in a changing society where men may no longer be in control of resources, they may resort to violence to enforce the status traditionally associated with their gender.

The Culture of Violence

This theory looks to the culture within a society to explain patterns of violence. Various forms of this perspective have been developed since it was first hypothesised by Wolfgang and Ferracuti (1967). This theory suggests that some subcultural groups develop norms and values that emphasise the use of violence. The implication is that physical punishment of children might be more common and considered more appropriate, or even more desirable, by certain groups than by others. Within societies there may be subcultures, or different sectors of that society which use violence to a greater extent than the dominant culture.

This theory has also been extended to explain the differences in the frequency of violence between different societies (Levinson & Malone, 1980).

Levinson would add: 'Just saying that some societies are more violent than others explains nothing. It does beg the question, however, of why this occurs' (Levinson, 1989, p. 16).

MODELS THAT LOOK TOWARDS FACTORS WITHIN THE FAMILY

The Psychiatric Model

Earlier models to explain intergenerational child maltreatment were strongly based on the psychiatric/psychoanalytic tradition (Kempe & Kempe, 1978). It was felt that the individual 'ego' of parents who abused their children had been damaged in their childhoods, rendering them in turn more likely to abuse their own children. Aggression was related to a subconscious 'inner drive'. An analysis of past histories would indicate lists of pathological influences. Insight or an understanding of how an individual's own past had influenced their present situation was central to therapy. Therapists were encouraged to focus attention on the mothers, and develop positive 'mothering' relationships with them. Some attention was paid to social issues, but the main focus was on the work with the mother (Parton, 1985).

Social Learning Theory

Social learning theorists reject the idea that aggression is an inner sub-conscious drive. They argue both that aggression is learned and that it takes place within a social context. According to the behaviourist perspective the child comes into the world as a *tabula rasa* or clean sheet and is moulded by the treatment he or she receives from their parents. The child following the abusive model of his parents learns that violence pays (Kalmuss, 1984; Pagelow, 1981; Ulbrich & Huber, 1981). Individuals are not only exposed to techniques of being violent, they also learn the moral justifications for their behaviour. Gelles and Cornell (1985, 1990) note that it is not uncommon for parents to justify abusing their child because the punishment was for the child's own good. They have found parents using the same punishments on their children as they experienced as a child and in some cases parents have even used the same instruments (Gelles & Cornell, 1990).

Related to social theory learning are the cost-benefit gains of *Exchange/ Control Theory* (Goode, 1971; Gelles, 1974). Gelles summarises this as:

'People hit and abuse other family members because they can' (Gelles, 1983, p. 157). The rewards from hitting outweigh the consequences, and family members will continue to use violence for as long as society, with its reluctance to intervene in family disputes, permits this behaviour.

Developments from the social learning theory include the *cognitive behavioural approach*. Azar and Siegal (1990) argue that unrealistic parental expectations and misattributions of negative intent (the child seeks to annoy) lead to abusive situations. Physical child abuse is related to the parental cognitions of the situation, the parental impulse control and parent–child interactions. Although Azar recognises the importance of social factors in setting the scene, lack of parenting skills, to cope with particular stages of their child's development, leads to patterns of child maltreatment.

It is also noted in a number of studies that physical child abusers have low self-esteem (Friedrich & Wheeler, 1982; Milner, 1988), and it is this low self-esteem in itself that can lead to unrealistic expectations of their children. This perhaps explains why some parents, despite deprivation and disadvantage, do not abuse their children. Low self-esteem can be related to the care parents themselves received as children, not only from their families but from the stigma of being looked after in the public care system that sought to protect them (Buchanan, Wheal, Walder, Macdonald & Coker, 1993).

Broadly speaking, those who believe in social learning approaches seek to change individual patterns of maladaptive learned behaviour by changing the cost/benefit of violence, re-educating parents into less violent methods of control by incident analysis, and by using techniques to improve self-control and self-esteem.

Attachment Theory

Attachment theory could be seen as another way to explain some of the concepts of social learning theory. Bowlby (1979), Ainsworth (1973), Crittenden and Ainsworth (1989), note that the early attachment relationships between the caregiver and the child are a prototype of later relationships. Egeland, Sroufe and Erickson (1988) have hypothesised that attachment theory may explain the cycle of abuse. During early life the infant, in order to survive, needs to make a strong attachment to its primary caregivers. From this early experience the child develops working models of him/herself and significant others, and creates a set of expectations about future relationships. Zeanah and Anders (1987) note that these early working models compel individuals to recreate their relationship experiences in their own lives. Violence may not be passed on *per se*, but rather the ongoing theme of the caregiving relationship, for example rejection, psychological unavailability. Egeland and Sroufe (1981) have found this form of maltreatment has devastating effects on the development of young children.

The difference between social learning and attachment theory is seen in the recommended type of intervention. Attachment theory relates back to earlier psychodynamic theory in stressing the importance of the abusing parents' gaining insight that their present parenting is the result of their early experiences.

Sociobiologists

Sociobiologists consider that all human beings are programmed to preserve themselves and their genes (Dawkins, 1976). This theory proposes that under certain conditions, particularly those of stress, abuse of offspring can be seen as consistent with the need for survival. Sociobiologists take a particular interest in step-parenting where there are clear examples of non-biological fathers grossly ill-treating the young of their partner because, it is argued, they have no particular investment in the genes of these offspring. As increasing numbers of marriages end in divorce, and more single and separated parents take new partners, society needs to act to preserve the sanctity of the natural family.

Biological Theories

Research has also returned to biological factors in individual perpetrators as contributory factors in explaining patterns of child abuse. Elliott (1988) considers that abusers' neurological handicaps have been overlooked. Cognitive deficits related to minimal brain dysfunction decrease parents' ability to cope adequately with child-rearing, increasing the likelihood of child maltreatment. There is considerable evidence on psychophysiological differences between abusers and non-abusers (Knutson, 1978; Wolfe, Fairbank, Kelly & Bradlyn, 1983; Crowe & Zeskind, 1992; Casanova, Dominic, McCann & Milner, 1992). Several researchers indicate that perpetrators have more health problems than non-abusers (Conger, Burgess & Barrett, 1979; Lahey, Conger, Atkeson & Treiber, 1984). These health problems which lower parents' ability to parent may have an intergenerational component. Alcohol consumption may have a familial base especially when associated with depressive tendencies, and this can affect parenting abilities. Biological characteristics in children may place them at greater risk (Buchanan & Oliver, 1977; Ackerman, 1988).

MULTI-FOCUS THEORIES

The inadequacy of single-focus models, to explain the complex relationship, led to the development of multi-focus theories. Straus (1980) suggested that our understanding how to change patterns of family violence would be enhanced if it were seen as a product of the interaction of social systems operating at individual, family and societal levels. In addition to Straus, major influences in this area have been the works of Garbarino (1977), Bronfenbrenner (1977), and in particular Belsky (1980). Garbarino (1977) proposed an 'ecological model' to explain the complex nature of child maltreatment. Garbarino's model, which was later developed by Belsky (1980), concerns the complex interrelations of the many social systems which overlap with family life and influence human development. The domains include individual factors (ontogenetic level), family factors (microsystem level), community factors (exosystem level) and cultural factors (macrosystem level). A similar theory known as the Transactional Model has been developed by Cicchetti and Rizley (1981).

These models brought together many of the factors highlighted by other theoretical approaches. From an intergenerational perspective, they are important because they demonstrate how factors both within and without a family can interact, resulting in repeated patterns of child maltreatment. These models suggest interventions should be focused at every level of the system. However, because of the size and complexity of the model they are difficult to test empirically: 'The complexity of the relations among the variables that affect the likelihood of transmission occurring undermine efforts to predict which individuals are most likely to repeat the pattern of abuse in subsequent generations' (Kaufman & Zigler, 1989, p. 141).

Summary

What sense should the practitioner make of the many theories that abound? Two thoughts emerge. Firstly, despite the often oppositional stances adopted by the different theoreticians, there is considerable common ground. Secondly, despite the growth in knowledge, there are still gaps in our understanding. Central to the whole debate, are the methodological difficulties academics in the field of family violence have experienced.

METHODOLOGICAL DIFFICULTIES

A particular limitation in most intergenerational research is that most of the quoted studies have been undertaken in the USA and UK. Child abuse is no longer a problem of the Western world alone, and we need to look beyond our shores for a wider world understanding. In particular, as we will see in Chapter 4, we have much to learn from cross-cultural studies. In this section we will, however, explore some of the dilemmas experienced by Western researchers.

At the heart of the difficulties for researchers, is the intense secrecy about what goes on in the privacy of family life. Personal experience of researching in this area (Buchanan & Oliver, 1977; Oliver & Buchanan, 1979) has demonstrated that, even with extensive record linkage, only partial knowledge is possible, and this knowledge in itself may be unreliable and lead to faulty conclusions. When looking for intergenerational patterns these difficulties are magnified. Variation in aspects of research design affects the findings derived from studies. As research methodology in the field of family violence develops, new research designs reveal new dilemmas.

Kaufman and Zigler indicate that findings from empirical studies will vary according to the following factors:

(1) The subjects studied (identified abusers vs high-risk populations)
(2) Retrospective vs prospective research designs
(3) The types of data sources utilised to substantiate claims of past and current abuse
(4) The duration of follow-up
(5) The definitions of a history of abuse and current abuse used
                                          (Kaufman & Zigler, 1993, p. 210).

Case History Studies

The early psychiatric studies were based on clinical studies of identified abusing parents (Kempe *et al.*, 1962). The central controversies here are how far findings could be 'generalised' to families in general. Families in the studies were already identified as abusing. They were not representative samples from a general population. Very often in these studies there were no comparison groups of non-abusing families to indicate how common the findings were to all families. The observers were not blind to the maltreatment status of their subjects and however objective they might try to be, there was the likelihood of bias reporting. These studies also used different definitions of abuse so it was difficult to make comparisons with other studies, there were usually no statistical checks on the significance of the findings, and sample numbers were often small. Others, however, would argue that the researchers' 'closeness' to their study families meant the clinician had a better chance of breaking through the veil of family secrecy (Oliver, 1993). The issue of definitions is also problematical, as types of abuse inflicted on children vary from generation to generation, and this may lead to an underestimation of the true extent of the phenomenon. A mother or father who had suffered physical violence, might not inflict the same level, or type, of maltreatment on their offspring, but the severe emotional abuse or sexual abuse which they might inflict could be harder to identify, and yet for their offspring more damaging.

Clinical Studies

One of the most influential early studies supporting intergenerational patterns of child maltreatment was that of Steele and Pollock (1968). This was a study of 60 abusing parents whose children had been treated for non-accidental injuries. Steele and Pollock noted that: 'This study group of parents was not to be thought of as useful statistical proof of any concepts' (Steele & Pollock, 1968). Their finding, that there was a strong pattern of intergenerational maltreatment, was very influential. There was a particular difficulty in what was considered as evidence of child abuse in the previous generation and some researchers felt (Kaufman & Zigler, 1989) that without an appropriate comparison group it was impossible to determine if the experiences were unique to abusive parents, or simply to parents receiving psychological treatment.

Agency Record Studies

Agency record studies have been criticised for having many of the same problems demonstrated in the clinical studies. These studies often depended on retrospective data which had not been systematically recorded (Oliver & Taylor, 1971). Agency recording of information could be patchy, biased and unreliable. There were bound to be data omissions, and information that was recorded was felt to give a false picture of the whole. Others would argue that a truer, yet still only a partial, picture emerges from agency case studies, especially where records from different agencies are linked (Oliver, 1993).

Social Surveys on the Extent of Child Abuse

One of the dilemmas in the early research was that there was little information available on the extent of child maltreatment in the general population. In 1967 David Gil (1970) conducted a nationwide inventory of reported cases of child abuse. He also undertook an opinion survey which asked a representative sample of 1520 adults if they knew families where child abuse had occurred. In his nationwide inventory he found 6000 confirmed cases of child abuse. From this, Gil estimated that between 2.53 and 4.07 million children were abused each year, or there were between 13.3 and 21.4 incidents of abuse per 1000 persons in the United States. In the UK, Oliver *et al.* (1974) undertook a study of children who were severely maltreated, using a case record linkage methodology in a defined population, and estimated that there was 1 child per 1000 aged under four years who suffered *very severe physical abuse* each year. The rate of reported abuse rose as practitioners became more aware of the problem. Other studies have demonstrated that the number of children known to child abuse agencies may severely underestimate those who are in fact maltreated. Nagi (1977) surveyed community agencies that had contact with abused children. He estimated that 167 000 cases of abuse are reported annually, while at least an additional 91 000 go unreported. Although it has been suggested that child abuse is over-reported (Besharov, 1990), most would concur with Finklehor (1990) and Newberger (1985) that it is more a question of whether there is a bias in reporting—that is, are families living in disadvantage more likely to come to the notice of authorities? The 'guesstimates' of the extent of child abuse are important in estimating the extent of intergenerational patterns of child abuse. Patterns of reporting child maltreatment may change over time and with greater awareness of the problem, and there may be biases in reporting, but it is still likely that large numbers of children who are maltreated will go unrecognised (Finkelhor, 1990).

Self-report Studies

In an effort to overcome some of these biases, researchers have developed standardised self-report measures. Straus and Gelles, using a self-report methodology, carried out two surveys, firstly in 1976 and again in 1985

(Straus, Gelles & Steinmetz, 1988). They used a nationally representative sample of 2143 individual family members in 1976 (Straus 1979) and 6002 family members in 1985 (Gelles & Straus, 1988). Parents were asked to report on their own 'conflict tactics techniques' with their children. Among the list of tactics were nine items that dealt with physical violence, ranging from 'threw something at child' to 'used a knife or gun'. Straus and Gelles estimated that 7 per 1000 children under 18 years of age were injured each year.

Other researchers latched on to the technique to explore intergenerational patterns (Altemeier, O'Connor, Vietze, Sandler & Sherrod, 1982; Egeland & Jacobvitz, 1984; Herrenkohl, Herrenkohl & Toedtler, 1983; Hunter & Kilstrom, 1979).

> In these studies, the terms 'history of abuse' and 'current abuse' were consistently defined, comparison groups were always employed, and multiple aetiological factors were always assessed. Measures of stress, social isolation, and child characteristics were often included, representing a shift from the earlier investigations that concentrated solely on detecting pathology in the parents who abused their children. (Kaufman & Zigler, 1989, p. 131)

In Straus's study in 1979, he used a self-report methodology using 1146 children, aged between 3 and 1 in two-parent families. Straus obtained an estimate of 18% for the rate of intergenerational transmission of abuse. This is likely to be an underestimate because much higher rates of abuse occur with younger children, and lone parents may be at greater risk of abusing their children than two-parent families.

Self-report studies do however have a number of difficulties. Firstly, in self-report studies how accurate is the adult recollection of earlier child abuse? There is considerable evidence that child maltreatment victims tend to blame themselves for abuse inflicted by their parents, and see it as normal or at least acceptable (Zeanah & Zeanah, 1989). There is also the tendency for them to idealise their past (Main & Goldwyn, 1984) in order to cope with the trauma of abuse and to dissociate themselves from their past. This 'psychogenic amnesia' (Egeland, 1993) was vividly illustrated in work with Oliver (Oliver & Buchanan, 1979) when the realities of abusive parents' past, as demonstrated in old records, bore little resemblance to their perceptions of their childhoods. In contrast to this, some parents who apparently had very positive experiences in their childhood retrospectively reported high rates of maltreatment. These findings in themselves raise a number of issues about the value of a child's perceptions of abusive behaviour, but also demonstrate how difficult it is to break into the secrecy of family life. As Altemeier, O'Connor, Sherrod & Tucker (1986) note:

perhaps this also reflects that recalled abuse and reported abuse are some-
what different forms of maltreatment . . . *feeling unloved and unwanted* by
one's own parents was a much stronger predictor for having a child reported as abused than a history of being abused as a child. (Altemeier *et al.*,
1986, p. 329)

THE RATE OF INTERGENERATIONAL CHILD MALTREATMENT

Given the difficulties and differences in research methodology, it is not
surprising that the rates of intergenerational transmission of child maltreatment range from 1% to nearly 100% (Oliver, 1993). To the practitioner faced with the reality of making life decisions on an abused child,
what value should be placed on an abusing parent's own history of
maltreatment? Table 1 summarises some of the findings.

The two central research figures in the debate take opposing positions.
Egeland (1993) argues that a history of abuse is a major risk factor for
abusing the next generation, whereas Kaufman & Zigler (1993) lead the
opposition in saying that the intergenerational transmission of abuse is
overstated.

Apart from the methodological difficulties stated above, Egeland, and
Kaufman and Zigler dispute as to how much evidence should be placed
on *retrospective* as against *prospective* studies. The bulk of empirical evidence in support of the intergenerational hypothesis has come from retrospective studies. The problem with this approach is that it cannot
determine what proportion of adults who were maltreated as children are
providing good-enough parenting for their own children. Looking back,
it appears that the majority of abusing parents were themselves abused.
Looking forward the rate is likely to be much lower. Egeland (1993)
argues that caution is needed in interpreting the findings of retrospective
studies, but because of the problems of recall discussed above, even these
may underestimate the extent of transmission. Egeland states that to date
there has never been a true prospective study on intergenerational child
maltreatment.

Hunter and Kilstrom (1979) found the same intergenerational transmission rate as that found by Straus (1979)—18%. In the case of Hunter and
Kilstrom's study this figure may also be an underestimate as they followed up families for only one year.

Kaufman and Zigler question Egeland's earlier controlled study (Egeland
& Jacobvitz, 1984) which, apart from the clinical studies, produced one of

Table 1: Rates of intergenerational child abuse

	YEAR	RATE IGT %	TYPE OF STUDY
Oliver & Taylor	1971	100	Retro agency record linkage severely abusive families
Steele & Pollock	1968	100	Retro clinical study of abusive parents. No controls. Wide definition of abuse
Hunter & Kilstrom	1979	90	Retro-element: Agency record/ self-report/controlled
Egeland & Jacobvitz	1984	70	Prospective Multiple interviews high-risk parents. Comparison abusive vs. non-abusive group/ various rating scales. Wide definition of abuse
Herrenkohl, Herrenkohl and Toedtler	1983	47	Retrospective. Self-report clinical study with comparison subjects
Egeland, Jacobvitz & Sroufe	1988	40	As 1984 study above but minus 'borderline' abuse categories
Straus	1979	18	Retrospective, self-report nationally representative sample
Hunter and Kilstrom (prospective)		18	Prospective self-report controlled
Gil	1970	14–7	Nationwide survey. Self-report
Altemeier *et al.*	1986	2–5	Prospective self-report controlled
Widom	1989	1	Prospective agency records for validated child abuse, controlled

the highest transmission rates (70%). This was a study of 160 high-risk first time pregnant single parents who were predominately low-income. The mothers were followed up for approximately five years. There were three categories for their children of current abuse, but not all these were severe, and some involved physical chastisement. Kaufman and Zigler believe that the rates of transmission are inflated in this study because of the high-risk nature of the parents, and the broader definitional criteria employed for current abuse. Straus (1983) has shown that 97% of all children in the United States had been physically punished. In a later study which eliminated the 'borderline abuse' category, Egeland found a rate of maltreatment of 40% across generations (Egeland, Jacobvitz & Sroufe, 1988). In this study he noted that 61% of the mothers who had reported being sexually abused as children were maltreating their own offspring.

At the other end of the scale, the very low figure found in Widom (1989) may reflect her reliance on official documents and her strict criteria that only child abuse and neglect cases that had been validated by a court were included in the sample. In Altemeier *et al.*'s study (1986), pregnant mothers were asked to 'recall' any abuse in their childhood. Altemeier himself questions, as we have seen, whether recalled maltreatment is the same as reported maltreatment. Research findings could be ser- iously corrupted by this. If parents who had been abused were unwill- ing or unable to recall abuse, and others who might have suffered minimal harm feel able to recall abusive incidents, this could totally reverse findings.

So where does this place the practitioner? Surprisingly, when it comes to the suggested rate of intergenerational child maltreatment there is now some consensus. Egeland (1993), Kaufman and Zigler (1993), Oliver (1993) all conclude that intergenerational transmission is far from inevit- able. When methodological considerations are taken into account, they conclude it is probable that between 30 and 40% of abusing parents will go on to abuse their children (Egeland, 1993; Kaufman & Zigler, 1993; Oliver, 1993). This is considerably more than the 2% to 3% seen in the general population. A danger in attempting to view the intergenerational hypothesis from a pro or con perspective is the idea that there are only two points of view. There are multiple causes of child maltreatment which have different effects on each parent. Viewed in an international perspective, we need to remember that we may have to adjust our views in applying the concepts to other parts of the world. As Kaufman and Zigler conclude:

> It is time to focus . . . on understanding the mechanisms involved in the transmission of abuse and the factors that decrease the likelihood of its occurrence. Undoubtedly a history of abuse is a considerable risk factor associated with the aetiology of child maltreatment, but the pathway to abusive parenting is far from inevitable and involves many complex inter- actions between genetic and environmental factors. (Kaufman & Zigler, 1993, p. 218)

The task of the following chapters is just that. The focus is on understand- ing these mechanisms involved in the transmission of abuse and finding the factors that may decrease the likelihood of its occurrence.

SUMMARY: FACTS AND FALLACIES IN INTERGENERATIONAL CHILD MALTREATMENT

- Intrafamilial research suggests that the majority of those parents who were abused as children will not repeat the patterns. However, research does suggest that having been abused is a significant risk factor for later parenting. There is a growing consensus that probably around one third of abused children will repeat the patterns of their childhood. These intrafamilial studies need, however, to be seen in the wider socio-political and cultural contexts.
- The whole area of intergenerational patterns of child maltreatment is fraught with sensitivities, difficulties, dilemmas and controversies.
- There are many methodological problems in undertaking research in this area.
- How studies are set up defines what they find. In particular, prospective studies will have very different findings from retrospective studies. The tendency for abused adults to 'idealise' their childhoods can seriously distort findings.
- Early single-focus theories may be of limited value.
- Theories of causation define what is looked for, what is found, and what it is felt should be done.
- There is a need to examine both extrafamilial and intrafamilial mechanisms of transmission.
- There is considerable research on socio-political and psychological causation factors.
- Cultural factors have only gained prominence in the last ten years.
- There has been an understandable reluctance to consider biological causation.
- However, these views are no longer tenable as recent evidence suggests that much can be done to limit the effects of biological risk.
- As the pathway from abuse in childhood to abusive parenting is far from inevitable, there is a need to take a holistic approach in understanding the complex interrelationships of mechanisms in order to plan effective interventions and prevent recurrence of abusive child-rearing patterns.

II

THE FOUR CYCLES

3

SOCIO-POLITICAL FACTORS IN INTERGENERATIONAL CHILD MALTREATMENT

A society lives and mirrors itself through its children. The Romanian people have always valued the family and its children . . . growing and protecting children is an integral part of our people's very spirituality. In opposition to this tradition, the totalitarian system savagely espoused a policy of forced birthrate, despising the woman-mother, the family and the underprivileged children, thus undertaking socially disadvantageous steps instead of protective ones, and creating deep perturbation in the normal development of the family equilibrium. Paradoxically instead of growing and educating children, families have come to the stage of not wanting their children . . . leading to an increasing number of abandoned and handicapped children, of orphaned and vagrant children, the very destruction of the family. (Radulian, 1992, p. 1)

INTRODUCTION

This chapter considers socio-political factors which affect the ability of parents to parent, and discusses the possible mechanisms that result, directly or indirectly, in cycles of child maltreatment. The above quotation by Professor Radulian, President of the Romanian National Committee for UNICEF, illustrates some of the central issues. This is an extreme example, but the twin prongs of social and political factors can, in many ways, foster situations which lead to cycles of child maltreatment.

In this chapter when we talk about intergenerational maltreatment, this relates either to whole populations of children where successive generations are brought up in abusive circumstances, for example street children, or we are referring to situations where the effect on one generation is so catastrophic that there is a carry over until the next.

As Rutter has said: 'If intergenerational child abuse continuities are found it cannot be assumed that the mechanisms of transmission necessarily involve family pathology' (Rutter, 1989, p. 320–321).

The Primacy of the Family as the Protector of the Child

Even in the most extreme circumstances most families do not maltreat their young. However, small changes in social conditions have important effects on parenting abilities, and the care of subsequent generations of children can be affected even after the original conditions have ceased to be in force.

Bronfenbrenner in the USA recognised that the family was a functional system, the operation of which will be altered by its *internal* composition and by *external* forces (Bronfenbrenner, 1979).

What do parents require if they are to perform the essential task of protecting their young? A paper from the Department of Health and Social Security in England and Wales suggests there are four main areas in which support and guidance may be needed. Parents need information and knowledge; parents need skills; parents need an understanding of themselves; and finally, the main issue in this chapter, parents need 'permitting circumstances' (DHSS, 1974). The interaction that takes place between economics, social factors, education and deprivation is complex, yet many families find it very hard to bring up their children adequately when their basic needs are not met. 'Permitting circumstances' relate not only to the family's financial well-being, housing and employment status, but also to whether family and friends are near enough for regular contact, the strength of community support and the extent of isolation. It is the environment both within and without the family that parents 'create' and are 'permitted' to create which crucially affects the development of the child.

Parents . . . create the environment that helps children achieve their maximum potential in terms of physical, intellectual, and psychological development. The child's job is to make use of the environment. Neither can accomplish the other's work; it is only in the context of the parent–child relationship that the child is able to move successfully through the stages of development. (Fahlberg, 1991, p. 15)

Given 'permitting circumstances', and the interpretation of this has wide cultural variations, most parents can create an adequate environment for their children. When the threshold is lowered, large numbers of children can be at risk.

The Role of Socio-economic Factors

The sociological model for child maltreatment outlined by Gil (1970) in the last chapter would suggest that society has a responsiblility to ensure all parents have the necessary 'permitting circumstances' to parent. Gil argues that as a direct or indirect consequence of policies, the welfare of millions of children is jeopardised. Poverty, inadequate nourishment, poor housing, inadequate education, poor health care, unemployment, decaying neighbourhoods and alienation permeate down from the societal level and determine, by complex interactions, how children fare in their own homes (Gil 1970).

Brown and Madge demonstrate the link between living in poverty and child abuse:

> Hopelessness and despair are commonly noted among families on very low incomes. . . . The monetary consequence of poverty which includes disconnection of fuel supply and acute shortages of cash to buy food or clothe the children adequately, must create situations where children are not properly cared for in a material sense. And the psychological consequences of chronic anxiety and despair are hardly conducive to happy child rearing. (Brown & Madge, 1982, pp. 160–161)

Although child abuse does cut across social and economic groups it does so unevenly. The risk of child abuse is greater among those who are poor, who are unemployed and who have poor paying jobs (Gelles & Straus, 1988, Straus; Gelles & Steinmetz, 1988).

The core of Gelles' sociological perspective (Gelles & Straus, 1988; Straus, Gelles & Steinmetz, 1980; Gelles, 1993) is that social structures affect people and their behaviour. The key variables in family violence are: 'Age, sex, position in the socioeconomic structure and race and ethnicity' (Gelles, 1993, p. 31). The rates of violence within the family are highest between the ages of 18 and 30 years (Straus, Gelles & Steinmetz, 1988; Gelles & Straus, 1988). Most extrafamilial violence takes place between men. Within the family, mothers are as likely, or more likely to maltreat their children than fathers. Gelles (1993) feels this sex difference is not as clear as it might appear. Mothers are more likely to be implicated in child abuse inquiries, and mothers, who are often sole or prime carers for children, are at greater risk of inflicting violence because they spend more time with their offspring. The stresses of living in poverty, as we have seen, are felt to explain why child maltreatment is more likely to occur in lower socio-economic groups. The findings of high levels of reported child abuse amongst Black and other minority racial groups may also reflect socio-economic factors. With this group, poverty may be more important than racial characteristics.

Gelles would also see the social institution of the family as a breeding group for family violence. The likelihood for example of being a victim of violence on the street at the hands of a stranger is measured in terms of risk per 100 000 people but the risk of family violence is measured in terms of a rate per 100 individuals (Gelles & Straus, 1988). Straus and Hotaling (1980) note that the particular characteristics that make the family a warm supportive environment also create the conditions for intrafamily violence.

Research on multiple victimisation (Farrell, 1992) indicates that a small proportion of the population experience a large proportion of all crime. Petrie and Garner (1990) add that much homicide and violence are distinguished by three characteristics: prior relationship between the victim and the offender, prior contact between victims and official agencies; and concentration of offences in time and by location.

Feminist theory, as we have discussed, would also look to faults in the continuing patriarchal structure of society, whereas Resource Theory might suggest that it is unemployment, and poor opportunities in life, which drive men to violence in the home to maintain their traditional dominance.

The difficulty with these single-focus theoretical approaches is that they do not explain the exceptions, the majority of families who do not abuse their children despite severe social disadvantage. Some of these issues are explained in Belsky's (1980) model. This model suggests four levels and at each level there are *compensatory* or *risk* factors. This model broadly links to the four cycles of child maltreatment. The Exosystem and the Macrosystem are extrafamilial and link to the socio-political and cultural cycles, whereas the ontogenetic and microsystems are intrafamilial and link to the psychological and biological cycle.

Quinton, Rutter and Liddle (1984) demonstrate that compensatory and risk factors are capable of producing bidirectional effects. In addition there is the 'roulette wheel' of life's chances (Rutter, 1984). We will return to this model in later chapters, when we consider intrafamilial patterns of child maltreatment. Belsky's model is, however, useful in understanding how social structures and political systems might raise the number of risk factors in the Exo and Macrosystems for groups of the population, and so indirectly increase the risk of intergenerational patterns.

THE POLITICS OF CHILD WELFARE

Most social groups with a distinct cultural awareness attempt to formalise, through policies and legislation, what to them are proper concepts

Table 2: Determinants of abuse: compensatory and risk factors

ONTOGENETIC LEVEL	MICROSYSTEM LEVEL	EXOSYSTEM LEVEL	MACROSYSTEM LEVEL
Compensatory factors			
High IQ	Healthy children	Good social	Culture that
Awareness of	Supportive	supports	promotes a sense
past abuse	spouse	Few stressful	of shared
History of a	Economic	events	responsibility in
positive	security/savings	Strong,	caring for the
relationship with	in the bank	supportive	community's
one parent		religious	children
Special talents		affiliation	Culture opposed
Physical		Positive school	to violence
attractiveness		experiences and	Economic
Good		peer relations as	prosperity
interpersonal		a child	
skills		Therapeutic	
		interventions	
Risk factors			
History of abuse	Marital discord	Unemployment	Cultural
Low self-esteem	Children with	Isolation: poor	acceptance of
Low IQ	behaviour	social supports	corporal
Poor	problems	Poor peer	punishment
interpersonal	Premature or	relations as a	View of children
skills	unhealthy	child	as possessions
	children		Economic
	Single parent		depression
	Poverty		

From Kaufman & Zigler (1989) in D. Cicchetti & Vicki Carlson (Eds), *Child Maltreatment*, p. 169. Reprinted with permission of Cambridge University Press.

of childhood and adulthood (Denzin, 1977). Central to this 'proper concept' is how childhood is defined (Aries, 1962). These policies have a direct bearing on the conditions under which children and families live. As we will see in the next chapter, different societies at different times can have very different ideas on what is the proper treatment of children.

Prevailing political ideology is a major influence on formalising notions of childhood, 'proper' parenting and parenting that falls below standards. The first issue is how a social condition gets defined or 'constructed' as a problem:

> A social problem is a condition which is defined by a considerable number of persons as a deviation from some social norm which they cherish. Every social problem thus consists of an objective condition and a subjective definition. The objective condition is a verifiable situation which can be checked

as to existence and magnitude (proportions) by impartial and trained observers. The subjective definition is the awareness of certain individuals that the condition is a threat to certain cherished values. (Fuller & Myers, 1941, p. 320)

Parton (1985) argues that concepts of ownership, causal responsibility and political responsibility are central to how child abuse has been constructed.

Gusfield (1981) and Wiener (1981) have demonstrated that the concepts of 'ownership' of the problem and 'responsibility' are important in specifying the structure of social problems. 'Ownership of public problems' implies that those who have identified the problem have power and influence; and they command public attention. Owners are crucial to identifying the facts of the problem. Parton would argue (1985) that Kempe in rediscovering child abuse was such a person.

'Causal responsibility' relates to the nature of the explanation given for that problem—the theory espoused to explain it. Hence in the early psychiatric studies, child abuse was explained by a medical model of family pathology and intergenerational transmission of abusive parenting. 'Political responsibility' is about policy and how it should respond to the identified problem.

Political responsibility is also linked to the prevailing ideologies. Although Gil (1970) was able to demonstrate that structural factors, such as poverty, were as important, or more important than individual pathology, in the political climate of the USA and UK, his research largely fell on deaf ears.

If, however, family pathology was responsible for child abuse, the next question is how far could the perpetrators be held responsible for their actions? If, in fact, a crime had been committed then the response should be penal measures. If, however, the perpetrator was 'sick', then they cannot be held responsible. They needed medical treatment.

How the problem is defined within prevailing political ideologies, and the causality given to explain it, are then framed in legal regulations. As Aber and Zigler (1981) suggested, modern societies have come to rely heavily on the law, as well as on the social and health sciences, to solve social problems.

Legal definitions of child maltreatment are used to guide judicial decision making about conditions that require reporting of maltreatment, conditions that warrant coercive state intervention, and conditions that warrant termination of parental rights to custody. Legal definitions provide the mandate for enforcing society's standards for child care. (Hutchison, 1994, p. 7)

Carter (1974) summarises the consequences of alternative child abuse ideologies in Table 3.

Table 3: Alternative child abuse ideologies

	PENAL	MEDICAL	SOCIAL WELFARE	
Framework	Legal	Scientific	Humanistic	
Presupposition	Individual has free will	Behaviour is determined	Traditional	Radical
Definition	Cruelty	Battered Baby Syndrome	Child abuse	Child abuse
Attitude to problem	Punitive: deviance is conscious defiance of rules: moralistic	Results from forces beyond control of individual	Compassionate individual/family cannot cope with situation	Relative but results from social processes
Social rationale	Justice: due process: individual rights	Cure: treatment of needs of the child	Prevention: rehabilitation by adjustment	Social liberation by reorganisation
Focus of attention	Act of abuse: deprivation	Disease process, pathology syndromes	The person: family, social situation 'cycle of deprivation'	Social processes, structural inequality
Tools	Legal code, courts	Medical expertise and technology	Counselling, therapeutic relationships, social experts	Social change
Conception	Responsible	Irresponsible or not responsible	Psychologically, emotionally and socially inadequate	Socially victimised
Stated purpose of	Punishment of guilt	Treatment of dysfunction	Personal, family rehabilitiation physical and emotional safety of child	Equality and redistribution
Some practising	Police, judiciary	Doctors, some psychiatrists	Social workers, some doctors e.g. paediatricians	Some social workers and some sociologists

From J. Carter (1985) in Parton, N. *The Politics of Child Abuse*, p. 17. Basingstoke: Macmillan. Reprinted by permission of Wayland Press.

Differing political climates will then dictate to what extent the possible approaches are acceptable. In the US and the UK, for example, the re-emergence of child abuse has largely coincided with conservative policies espousing individualism and individual responsibility for the family.

The politics of child abuse are also deeply rooted within the traditions of a society. Cooper *et al.* (1995) have illustrated that English society is power-fully shaped by the tradition of *individualism*. Individual rights are para-mount. Our courts are adversarial in order to protect individual rights. In contrast the politics of France since the revolution are focused on *collectiv-ism*. *Liberté, égalité, fraternité* with social education for those whose behaviour falls below acceptable standards so that they may be re-included into society. In many cases justice, especially in child protection issues, is dispensed by negotiation (Cooper *et al.*, 1995).

In the wider world, similar forces are evident. In the fast emerging econ-omies of the Pacific bowl, there is a reluctance to undermine the strong 'filial' tradition of family responsibility by implementing more extensive welfare programmes (Singapore Children's Society 1994).

In the more open climate of post-communist countries, the emergence of social problems, where they had previously been denied, and the re-establishment of individual rights have also led to a reluctance to inter-vene in family life (Maclean & Kurczewski, 1994).

Politics and Social Welfare Policies

Social policies are therefore moulded by these political forces. Models of welfare are closely linked to how these political forces 'construct', or explain the problems and consequently what they do about them. Hard-iker, Exton and Barker (1991) outline some of these models and their consequences on how the state sees the provision of welfare. In the *'residual'* model, the individual or family is seen to carry the burden of providing for all their needs. The family has the right to choose and the duty to provide. Social problems are the result of pathologies within individuals and families. The state as a result only provides the 'basic social minimum' as a last resort or as a safety net. In an *'institutional'* model social problems are seen to result from the faulty functioning of either individuals or social institutions. As a result, the state has a duty to ensure the needs of the most disadvantaged members of society are met. The state discharges its duty by coordinating a mixed economy of welfare in which it plays a significant role. In a *'developmental'* model, individual difficulties arise from the unequal distribution of power and resources in society. The state therefore has a duty to guarantee social rights and accept the predominant responsibility for meeting social needs via universal social services and redistributive social policies. The state actively intervenes to create a fairer and more equal society. The 'radical' model seeks to mount an irrevocable challenge to the existing system, leading to its replacement by a new order. The capitalist state is seen as dominated by the interests of the powerful ruling groups within society. The object of welfare is to work towards social transformation (Hardiker, Exton & Barker, 1991; Titmuss, 1974). Hardiker links these models to how the state seeks to intervene to *prevent* social problems at the primary, secondary, tertiary and quaternary levels. This will be discussed in Part 3.

Other Factors Influencing State Policies

State policies may also be influenced by other less well defined factors. Firstly, the policies do not always have the expected outcomes. Secondly, in non-democratic societies, the population as a whole may not share the values of the legislators. For instance, the Romanian decree in 1966 which banned abortion (Radulian, 1992). Even in democratic societies, there may also be substantial minorities, such as in Northern Ireland, who do not have an effective political voice.

Thirdly, child welfare policies reflect the resources and priorities that a particular society, at a particular time, is able or willing to devote to the future of its children. In the developing world, the main focus will be on survival, and policies that foster healthy babies and children. In an advanced economy, there may be a greater emphasis on the child's emotional health. Policies a country can resource may relate not only to its own economic status but to the prevailing international economy. Even in the relative economic security of the first world, when politicians choose to go to war, or are forced to engage in war to defend their state, the priority a society places on child welfare can change dramatically. Majlajlic (1993) notes, for example, that in Croatia they felt that they had one of the best child welfare systems in the world. With the emergence of conflict, however, there were suddenly 60 000 refugees and no resources to respond to the emergency (Majlajlic, 1993).

Socio-political policies can influence the role of the family and rates of intergenerational maltreatment in a number of ways. Some policies have direct consequences, such as those resulting in war or national disaster, but there are other less obvious policies which can insidiously undermine the role of the family.

More usually, socio-political factors resulting in cycles of child abuse affect families indirectly. They are the consequences of omission. A lack of policies or effective policies to identify and protect children at risk; a lack of policies or lack of effective policies, both nationally and internationally, to respond to the tragedies of street children risking their lives on the streets, or child prostitutes selling their bodies to provide for the essentials of life. This lack of policies may reflect a lack of knowledge on how best to respond to the issues. Economic policies may set priorities whereby thousands of families and young children live on the brink of poverty and hence child abuse; policies or lack of policies whereby women are so debilitated by ill-health or abuse that they cannot protect their young, or policies resulting in direct or indirect discrimination whereby certain racial and ethnic minorities groups are forever kept at the threshold of violence. Such economic policies are not wholly dependent on resources. They relate, as we have discussed, to political constructions, choices and the welfare policies enacted as a result of these politics. The effects of such policies, or lack of policies, are multidimensional, affecting the health, education and future opportunities of both the children themselves and their children in turn.

And yet, however, social problems are constructed, when children are at risk: 'It makes both economic and human sense to protect young children from the worst effects of the mistakes and misadventures of the adult world.' It also makes sense: 'No matter how difficult the circumstances . . . to protect the young if their problems are not to be perpetuated into the next generation' (UNICEF, 1993, p. 56).

DIRECT CONSEQUENCES

War

UNICEF describes a category of children who live in what are termed as 'especially difficult circumstances' (UNICEF, 1990, 1993). Within this category are 1.5 million children who from 1945 to 1990 had died as a direct result of war, a further 4 million children who have been physically disabled, and 10 million who have been psychologically traumatised. Most armed conflicts in recent times have taken place in third world countries. However, in January 1993 the *Sunday Times* estimated that 1.4 million children were victims of the Balkan War alone (Kahan, 1993). Before the First World War, under 10% of deaths and casualties in a war situation related to civilians. In the last decade this figure has jumped to over 75% (UNICEF, 1990).

State policies may lead to war, but industrialised countries allow the provision of over 80% of the military expenditure and 90% of all arms exports (UNICEF, 1993). War leads to child maltreatment in a number of ways. However, such is the paradox of human nature, that even in extreme cases, individual responses and social contexts govern the day (Ayalon & Van Tassel, 1987). Conflicts which span more than 20 years inflict their abuse on successive populations of children. But even shorter conflicts can lead to patterns of child abuse. Studies carried out since the Second World War suggest that war-related trauma is unlikely to heal for at least two generations (Freud & Burlingham, 1943). Richman (1993) notes that psychological effects can resurface after apparent recovery. She also stresses the related secondary consequences of political conflict:

> From the preventive point of view we also need to understand how many of these long term effects are related to secondary consequences of conflict, such as loss of family, inadequate child care, poverty, marginalisation, continued repression, rather than violence per se. (Richman, 1993, p. 1302)

Of necessity, many children of war adopt defiance and violence as a way of life, thus perpetuating the probability of future armed conflict (UNICEF, 1990). These children who have experienced the stress of having lived through conflict, the prospect and reality of death, injury, and emotional brutality are then at risk of inflicting their post-traumatic distress on their own children (Clark, 1992).

War can also override the basic human instinct of the family to ensure the survival of the species, because of some 'higher' need. In recent years, child soldiers are to be found in Beirut, Kampuchea, Ulster, Nicaragua, Iran and Peru (Moorhead, 1989). Cairns (1989), for example, argues that in Northern Ireland, for some families, the common good is more important than the rights of their individual child. Such families cultivate particular cultural values even when this may be threatening the actual physical survival of some, if not all, of their children. They actually encourage their offspring to take part in life-threatening activities. In a conflict spanning more than 20 years, some 150–200 children under the age of 14 have been killed or injured in Northern Ireland (Cairns, 1987). Similarly in the former Yugoslavia, between April and October 1992, 1000 children have been killed (National Children's Bureau, 1992). Those who survive are victims in other ways: psychologically, educationally and economically. The processes can be seen in many societies in conflict. Families pass on their cultural values. Where this is a culture of violence, they may be indoctrinating their children to become victims, and yet they would argue it is all done: 'For the sake of the children if not for the sake of the children's children' (Cairns, 1989, p. 126).

Specific Policies

Specific policies may have unintended consequences. Evidence is growing that children from unwanted pregnancies, following a request for an abortion, do less well than planned children. For the past 20 years researchers in Prague have been undertaking a longitudinal study on children born from unwanted pregnancies. In 1957 abortion in the first three months of pregnancy on medical and social grounds was legalised in Czechoslovakia with about 50 abortions taking place for every 100 births. However, about 2 to 3% of abortion requests were denied by the district commissioners and upheld on appeal. The resulting children have been followed up over 20 years or more. The findings show that the 'unwanted' children have experienced more problems than the comparison group of 'wanted children'. Some of these children have now themselves become parents, and the indicators are that child maltreatment patterns are recurring (Dytrych, 1992). Following the findings from this research the regulations in the Czech Republic relating to abortion have been relaxed.

In Romania, in 1966, 'Decree 770' denied women the right that they had previously enjoyed under the regime of abortion on demand. The policy was deliberately intended to increase the declining population. Previously abortion had been widely used for family planning purposes. Under the decree of 1966, prosecutors, rather than doctors, decided who should have a termination. In most cases it applied only to women over 45 years of age who had had at least four other confinements, or in cases where confinement could represent a risk for the woman. A woman under 45 could find that she had no right to abortion, or indeed any effective family planning even although she may have had numerous children. More serious were the many disabled children who were born after mothers tried to have an illegal abortion. Of those that survived, many children, even when brought up by their families, suffered from diseases of malnutrition and hygiene (Radulian, 1992). Other factors undoubtedly played a part. In the 1960s there were 6 million urban inhabitants in Romania, and 14 million rural inhabitants. Late in 1980 there were 12 million urban inhabitants and 11 million rural inhabitants. Radulian indicates that in radical and rapid transformations the first victims are always the children (Radulian, 1992).

The Romanian situation, in this respect, reflects findings from other areas where socio-cultural and socio-economic change have been shown to have an impact on parent–child relations, increasing the risk for maltreatment (Korbin, 1981, 1991; Hiew, 1992). Radulian also mentions an increase in vagrancy amongst young people, prostitution and drug addiction amongst young people, as well as an increase in the rate of divorce, a third of these divorces taking place before five years of marriage.

With hindsight it is easy to reflect on the outcomes of socio-political policies in areas undergoing rapid change. It is easy to be critical, but how well would British policies stand up under such scrutiny?

100 000 people started the year in Bed and Breakfast and other temporary accommodation in London. Families of four or more children spend 15 months in temporary accommodation on average. Figures also show that homelessness is becoming an increasing problem outside London.

British Youth Council links rising suicide to increasing unemployment and homeless amongst young people. . . .

Centrepoint survey reveals large increase in the number of homeless 16 and 17 year olds. Centrepoint blames withdrawal of income support payments for those under the age of 18.

Campaign for Homeless and Rootless research indicates that four out of ten homeless young women have left home because of sexual abuse. The absence of adequate services for the homeless leads to prostitution and crime.

National Children's Home report estimates almost 100 000 occurrences of children running away each year.
(National Children's Bureau (1992), *Children Now*, extracts pp. 47–53)

In the relative prosperity of the US, similar patterns can be elicited. Estimates of homeless young people in New York have been as high as 12 000 children in the shelter system and 10 000 adolescents on the streets (Alperstein & Arnstein, 1988).

INDIRECT CONSEQUENCES

The Need for Policies to Protect Children

UNICEF notes that for many children in the world today protection is manifestly inadequate (UNICEF, 1993). The United Nations Convention on the Rights of the Child offers a starting point. Nations that both sign and ratify the convention will put their name to Article 19 which states that they will take all appropriate legislative, administrative, social and educational measures to protect the child from all forms of abuse.

Those who have signed have the challenge of applying the principles. At the Third Asian Conference on Child Abuse and Neglect in 1993, it was noted that Asia was home to half of the world's children, and contained the majority of the world's absolute poor (UNICEF, 1989). The problems of abuse, exploitation and prostitution of children in Asia have also been aggravated by rapid social and economic changes. Munir feels that Asian governments have not conscientiously incorporated the welfare of children as an integral part of their economic and social development plans. Children have no political power (Munir, 1993). It is a cultural as well as a political issue made more complicated by the rapid pace of change.

Child Prostitution, Street Children and AIDS

In Thailand, a government survey of child and adolescent development in 1988 reported the number of child prostitutes under 16 years of age in Thailand to be 30 000 (cited in Hiew, 1992). Child prostitution exists on a large scale in many parts of the world. In the Philippines, a conservative estimate by UNICEF of the number of child prostitutes is about 20 000, two-thirds of whom are street children and runaways used by paedophiles (Hiew, 1992). Various laws and international covenants designed to check it have had very little effect. It is estimated that the numbers are increasing, particularly amongst boys. Child prostitution is not confined to South East Asia, but is common in all countries where other forms of prostitution exists. In Western countries, child prostitutes tend to be runaways (Moorhead, 1989); in poorer countries, they tend to be street children who turn to sex as a way of earning their living. Sex tours are advertised in Western travel guides for paedophile and homosexual rings and give advice on how to find a child prostitute and how much to pay him or her. Caroline Moorhead suggests that child prostitution exists because it answers a demand, and in answering that demand many people make a lot of money. Child prostitution is thereby an international responsibility.

There are thought to be some 100 million children living on the streets of the world's cities today (Moorhead, 1989). Street children are not a homogeneous group. Tyler, Tyler, Tommasello and Connolly (1992) interviewed two groups of so-called 'street children' in Bogota, Columbia and in Washington, DC, USA. The Bogota children had generally left their homes and institutions and survived by a combination of legal and illegal activities. In Washington, DC more than two thirds of the children reported that others were responsible for them, including parents, friends, and siblings. Many of the young people were immigrants, some without papers, who although living with relatives or parents were still responsible for themselves (Tyler et al., 1992).

Child prostitutes and street children are particularly vulnerable to the new threat affecting the well-being of children—AIDS—but they are not the only ones to be affected. In countries where there have been no major educative polices the results can be devastating (Kramer, 1992). In Rakai, a county in Uganda of about 300 000 people, AIDS kills the breadwinners and leaves behind the most helpless. It is reported that up to 40 000 children in this county have been orphaned by the disease (Perlez, 1990). The family functioning and structure is threatened by infection and the loss of parents, and the children are usually taken in by less prosperous and ageing grandparents only to fall prey to the disease themselves in their middle years. AIDS demands new measures to protect the well-being of children (Kramer, 1992).

Poverty

The World Health Organisation has underscored the dramatic increase in poverty in the developing countries: 'Absolute poverty traps almost one thousand million people' (WHO, 1987). The risk of disease and disablement is much greater for the poverty-stricken, threatening families with further demands on their limited resources and thus creating even deeper poverty. Poverty's most savage toll is measured in the lives of children. As income declines, family size increases. The prospects for these young people are worse than for their parents. Disease, and lack of proper nourishment, mean that one third of these children die before their fifth birthday. Many of those who survive are physically stunted and mentally impaired (Durning, 1992).

Absolute poverty is rare in the first world, but during the 1980s levels of poverty rose, particularly in the United States, the United Kingdom and Eastern Europe. In the United States, the last decade saw more people living below the poverty line than at any time since the 1960s. In 1987, the Census Bureau reported that 13.6% of all persons in the United States and 22% of all children under the age of six were living below the Poverty Level (US Bureau of Census, 1989). In 1989, it was recorded that 16.2% of *all* families with children lived below the Poverty Level. Kramer (1992) notes that these rates have not shown any marked change since 1981.

In the UK in 1979, 17.9% of all children were living in families with incomes around the Supplementary Benefit level. By 1985 this had risen to 28.6%. Economic trends, demographic changes, fiscal and social policies have been blamed (Bradshaw, 1990).

The correlates of poverty, including stress, drug abuse and inadequate food and medical care, increase the likelihood of maltreatment. Lack of basic skills, educational failure, teenage pregnancy, infant prematurity and low birth weight are also associated both with poverty and with maltreatment (Willis, Holden & Rosenberg, 1992). Lowering poverty rates will not only improve the general well-being of children but will also have an impact on the rates of maltreatment (Kaufman & Zigler, 1993).

The macro-system perspective is helpful in understanding the role of social conditions in intergenerational child maltreatment, but it does not tell the whole story. Nevertheless, because of the very large numbers of children involved, policies that improve the conditions of their parents will also improve the conditions of children and their children in turn.

The Role of Discrimination

'It may be that blacks are in the same boat as whites but we are on different decks' (Grant, 1987, p. 21). Because of their very 'difference', be it religious, cultural or the colour of their skin, different minority groups all over the world suffer from prejudice and discrimination. Although cultural factors have a role to play, the mechanisms that enforce inter-generational second-class citizenship are also socio-political.

In Western societies, quite apart from the daily grind of living with ha-rassment and prejudice, black and other minority and ethnic groups are likely to have the lowest paid jobs, poorest housing, limited opportunities for education and poorer health care (Kramer, 1992). These very condi-tions could increase the risk of child maltreatment.

In the US in 1989, 37% of black families with children lived below the poverty level, compared to 32% of Hispanic and 12% of white. A growing number of these families were headed by single female householders. Amongst such black families the rate was 59.5%, Hispanic 60.7% and white 38.7% (US Bureau of Census, 1989). The stress of being such a householder places these mothers at higher risk of developing an MNP (mental, neurological, psychosocial) disorder (Kramer, 1992).

Poor health care, even under the free National Health Service in the UK, can mean that babies born to minority groups start life at a disadvantage and may therefore be harder to rear. The perinatal mortality rate (PMR) among babies born to women of Asian origin remains 30 to 50% above those born to women of English origin. The incidence of low birth weight babies, congenital abnormalities and maternal complication is also higher (National Children's Bureau, 1992).

It is not surprising that the stresses may result in situations where chil-dren are at risk. Mama notes that there is evidence to suggest that socially oppressive conditions produce more intracommunal violence including wife-beating and other abusive behaviours (Mama, 1989). Difficult social circumstances are likely to exacerbate relationship problems, thereby increasing the likelihood of them degenerating into physical violence (Mama, 1989).

For some minority groups, child maltreatment can result from excessive discipline, as parents become concerned about the 'enculturing' of their offspring in opposition to their own morals and values (Stainton Rogers, 1989). Where family violence does occur, black families in the UK may be more reluctant to ask for help from welfare services; when they do, they may find that help inappropriate to their needs (Swarup & Hayden, 1994).

Differential rates of child abuse have been found between different racial groups living in one county in the USA, but socio-economic status, and whether families live in towns are also important factors (Spearly & Lauderdale, 1983). Single-focus analysis would appear unreliable, as there is evidence that black children are more likely to be diagnosed abused than white (Turbett & O'Toole, 1980).

In the developed world, there is an intergenerational pattern that social factors and discrimination can place black and ethnic minority families in situations of social stress. Nevertheless, the majority of such families do not abuse their children. There is increasing evidence that even with all the difficulties, some young people are very effective in overcoming the effects of prejudice and disadvantage (Simeonsson & Thomas, 1994).

The Role of Women

In most countries today, the girl child has a lower status and enjoys fewer of the rights, opportunities and benefits of childhood than the boy child. The double disadvantage of being born poor and female is vividly illustrated by UNICEF in their booklet *The Girl Child* (1991). The actual figures are strongly suggestive of a child maltreatment epidemic. Not only are there gross inequalities in health care and education but girl deaths are far more common than those for boys (UNICEF, 1991).

Children's well-being and women's well-being are inextricably linked. Women cannot effectively produce and rear healthy babies if they themselves are ill, malnourished, overworked, insecure within their families and treated by society as a disadvantaged group. Figure 1 illustrates the issues. The role of women is linked, as we will see in the next chapter, to violence against women in the home.

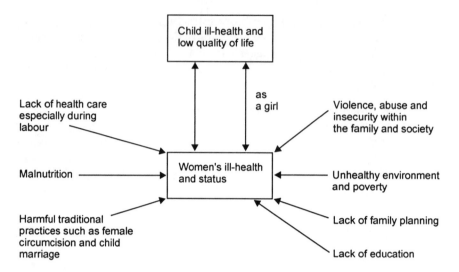

Figure 1: The relationship between the health of children and the health and status of women

From El-Mouelhy, M. (1992) in G. Albee, L. Bond & C. T. Monsey (Eds), *Improving Children's Lives*, p. 84. Reprinted by permission of Sage Publications, Inc.

Even when the law is extremely discriminatory in other ways, most religious and customary legal systems accept physical abuse as grounds for a woman to divorce the perpetrator (Mama, 1989), but to many women, particularly in the third world, this is not a realistic option. In the Western world, where presumably there is a chance of another life, studies of women who have suffered violence in the home paint a picture of amazing endurance. They stay for the sake of the children and yet in many cases children too are the subjects of abuse, and/or experience psychological trauma as a result of enduring their parent being abused (Jaffe, Wolfe & Wilson, 1990).

Lewis, Mallouh and Webb (1989), in a review of research on the links between child abuse, delinquency and violent criminality, illustrate that although most children witnessing family violence do not become violent delinquents, studies of young people involved in violent delinquency show that for some children there may be important links between *witnessing* family violence as a child and later violent acts. The very act of witnessing the family violence may, on its own, act as a mechanism for the transmission of maltreatment.

Linking into these ideas are those from a self-report community study from Dunedin in New Zealand (Mullen *et al.*, 1996). This examined the long-term impact of the physical, emotional and sexual abuse of children.

The similarities between the three forms of abuse in terms of their association with negative adult outcomes were more apparent than any differences. Logistic regression analyses indicated that the associations between abuse and adult difficulties in some cases, though not all, could have been accounted for, not by the abuse itself, but by those factors connected to the increased risks of abuse, that is, the matrix of childhood disadvantage from which abuse so often emerges.

Unintended Consequences from Protection Procedures

The rapid development of knowledge about the causes and consequences of child maltreatment during the 1970s and 1980s led, in developed economies, to a range of policies and procedures and social interventions to protect children. Loseke and Gelles (1993) note that although we did not know what worked, social interventions could not wait until the debates were settled.

In the 1990s, these policies, procedures, interventions and outcomes are being re-evaluated. The uncomfortable result from such findings is that some things that were being done to protect children may not always have been in their best interests.

In the US, following mandatory reporting of child abuse and neglect, and the associated public awareness campaigns, there was a rapid rise in reporting. In 1974 the United States passed the Child Abuse Prevention and Treatment Act (CAPTA), whereby professionals were obliged by statute to report cases of child abuse and neglect. Besharov in 1990 reported that in 40% of states, laws also require citizens to report suspected cases of abuse. It has been suggested that the relative ease with which the initial federal legislation was passed was because child maltreatment was represented as a classless phenomenon and therefore apart from unpopular poverty legislation (Nelson, 1984). Although the legislators intended to limit the legislation to physical abuse, a wider definition was included encompassing mental injury, sexual abuse, negligent treatment or maltreatment (USA Child Abuse Prevention and Treatment Act, 1974).

In 1963, about 15 000 children came to the attention of public authorities because of suspected abuse or neglect. By 1987 it was estimated that 2 178 000 children were reported (Besharov, 1993). Besharov estimates that some 55 to 65% of these reports were 'unfounded', and such unfounded reports are unfair to both children and parents involved. Finkelhor would argue that 'unfounded' does not mean 'false' but rather 'not substantiated' (Finkelhor, 1993).

Such anxieties were further fuelled by parental groups in the US such as VOCAL (Victims of Child Abuse Laws), and in the UK, PAIN (Parents Against INjustice) (Amphlett, 1991), as well as the Family Rights Group (1991).

In the UK, although mandatory reporting was not required (Dingwall, Eekelaar & Murray, 1983), there were the twin dilemmas arising in the 1980s that on one hand some children were not being protected despite the procedures (DHSS, 1982, Study of Inquiry Reports), while on the other hand social workers were overstepping their duties by unnecessarily intervening in family life, for example in the Cleveland Child Care Crisis (Butler Sloss, 1988). In the US, despite federal legislation that requires states to make 'reasonable efforts' to keep families together by providing family-based services (Wisendale, 1993), there was also concern that some children were unnecessarily being removed from their families (Edna McConnell Clark Foundation, 1985).

In the developing world, Gurry has noted: 'Simply sending a child to a welfare home in a developing country represented further abuse' (Gurry, 1993). In the developed world, although many children are fostered, the studies in the UK on Social Work Decisions on Child Care (DHSS, 1985) and Patterns and Outcomes in Child Placement (DoH, 1991b), also raised concerns about the outcomes of children being cared for by the state.

There was evidence that there were difficulties of ensuring placement stability for children who were unable to live at home (Berridge & Cleaver, 1987; Tatara, 1989, 1994). Some children, however, did thrive under 'permanence' planning (Thorburn, Murdoch & O'Brien, 1986; Maluccio & Fein, 1983) and this could be very successful, particularly in some cases of late adoption of children with disabilities (Macaskill, 1985). In the US and UK one of the foremost goals of 'permanence' planning is to achieve 'permanence' within their *own* families by providing family maintenance services but if they cannot live at home, to retain links with the birth family, and to later reunite children in foster care with their birth or extended families. If children are unlikely to be able to return to their families adoption is believed to provide the most permanent of homes (Barth & Berry, 1994).

In the US the rise in child abuse reporting correlated until 1989 with the rise in foster care entry (Barth & Berry, 1994). In 1989, of the more than 800 000 'substantiated' reports, around 250 000 were fostered. By 1992, despite more than 1 million 'substantiated' reports, approximately the same number—250 000 were fostered. Of the 178 000 children who left substitute care during the year 1983, over 56% were discharged to their biological families (Tatara, 1989). However, leaving foster care is becoming slower and less likely (Wulczyn & Goerge, 1992).

Another concern about social interventions in child protection was the growing evidence of weaknesses in the social work decision-making in both the US and UK (Fanshel & Shinn, 1978; Packman, Randall & Jacques, 1986; Vernon & Fruin, 1986), and the difficulties of offering children who could not be fostered a good quality of life in residential care (Berridge, 1985; Tatara, 1994). This was further fuelled by the scandals in residential care in the UK. The Staffordshire Pindown Inquiry highlighted four residential units where children were isolated, and otherwise treated in ways which were 'intrinsically unethical, unprofessional and unacceptable' (Levy & Kahan, 1991). The Williams Report (Williams & McCreadie, 1992) on the Ty Mawr home in Wales investigated reports of physical and emotional abuse. The Leicestershire inquiry (Kirkwood, 1993) investigated the case of Frank Beck who was convicted in 1991 on many charges of abusing children in his care.

In the UK, the Warner Inquiry (1993) in examining the selection, criteria and recruitment methods following the Beck inquiry highlighted that an increasing number of difficult children were being cared for in homes where the staff were largely unqualified. The picture confirmed that much (although not all) residential care in the UK was of poor quality and staff morale was generally low. Despite such concerns, however, there is still a need for high-quality residential care for a core of children, as Cliffe (1990) discovered in the Warwickshire experiment where the last children's home in the county was closed in 1989.

In the US, approximately 30% of children placed outside the home are in group homes or institutions (Howing, Kohn, Gaudin, Kurtz & Wodarski, 1992). Several studies have focused on institutional abuse and neglect of children (Rabb & Rindfleisch, 1985; Rindfleisch & Hicho, 1987). These studies found that few state laws specifically addressed institutional maltreatment. Child protective agencies also showed little awareness of, or interest in, the problem and few workers are trained in investigating institutional maltreatment.

In the UK, the final fire to the flame has come from the 20 research reports recently published by the Department of Health on the *processes* and outcomes of child protection procedures (1995). Some of these studies relate to sexual abuse, which is not the focus of this book. The disquieting finding, however, was that between a quarter and a third of children were known to have been reabused after they came to the notice of the child protection agencies (Cleaver & Freeman, 1995; Farmer & Owen, 1995; Thorburn, Lewis & Shemmings, 1995; Gibbons, Gallagher, Bell & Gordon,

1995). It was also disquieting that a study of outcomes ten years after original registration in the Child Protection system revealed that:

> We could find no evidence that children who were legally protected (by Care or other orders) did significantly better. Nor did those removed from their abusers, and placed in new permanent or long-term families, have significantly better outcomes than those who remained with their original carers. (Gibbons et al., 1995, quoted p. 50, Department of Health, Child Protection, Messages from Research)

These findings suggest that, although some children prospered, a better quality of life could not be guaranteed by 'rescuing' a child to a non-abusing family. There is also the suggestion that the very process of investigation may in some cases be abusive, and that after the investigation children's overall welfare needs are not being met (Sharland, Seal, Croucher, Aldgate & Jones, 1993; Thorburn, Lewis & Shemmings, 1995). In the UK the dilemma may be, because of media pressure among other factors, that there has been an overfocus on child protection investigative strategies and an underfocus on family support and family preservation. The research report published by the Department of Health (1995) suggests the need to move the *thresholds* of child protection investigations, and develop further strategies that promote *the overall* well-being of children by providing more family support. These moves are echoed in the USA:

> There is an urgent need in the United States for a comprehensive family policy that supports rather than controls caregivers and for an improvement in general social services . . . [this] would assist families to respond in more nurturing ways to children's needs while not eliminating the necessity for protective services. (Hutchison, 1994, p. 23)

It cannot, therefore, be assumed, without *monitoring outcomes*, that everything that is done in the name of protecting children will, indeed, promote their welfare.

THE NEED FOR A POSITIVE APPROACH

In this chapter it has been possible to give only a broad overview of how socio-political factors affect intergenerational patterns of child maltreatment. There is considerable support for the theories outlined earlier. These theories help to explain why family violence in its sociological context occurs, but they do not necessarily offer appropriate, or even possible solutions. As Munir says, countless children around the world are exposed to dangers that hamper their growth and development. The protection of children requires a framework and standard agreed by the world (Munir, 1993), but it is important that by monitoring outcomes, we know that these frameworks do indeed promote the welfare of children.

In an international context, the danger is that the sheer size of the problem leads to a feeling of hopelessness. Here too, rather than focusing on maltreatment maybe we need to focus on promoting the welfare of specific children and families who are at risk. Promoting the welfare of children and families across generations is both a national and an international challenge and calls for national and international action. Better monitoring of social programmes and social outcomes will demonstrate our successes as well as our failures, increase our knowledge base, and encourage positive action to break into the cycles of child maltreatment. Possible strategies to achieve this will be discussed in the second half of this book.

SUMMARY: SOCIO-POLITICAL MECHANISMS IN INTERGENERATIONAL CHILD MALTREATMENT

- It cannot be assumed that mechanisms of transmission involve family pathology
- The function of the family is altered by external forces
- Families need 'permitting circumstances' in order to parent effectively
- Social factors profoundly influence the effectiveness of the family and child-rearing
- Politics and policies have a direct bearing on the conditions under which child and family live
- Politics and policies in each country define, to some extent, notions of 'appropriate' parenting
- Politics influence the extent and type of welfare provision
- Policies in each country reflect the availability of resources and define priorities
- Policies can have unintended consequences
- Families also suffer from lack of appropriate policies to support them in their parenting task
- Some policies directly result in conditions where families are unable to parent effectively
- Other policies directly lead to a child living in 'especially difficult circumstances'
- The international community indirectly fosters some of these circumstances

- Some specific issues are: the role of poverty, discrimination, and the role of women
- Lack of policies can leave children unprotected
- It cannot be assumed that all child protection policies necessarily ensure a better quality of life for children

4

CULTURAL FACTORS IN INTERGENERATIONAL CHILD MALTREATMENT

Spare the rod and spoil the child
(Traditional saying)

Parents around the world are faced with a similar task when rearing children. In all societies the helpless infant must be protected from the risks threatening survival and turned into a responsible adult obeying the rules of his or her community.

> Children born in diverse cultures appear to enter the world with similar endowments. Both as elicitors and actors, they share panhuman characteristics that equip them for survival. . . . yet cultural forces do modulate social development and lead to increasing differences in the kinds of behaviour which adults expect in children, which they give children the most opportunity to practice, and which they make meaningful to them in terms of central cultural goals and values. (Whiting & Edwards, 1988, p. 266)

These cultural patterns of child-rearing are passed from generation to generation (Whiting & Edwards, 1988; Levinson, 1989). Although intergenerational child maltreatment is the result of complex interactions within and without the family, cultural factors have an important part to play. Just as parents need 'permitting (social and environmental) circumstances' in order to rear children effectively, cultural factors can be the 'permitting circumstances' which for one reason or another can result in, or condone, pain and suffering for children.

Culture comprises a number of elements including religion, different concepts of childhood and parenting, different practices associated with these concepts, and different values attached to particular children (Korbin, 1987).

Culture exerts a powerful influence on parental behaviour (EPOCH-WORLDWIDE, 1992), but this influence, although transcending the generations, is not static. History is evidence that concepts relating to the proper treatment of children can change within cultures over time. If we are to break intergenerational patterns of child maltreatment, we need to understand the meaning of these cultural factors and the mechanisms involved in change.

This chapter starts by examining the social construction of childhood, as well as the changing concepts of good-enough parenting, and the factors across societies that influence these changes. It will then consider risks faced by children across cultures, but will argue that if we are to move from a position of ethnocentricism, we need to understand the context in which child maltreatment, if that is what it is, occurs. The controversies surrounding differential rates of child maltreatment by ethnicity within Western world societies will also be discussed. In the final section, the chapter will conclude with some of the messages from the research, and some of the dilemmas posed.

The aim, in this chapter, is to highlight the central themes rather than give a comprehensive account of all the research. Three broad categories of literature have been used. Firstly, cross-cultural anthropological studies and reviews by anthropologists on parenting behaviour and family violence. Although there is a growing interest in anthropological studies of family violence, because child maltreatment is a low base rate behaviour, studies in this area have been limited. This section will, therefore, draw heavily on the work of Korbin and Levinson. Secondly, this chapter will highlight socio-medical studies and reviews on child abuse and ethnic differences from the Western world and thirdly, examples will be given from small-scale socio-medical studies internationally. All these approaches have their methodological limitations. Anthropological research generally focuses on the regularities of culture rather than on the departures from normative behaviour. Traditionally anthropologists spend approximately one full year observing a society, and during this time span, it may not be possible to gather more than anecdotal data on relatively uncommon behaviours such as child maltreatment. It is, in addition, often difficult to obtain systematic cross-cultural comparisons from ethnographic data. (Levinson, 1989; Korbin, 1991). Thirdly, traditional socio-medical research may be more systematic, but much of this has originated from industrialised societies who do not constitute a sufficient sample from which to draw conclusions about all of human behaviour. The growing number of interesting studies from other parts of the world are still, as yet, mostly small-scale and localised.

THE SOCIAL CONSTRUCTION OF CHILDHOOD

As we have seen, every nation with a distinct cultural identity attempts to formalise what they consider to be a proper concept of childhood (Denzin, 1977). These concepts become social constructions; different social realities or world views, which imply different taken-for-granted ground rules. The more distant people are from one another in terms of historical time, geographical location, culture or class, the more likely they are to have different social realities (Berger & Luckmann, 1967; Stainton Rogers, 1992). Social constructionists would also claim that the child and childhood have no existence independent of a person's way of thinking, and it is their very actions which bring them into being.

Historical Constructions of Childhood

Childhood, as distinct from infancy, adolescence or young adulthood, was unknown in historical periods (Aries, 1962). Young boys dressed as little versions of their fathers, they played as their fathers 'and were hung by their neck' like their fathers (Illich, 1973). Stainton Rogers (1992) argues that the fact that we no longer burn children as witches or brand them as vagrants is not the work of the social reformers, it is the result of a whole society constructing a new social reality about children and childhood.

At the turn of the century, a trade catalogue advertised *appareils contre l'onaisme* for both boys and girls in silver or metal (Stainton Rogers, 1989). Medical opinion at that time taught that self-abuse or masturbation caused a range of physical and mental problems including insanity (Szasz, 1970; Mountjoy, 1974). Given such 'a reality', it was understandable that parents would seek to find an effective way to protect their young. That we might view using such a device as abuse of the child, is evidence that our social reality has changed.

Historically, children reflecting the social constructions of their time have been severely ill-treated and even killed. In many cases these maltreatments have been condoned and permitted by the society in which they lived (Radbill, 1968). Lloyd de Mause (1974) in a Western history of childhood, suggests the child was a permanent reminder of original sin.

A whole area of history is concerned with social constructions of children and families and the resultant theories of childcare (Aries, 1962). In recent years Freud's theories and Bowlby's concept of maternal deprivation have fed what has been known as the *mal-de-mère* syndrome, or everything that happens to a child is the fault of the mother. These constructions may in turn feed into social policy; for example, giving in the last 30 years in the UK, a low profile to nursery schooling (Jackson, 1993). One of the dangers is that these theorists can also be accused of constructing ethnocentric notions which presuppose the superiority of their American middle-class rearing practices.

The central message from the different historical constructions of childhood is that there are intergenerational continuities and discontinuities in how children should be treated. Past 'realities' can change over time. We need to understand why these constructions existed, and what caused them to change. Further clues on what the mechanisms were can be gained from recent cross-cultural analyses.

Cross-cultural Constructions

Behaviour that is acceptable in one culture, is deemed unacceptable in another. The concept of 'badness' is culturally bound. The same parental behaviour in one society may have quite different meanings in another. The examples often cited are, firstly, the Turkish practice of calming babies by rubbing their genitals, which might be felt to be sexual abuse in another society, and secondly, the Western practice of putting babies alone into cots, which could be seen as grossly rejecting in some third world societies. Differing methods of birth control also excite controversy. Infanticide as a method of family planning is abhorrent to the Western world, yet foeticide (abortion) is widely practised. Different human groups vary in how they define life.

Lynch points out that the recognition by physicians of child abuse as a social problem long pre-dates Kempe. In AD 900 a Persian physician noted that an 'infant may have been struck accidentally', and Soranus warned of the dangers of the wet nurse (Lynch, 1985).

Despite the long recognition of child abuse, there is less agreement cross-culturally on what actually constitutes child maltreatment. Every society has to develop concepts of 'good-enough parenting' and controls against parenting that falls below the accepted norms because its very survival depends upon this, but these concepts can also vary within the larger society, between classes, between communities, and even between streets. This is vividly illustrated in the Newsoms' (Newson & Newson, 1965) study of child-rearing practices in the United Kingdom. Research from Quinton, Rutter and Liddle (1984), also in the UK, has shown that cultural traditions also influence the wider scene which in turn influences patterns of parenting; for example, when a young person marries, at what age they have children, what type of relationship they have with their partners, and consequent upon all this, what type of relationship they have with their children. Anthropological studies are particularly interesting, because they offer useful observations on different types of parenting and the possible reasons for these differences.

PARENTING CROSS-CULTURALLY

Mothers and other caregivers throughout the world have the task of ensuring the future of the society. In every society the tasks are broadly similar (Whiting & Edwards, 1988). The carer must:

(1) See to physical well-being of children by attention to nutritional and other health needs and protect from discomfort and harm.
(2) Relieve from anxiety and fear by offering emotional comfort.
(3) See the infant learns sphincter control and proper hygiene.
(4) Help the child learn the culturally approved forms of etiquette and norms of social behaviour.
(5) Teach child skills in the early years. (Whiting and Edwards, 1988, pp. 86–87)

Since many of these behaviours and skills are prerequisites for acceptance and survival as a viable member of society the behaviour of caretakers the world over is broadly similar. Different societies, however, have different patterns for living. Some important factors are differences in household composition, gender patterns of workload, available support networks and beliefs about the nature of children. These factors all crucially influence how different societies seek to modulate the behaviour of their young (Whiting & Edwards, 1988). These modulations relate to their particular circumstances, and may be important at one end of the scale to ensure basic survival, or at the other to improve the quality of life.

Whiting and Edwards, in studies of 12 societies, highlight three profiles of maternal behaviour and illustrate how these appear to be related to ecological constraints on the mothers. They observed 23 maternal behaviours, coded them and then allocated them into five categories: nurturing, training, controlling, socialising, responding. An analysis was then made between the different societies to see how often training, controlling and socialising maternal behaviour occurred. Mothers in sub-Saharan agriculturalist communities used the most training behaviours. Children from an early age were taught how to undertake household tasks, gardening, animal husbandry skills. Mothers in Negaca, for example, punished their children for failure to perform these tasks responsibly or for refusing to do what their elders asked of them. Much of the training was through observation and imitation, often of older siblings. 'In general the polite command' was the most common style used by such parents but these commands might be imbued by explaining why such action was necessary. Whiting and Edwards suggest that *training* is important where mothers undertake workloads over and above household tasks. The training mothers are major producers of food for the family. In general these mothers expect more help from their children and consequently demonstrate more training maternal behaviour.

Mothers who used most *controlling* behaviour had a different set of needs. Whiting and Edwards demonstrate that these mothers lived in situations of social density, for example in the extended-family households of North India. In these households as many as 24 people may live together. The one way the mothers appear to cope with the noise and confusion of the large household is through a relatively dominant style of dealing with their children. Another factor may also be important. In contrast to the sub-Saharan mothers, there is greater sharing of workloads with husbands and other women within the house, and in general these families did not work outside the home. In effect there is less need to train children as the workload is shared between adults. However, in the densely populated homes, there is a greater need to control the children. Children have fewer specific tasks to do, and are therefore constantly underfoot and playing in areas where adults are trying to work and to talk to one another. Mothers feel responsible for socialising their children but are less specific about what they teach, and therefore constant reprimands to the children are common.

The third type of maternal profile observed was the *socialising* mother. These mothers, for example in Orchard Town in the USA, were residentially the most isolated and spent most of their day in the company of their young children. Generally they did not work outside the home, and had comparatively few household tasks to perform. These mothers relied on their children more for social interaction than for help with the work. Orchard Town mothers treated their children at times as if they were their status equal.

Whiting and Edwards also illustrate that children's age and sex have a strong influence in determining the kinds of behaviour that they elicited from their mothers. In most societies, girls are more likely to elicit training behaviours from their mothers, while boys are more likely to elicit controlling behaviour. Different ages in children similarly elicit different types of behaviour from mothers but these characteristics in the children are modulated by the existing maternal profiles of that society.

Cultural differences are also seen in the way mothers encourage or limit the expression of their children's wants and demands. In cultures where mothers engage in relatively high levels of controlling behaviours they encourage their children to express their needs in dominant/aggressive modes.

These anthropological studies give clues on how ecological settings, as long as they remain static, influence intergenerational cultural patterns of parenting, and indirectly of abuse. Cross-cultural studies also give interesting insights into patterns of family violence.

FAMILY VIOLENCE CROSS-CULTURALLY

Children around the world are at risk from a wide variety of violence which is generally carried out by their parents or with their parents' tacit approval. In Levinson's study of 90 societies, he charts a lifespan perspective of potential family violence, highlighting ways that family members have been known to harm or allow others to harm members of their family. Most types of culturally condoned violence directed at children occur only in a few societies. The major exception is the use of physical punishment in child-rearing and fighting between siblings. (Levinson, 1989).

The sheer number and variety of family violence types listed in Table 4 indicates that family violence of one form or another is something that is witnessed or experienced by most human beings at some point in their lives.

Infants

Although infanticide is reported as occurring in 78.5% of the 90 societies studied, in all of these societies it only occurs rarely (Divale & Harris, 1976; Whyte, 1978). Infanticide is not carried out lightly. It is usually performed by the mother or another relative in a situation where there appears to be no other choice. Infanticide can be a mechanism through which societies dispose of infants whose birth or condition makes them a liability to the family or social group. The infant may pose a threat to the family because he or she is illegitimate, or is the result of rape, is deformed, is unusual—such as a twin birth—or is unwanted. Between 40 and 50% of Levinson's societies permitted infanticide in such circumstances. An infant may be unwanted when of the wrong sex (16% of societies) or because the care of existing children could be hampered by the presence of additional children (Langer, 1974; Granzberg, 1973). Infanticide of girls has a further role in controlling population because they

Table 4: Types of family violence in a life-span perspective

Infants
      infanticide
      sale of infants for sacrifice
      binding body parts (head, feet and so on)
      force feeding
      hard disciplinary techniques
Childhood
      organized fighting promoted by adults
      ritual defloration
      physical punishment
      child marriage
      child slavery
      child prostitution
      drugging with hallucinogens
      parent–child homicide/suicide
      child labour
      sibling fighting
      nutritional deprivation
      corporal punishment in schools
      mutilation for begging
      child pawning
Adolescence
      painful initiation rites (circumcision, superincision, cliterodectomy, scari-
      fication, etc.)
      forced homosexual relations
      physical punishment
      gang rape of girls
Adulthood
      killing young brides
      forced suicide by young brides
      wife-beating
      husband-beating
      husband–wife brawling
      matricide
      patricide
      forced suicide of wives
      wife raiding
      marital rape
      parent-beating
      co-wife-fighting
      sister-beating
Old Age
      forsaking the aged
      abandonment of the aged
      beating the aged
      killing the aged
      forcing the aged to commit suicide

From Levinson, D. (1989), *Family Violence in Cross-cultural Perspective*, p. 26. Reprinted by permission of Sage Publications, Inc.

will not then reproduce. It also has a role in polygynous societies as a means of balancing the sex ratio.

Sale of infants for sacrifice is very rare. In most societies, the excruciating pain caused to the infant from the binding of body parts, such as the feet in China, is now a thing of the past, but in a few societies body binding is still acceptable and even expected by other members of the society (Levinson, 1989). With girls this may be seen to enhance their beauty and future value as a bride.

Childhood

Physical punishment is the most common form of culturally condoned violence to children. Levinson indicates that it occurs in 74% of his 90 societies, but the frequency with which it is used varies. Physical punishment is only used regularly in 13.3% of these societies, frequently in 21.1%, infrequently in 40% and rarely or never in 26.5%.

In the UK there is the common law defence of 'reasonable chastisement' against charges of cruelty to children. Newell, a member of the working party set up by the Gulbenkian Foundation to look at comprehensive protection of children in all settings, and others would argue: 'The built-in concept of "reasonable chastisement" has continued to permit a high level of violence and humiliation to children in their homes and in institutions' (Gulbenkian Foundation, 1993, p. 20). Levinson (1989) feels that another common form of violence, that of fighting between siblings, may be underreported in ethnographic literature. In societies where older children have an important role in caring for younger siblings, it is likely they will model their parents' child-rearing patterns. In the UK and USA there is growing evidence that the abuse most feared by children is that of bullying. This too can have a cultural component, as is evidenced from stories of life in British public schools in the last century. Patterns of bullying behaviour can occur within the family, within institutions and schools, and children with special needs can be especially at risk (Commission for Racial Equality, 1988; La Fontaine, 1991; Finkelhor, 1992; Buchanan et al., 1993; Rivers & Smith, 1994; Morrison, Furlong & Smith, 1994).

Adolescence

Adolescence as a distinct developmental stage is largely a Western phenomenon. In developing countries, the marking of adulthood often involves the pain of initiation ceremonies. Initiation ceremonies are prevalent in 55% of Levinson's societies. In 47% of these, painful procedures will be involved, such as scarification, tattooing, tooth extraction and other activities to change appearance, whippings, cold baths, forced starvation, and similar activities, as part of the training operation. Genital operations such as clitoridectomy for girls and subincision for boys can be carried out by the adults in the community with the support of the child's family. In such societies, parents could be said to have no choice. Their child cannot function as an adult without going through such procedures.

It is also relevant, perhaps as an example of Western duplicity, that although the Prohibition of Female Circumcisions Act 1985 makes this illegal in the UK, non-medical male circumcision is legally and culturally acceptable. It is estimated that around 10 000 girls in the UK are at risk of one form or another of female circumcision (Lewis, 1991). Both boys and girls undergoing circumcision operations can bleed to death, experience post-operative shock, or suffer from unsterilised instruments. With girls there is the additional risk that menstrual blood trapped by too small a hole can collect in the abdomen, causing it to swell. There are tales of young girls being killed because it was believed they were pregnant. Sex and childbirth can also be difficult as a result. Bruce-Chwatt (1976) in discussing the relevance of the medically indefensible female circumcision amongst the African Kikuyu, quotes a passage from Kenyatta's studies of Kikuyu life and custom (1938):

> The real argument lies not in the defence of the surgical operation or its details but in the understanding . . . that the operation is still regarded as the very essence of an institution which has enormous educational, social, moral and religious implications, quite apart from the operation itself. (Kenyatta, 1938, quoted in Bruce-Chwatt, 1976, p. 47)

Whether it is male or female circumcision, or any other initiation rites, parents may feel they have no choice, but in many societies parents do not feel they have to inflict pain in order for their children to become adult.

The Importance of Cross-cultural Analyses of Family Violence

Levinson's study is useful because he shows the relationship between different types of family violence—wife beating, child punishment, sibling aggression, husband-beating and infanticide. He noted a significant correlation between wife-beating, child punishment and sibling aggression.

He concludes that this does not bear directly on the intergenerational transmission hypothesis, but does provide indirect support for its validity:

> If the intergenerational hypothesis were entirely without merit, we would expect to find no relationships between these five types of family violence at the societal level. That there are statistical relationships among some of the variables suggests that there may well be both a cultural patterning of family violence as well as a cyclical pattern of intergenerational transmission in families of those societies. (Levinson, 1989, p. 37)

THE THEORETICAL BACKGROUND: *EMIC–ETIC* PERSPECTIVES

There is a need to find a humane standard for the treatment of all children, but this cannot be undertaken by adopting a Western ethnocentric perspective which catalogues a list of practices considered to be maltreatment. Korbin (1981) talks about the need for an *emic* perspective, that is the perspective that comes from within, or what might be called a society's 'social construction'. She also talks about the need for an *etic* perspective, that which comes from looking from outside, where particular behaviours, for example, are viewed in an international context. *Emic–etic* theories were first used by linguists to make a distinction between phonetics and phonemics (Smith & Bond Harris, 1993). While phonetics has to do with the universal properties of spoken sound, phonemics concerns the ways in which such sounds are formulated within the context of particular words and languages. Berry (1969, 1989) argues that many attempts to replicate US studies in other parts of the world can be classified as 'imposed *etic*'. That is, there is an assumption that the situation being studied has the same meaning to the new participants as it did in those settings where the measures were originally derived. Further discussion on the *emic* and *etic*, the insider and outsider perspective, is highlighted in a recent book by Headland, Pike, and Harris (1990).

Korbin suggests that in analysing practices which could be construed as maltreatment, there is a need to be aware of both *emic* and *etic* approaches and their potential for both agreement and disagreement. Not infrequently, cultural rationalisation of harmful behaviour is accepted blindly as proof that this treatment is neither harmful or abusive.

Korbin (1981, 1987, 1991) suggests three levels in formulating culturally appropriate definitions of child maltreatment.

(1) *Cultural differences in child-rearing practices and beliefs.* These are practices which are viewed as acceptable in the culture where they occur
but as abusive and neglectful by outsiders. Here there will be disagreement between the *emic* and *etic* perspective.
(2) *Idiosyncratic departures from one's cultural continuum of acceptable behaviour to children.* While all societies differ in what they define as
maltreatment, all societies have criteria for behaviour that is outside
the range of acceptability. Here there is likely to be some agreement
between the *emic* and the *etic* perspective.
(3) *Societal harm to children.* This relates to conditions such as poverty,
lack of material resources, health care and nutrition which seriously
compromise the well-being of children and yet are beyond individual
parental control.

The starting point must be to come to an internationally acceptable definition of what is, or is not, child abuse. Considerable dilemmas are posed in
coming to such a decision. Answers will have to be found to the following
questions. What, for example, is the spectrum of caretaker behaviour
accepted by different cultures? When does a caretaker act exceed the
cultural continuum of acceptability? What is more important in determining whether an act is abusive—the caretaker behaviour or the consequence to the child? How much overlap exists among cultures? These
dilemmas will be examined in depth in Chapter 9.

One of the major contributions from cross-cultural research has been the
insight it has given us to the types and categories of children who are at
risk of maltreatment, and the conditions in which they are likely to be
abused. Finkelhor and Korbin (1988) list the following categories of vulnerable children.

Vulnerable Children

These are children who are not valued for their economic utility, for
perpetuating the family line and cultural heritage and/or as sources of
emotional pleasure and satisfaction. Such children are at risk of a range
of physical and/or sexual abuse, neglect and even death. Vulnerable
children may be those with an *inferior health status* to their siblings. In a
study in the UK by Buchanan and Oliver (1977), children with disabilities, especially those with marginal disabilities, were at a greater
risk of maltreatment than children without disabilities. In poorer communities in developing countries, sickly children may be considered
'too risky for substantial caretaking investment' (Korbin, 1991).

Malnourished children who fail to elicit the necessary parental care may also be at risk and this can be reinforced by cultural beliefs. Related to this, the care of *deformed or handicapped children* varies between cultures. In some societies, such children are protected as they are seen to hold supernatural gifts. More usually they are regarded as a burden and unworthy of protection. Similarly *excess or unwanted children* who stress family resources may be subject to maltreatment. *Children born under unusual, stigmatised or difficult circumstances* may increase their risk of maltreatment. In certain cultures, unusual births are seen as an ill omen with the resultant effect on parental care. Different *developmental stages* may mean children are at greater or lesser risk of maltreatment. Toddlers and adolescents may be especially at risk but this, as we have discussed earlier, may relate to the type of living arrangement within the society. Toilet training is another developmental stage which can bode ill for a child, but again, not in all societies (Buchanan, 1992). Cultural beliefs about *gender* can in many countries compromise the health and survival of the girl child (UNICEF, 1991), while in Greece higher expectations for the boy can place him at risk of physical abuse (Agathonos-Georgopoulou, 1992). Particular *behaviours and personality* types in children may be devalued or undervalued but there is inconsistency between cultures. For example, among the Yanomamo aggressiveness is highly valued, but similar behaviour amongst the Machiguenga in young children would be disapproved of (Finklehor & Korbin, 1988). *Children with socially diminished supports* are also at risk. In a study in East Africa children born out of wedlock accounted for 2.5% of the population but 25% of the malnourished children. Similarly children from intertribal marriages were at risk (Finklehor & Korbin, 1988). In a number of cultures, *stepchildren* are at risk as are children without parents.

The Protective Role of Networks

It is hard to make generalisations about vulnerable children across societies, because where societies have good social networks and a community pattern of rearing this can decrease the risk to these children. Social networks offer assistance with child care; children at risk of abuse from their parents can be redistributed within the community. If child care is a shared responsibility there is likely to be greater consensus concerning the acceptable boundaries of child-rearing methods and goals. In contrast to this community pattern of rearing is the social isolation seen amongst mothers in the West which can place children at risk of maltreatment (Roberts, 1988).

The Effect of Social Change

In situations of rapid socio-economic change, many traditional values and practices, as well as the supportive network which may have in the past protected children from the extremes of abuse, may no longer be there (Korbin, 1981). As families adjust from rural to urban status, children may no longer be *producers* but *consumers*. Through school, immigrant children learn to become less compliant and their new knowledge increases the opportunities for parent–child conflict. Families may also be isolated from their kin. Without traditional protective practices, children may suffer maltreatment which may have intergenerational affects. Change can be positive as well as negative (Korbin 1991). In a 20-year perspective on an Indian community, Minturn (1982) found that improvements in locally available medical care promoted the survival and health of female children. Although boys were still favoured, if health care was readily and easily available, girls benefited. Korbin (1991) summarises the effects of socio-economic change as follows:

> Change may eradicate cultural practices perceived as abusive from outside the culture in question, but increase idiosyncratic maltreatment. Painful practices such as initiation rites or footbinding may be eradicated, but in the absence of protective networks, children may be more vulnerable to physical or sexual assault by their parents. (Korbin, 1991, p. 74)

Levinson, in considering the wider remit of family violence, also considers this issue (Levinson, 1989). His central conclusion is that structural features alone do not cause family violence but they do affect family violence. For example, where children immigrate into complex socio-economic systems, they are more likely to be physically chastised because there will be a greater need for them to be obedient and compliant.

The Relevance of Theories to Explain Family Violence in a Cross-cultural Context

Levinson's main focus in his analysis of 90 societies was to consider whether there was empirical support for existing theoretical perspectives which are associated with family violence. Some of these perspectives were outlined in Chapter 2.

Resource theory, as we have seen, depends on the idea that decision-making power in family relationships lies in the value of resources each person brings to the relationship. Where men control the economic resources, they hold the decision-making power. Levinson found male dominance was a powerful predictor of wife-beating frequency. Wife-beating was significantly associated with physical punishment of children.

Exchange theory, as outlined by Gelles' work (1983), suggests that people will use violence to achieve their goals, because there are inadequate social controls in their societies to inhibit or prevent them. At the cross-cultural level, Levinson found a more complex picture. It was economic inequality rather than sexual inequality and a tradition of violent conflict resolution which allowed men (at low cost to themselves) to hit their wives (and children). He found less evidence of the effect of socially isolated nuclear families but this may be because of sample bias.

Culture of violence theory is related to the norms and values within a society or micro-society which emphasise/permit physical violence. There are wide-ranging differences between societies and micro-societies on the levels of violence seen. Levinson, however, showed that in societies where extrafamilial violence was acceptable, this did not necessarily predict intrafamilial violence. However, if more complex urban societies had been included in his sample this might have led to a different conclusion.

Patriarchal theory indicates that in male-dominated societies where women are classified as possessions of men, men will use violence to control women and children. Although it was only possible to test limited aspects of the theory, Levinson found that economic inequality, male decision-making and restrictions on the freedom of women to divorce their husbands, strongly predicted family violence.

Social learning theory suggests that children learn violent behaviours by observation, experience, or modelling their behaviour on that of those immediately around them. Where a society requires obedient, compliant children, there will be more physical punishment of children. Similarly siblings caring for young children will model their care on that of their parents. Levinson's work demonstrated each form of family violence was generally associated with other forms. This indirectly supports the inter-generational transmission theory.

Under *ecological theory* family violence is explained by the links between intrafamilial factors and extrafamilial factors within the wider ecological framework. Children are, therefore, more likely to be at risk of child maltreatment in societies where families are socially isolated or where their belief system legitimates violence against children. Levinson found considerable evidence of the interaction between what occurs at a societal level and what occurs in the family setting.

Three further theories were consider by Levinson. Firstly he considers *evolutionary theory*. As human societies change over time, they follow an evolutionary pattern from the simple to the complex. Settlements become larger and more densely populated, social and economic equality becomes more pronounced, families become smaller. Caretakers in a more complex society often use physical violence as a means of rearing children to be obedient, compliant, and responsible. There was some evidence of this process in his analysis.

Finally Levinson tested Straus's (1980) *general systems theory,* which suggests that family violence is the product of interlinking systems at the individual, family and societal levels for cross-cultural analysis. From this he developed a simplified version of Straus's model to explain wife-beating in a cross-cultural perspective (Figure 2).

Levinson concludes that family violence is less common in societies in which family life is characterised by cooperation, commitment, sharing and equality. From his 90 societies he found 16 where there was little or no family violence. These 16 societies were representative of all seven major geographical regions of the world, and representative of a range of economic systems (Hunter-gatherers, horticulturalists, herders, agriculturalists). Levinson's work gives important indicators to some of the mechanisms behind intergenerational patterns of child maltreatment. However, a major limitation of his work is that few complex inner-urban societies were included. In his work he is also dealing with generalities rather than specifics. The following section is based on socio-medical studies from individual societies, and highlights more specific mechanisms in the transmission of cultural patterns of patterning.

THE PROCESS OF 'DISCOVERING' CHILD ABUSE

'Child abuse' arose as a label of consequence in the United States in the early 1960s. . . . Questions inevitably arose as to whether child abuse was universal or unique to the United States. Attention first focused on societies most similar to the United States as European nations underwent similar transformations from initial denial that child maltreatment existed within their boundaries to a recognition of its multiple manifestations. Repeated experience with nations that first denied the existence of child abuse only to 'discover' it, promoted skepticism that child abuse and neglect could be absent anywhere. (Korbin, 1987, p. 31)

Throughout the 1980s there was a growing recognition that child abuse existed in all societies to a lesser or greater degree (Korbin, 1987; Ikeda, 1982; Mejiuni, 1991; Kokkevi & Agathonos, 1987); that child abuse was

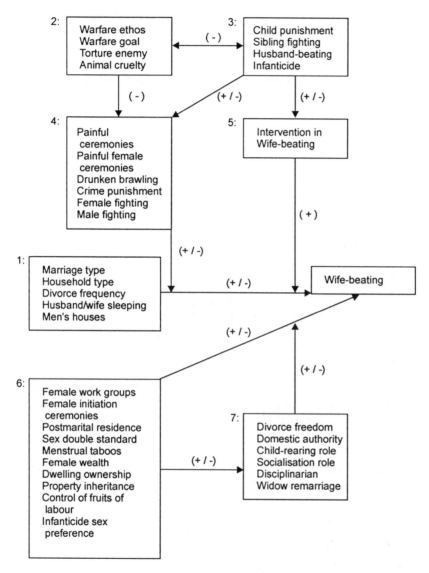

Figure 2: The Straus model in cross-cultural perspective
From Levinson, D. (1989), *Family Violence in Cross-cultural Perspective*, p. 86.
Reprinted by permission of Sage Publications, Inc.

not a new phenomenon (Lynch, 1985), and that specific cultural factors in addition to social and individual psycho-pathology were important in perpetuating a cycle of maltreatment (Mejiuni, 1991; Kokkevi & Agathonos, 1987). The dilemma of definition, in what was, and what was not, child abuse is vividly illustrated by the studies, as well as the related dilemma in deciding the priorities for intervention. At much the same time there was a growing literature on minority groups living in a dominant culture: their parenting styles, their concepts of abuse and their cultural adaptation to the new environment (Spearly & Lauderdale, 1983; Reid, 1984; Gray & Cosgrove, 1985; Lauderdale, Valiunas & Anderson, 1980). These studies give interesting clues on how cultural patterns change for better or worse in adjusting to the new cultural environment, and the mechanisms of this change process.

The Process of Recognition

The first mechanism for change is the recognition that child abuse is a problem for a particular society.

> There are many myths about child abuse in Japan. Many Japanese along with foreigners tend to think that there is no child abuse in Japanese culture because the family ties are still strong and parents tend to overprotect and overindulge their children. (Ikeda, 1982, p. 487)

The denial of child maltreatment also affects professionals:

> Culturally defined attitudes towards parental roles contributed to the strong resistance, not only of the general public but of the professionals as well, in recognising that appropriate parenting is not an infallible innate attribute of all parents. (Kokkevi & Agathonos, 1987, p. 94)

In the process of recognition, mass media play an important role. Although there is nothing new about child abuse, in the United States it was not until Kempe shocked both the public and the professionals with his images of the classless 'battered baby syndrome', that necessary action followed. The potential 'classlessness' of Kempe's original maltreated child was important in combating suppositions that child abuse was limited to 'multi-problem' families. In other countries around the world, the press have been equally important, for example Mejiuni (1991) in Nigeria, Ikeda (1982) in Japan and Agathonos-Georgopoulou (1992) in Greece. In each country, a similar pattern emerges. Child abuse is first seen as the problem of a few 'deviants'; then it is recognised as a larger social problem which is related to adverse social conditions; and finally, there is the recognition that cultural factors endemic in the society also play a part:

> Although certain psychological and economic factors may lead to and precipitate the maltreatment of children in Nigeria, they all find a support

system in the Nigerian cultures that permits and encourages some of these acts. (Mejiuni, 1991, p. 139)

In effect this process constructs a new social reality of what is and is not 'good-enough' parenting, and this construction is then formalised in legislation. There are considerable dilemmas in this process.

The Need for Specificity

As we have seen earlier, although all parents have, broadly speaking, the same role to perform in rearing children, different living situations modify the type of treatment, and different societies have different values, mores and beliefs. In developing mandatory standards, societies have to take both an *emic* and an *etic* approach. One way of doing this is to undertake a survey of the prevalence of Western types of abuse (*etic* approach). Another way is to ask the communities what they feel constitutes child abuse (*emic* approach).

Obikeze (1984), in asking 2000 parents in Nigeria what types of behaviour by parents they considered abusive, received the replies listed in Table 5.

In this survey parents identified important types of abuse not seen in the West, such as child pawning. This is where a child is effectively pawned to pay loans for land, goods, or medical services for another child. At best these children become second-rate temporary members of another family. At worst, if the credit is not redeemed by the child's maturity, they become concubines or slaves. There were different patterns between different Nigerian states on how acceptable child pawning was felt to be. In some states nearly 50% of the parents felt child pawning was an

Table 5: Types of behaviour regarded as abusive by Nigerians

	AFFIRMATIVE RESPONSE %
Economic exploitation	29
Starving or denial of food	21
Frequent or severe beating	12
General neglect	10
Excessive hard labour	6
Frequent bullying or nagging	5
Pawning or slavery	5
Don't know	8

From Obikeze, D. S. (1984), 'Perspectives of child abuse in Nigeria', *International Child Welfare Review*, **63**, 25–33.

acceptable practice, while in most states, over 80% of parents felt this was an unacceptable practice. This study highlights the dilemmas in coming to a nationally accepted definition of child abuse, let alone an international one.

Apart from child pawning in Nigeria, there were amongst the Igbo tribe traditionally two categories of slaves: those of men—'Oho'—and those of the Gods—'Osu'. Although slavery was outlawed many years previously, descendants of these families were still regarded as 'not free-born' and were denied full citizenship status on this account and they and their children suffered from severe discrimination.

In Obikeze's study more Western ideas of child maltreatment such as physical injury, sexual abuse, and emotional neglect hardly featured amongst the replies of his Nigerian parents. Physical discipline, except in the extreme, was seen as an acceptable part of parenting, and emotional abuse, which existed particularly amongst middle-class families where children were left for long hours with inadequate stimulation, was not recognised as abusive in any way. Mejiuni (1991) quotes a case where a father cut off the leg of his daughter who had run away, having refused to enter into an arranged marriage. The father took refuge in the traditional laws which permit such actions. Mejiuni adds: 'Forcing a child to marry a man she does not know and perhaps does not love is emotional abuse in itself; to cut off her leg is a crime against humanity' (Mejiuni, 1991, p. 141). Such *emotional* abuse may not in the national cultural and socio-economic climate be considered maltreatment, but there is likely to be an international consensus and pressure that such *physical* abuse should be eliminated.

These two studies in Nigeria illustrate the need for an internationally accepted definition of child abuse (the *etic* approach) and also the importance of each society prioritising within broad bands specific behaviours that they consider should be the focus of child protection programmes (the *emic* approach).

Minority Groups Living in a Dominant Culture

In recent years there have also been a number of studies which examine child abuse amongst minority groups living in dominant cultures (Lauderdale, Valiunas & Anderson, 1980; Reid, 1984; Spearly & Lauderdale, 1983; Gray & Cosgrove, 1985; Mtezuka, 1989). These studies bring together some of the issues already discussed in this chapter and highlight the dangers of an ethnocentric approach to child maltreatment.

Lauderdale, Valiunas and Anderson (1980) in Texas USA, using data from 36 945 validated cases of abuse and neglect from the state's central register, found the annual rates listed in Table 6. Lauderdale indicates that the differences in rates of abuse and neglect are suggestive of cultural factors being operational. But these differences could be related to a number of different factors. They could indeed reflect different cultural patterns of child-rearing and/or different cultural levels of interfamily violence; or they could reflect differential labelling by a dominant culture which is more prepared to report a black child as being abused; economic differentials and affordable amenities; or different life styles in particular whether the family live in a rural or urban setting and/or different levels of support networks. When the figures were broken down, it was found that the lowest rate of abuse for all ethnic groups was found amongst the rural black population, even though this ethnic group was found to have the highest maltreatment rates in comparison to the other ethnic groups.

Table 6: Annual rates of abuse and neglect per 1000 under 18 population by ethnicity, Texas 1975–77

INCIDENCE TYPE	ANGLOS	BLACKS	MEXICAN-AMERICANS
All abuse and neglect	2.87	3.94	3.17

Reprinted from *Child Abuse and Neglect*, **4**, Lauderdale, M., Valiunas, A. & Anderson, R. (1980), 'Race, ethnicity and child maltreatment: an empirical analysis, 166, with kind permission from Elsevier Science Ltd, The Boulevard, Langford Lane, Kidlington, OX5 1GB, UK.

In a second paper in 1983, Spearly and Lauderdale found that higher abuse rates were significantly associated with a greater proportion of single mothers, while higher neglect rates were significantly associated with a greater proportion of absent mothers due to employment. Nonwhite, especially black families had a higher incidence of poverty, fatherless homes and working mothers. Although blacks in towns were generally better off than rural blacks, there was a higher incidence of abuse amongst urban blacks suggesting that the loss of rural supportive networks could be a factor.

> The urban environment has had an inhibiting and even destructive effect on the supportive functions of the black extended family . . . given the proportions of higher income black families are greater in urban than rural areas, these factors suggest that factors other than availability of economic resources *per se* are responsible for the observed differences in maltreatment rates. (Spearly & Lauderdale, 1983, p. 101)

Cultural conflict and language may also have contributed to the stress levels in the urban areas, resulting in higher maltreatment rates. Spearly and Lauderdale's conclusion is that when considering ethnic specific rates of maltreatment, research should also include the physical and social dimensions of the community environment.

In another interesting paper, Gray and Cosgrove (1985) compared perceptions of subculture child-rearing practices by subcultures living in a dominant culture (Chicago, USA). Their particular concern was that ethnocentric perceptions in the protective services of subculture child care practices could lead to a form of institutional abuse of minority families. Interviews were conducted in person with members of six minority groups: Mexican, Japanese, Vietnamese, Filipino, Blackfeet Indians and Samoan. It is important to remember that these minority groups were also all Americans. The study is therefore a useful description of cultures in transition.

The Mexican-Americans, who had had the longest history of contact with the dominant culture, reported a relatively high number of examples where practices could be misconstrued. Neglect was mentioned more than other types of harm. There was particular concern that lack of supervision of children could be misconstrued as neglect. This, according to the respondents, usually represented the breakdown of traditional practices involving the care of children by older siblings. The findings here link with another paper by Reid (1984) who wrote on her work with undocumented, or illegal Mexican immigrants in Los Angeles. She notes that as families expected the community to supervise their children, they did not feel they were neglecting their children when they were not there. She also notes that despite their poverty and unenviable legal status (they could be deported at any time), there was a resistance to assimilating the child-rearing practices of the dominant culture. They all wanted to stay in the USA, and they knew that complaints about their child care could jeopardise this. They were, however, critical of the Anglo-American child care practices. The values of the Spanish-speaking families in Reid's study included a strong respect for parental authority, with children being taught to care for each other in preparation for the responsibilities of adulthood. Such families looked to the all-American children in Los Angeles urban schools and saw children exposed to licentiousness, drugs, and gang behaviour. Consequently they were reluctant to compromise their own values, even if this meant using severe physical discipline with their children to maintain discipline. In Gray and Cosgrove's study in Chicago (1985), the Spanish-American respondents also highlighted child-rearing practices which *they* felt were abusive but which the protective services dismissed as cultural adaptations to poverty.

The Samoan-Americans in this study also showed marked differences in their concepts of maltreatment. Within this subculture physical discipline is used quite readily with children of all ages to train and discipline them. Beatings that fall just short of medical attention are considered quite acceptable. However, respondents noted a trend to moderation as Samoan-Americans became more acculturated.

In the same study, the Vietnamese-Americans were concerned that their folk remedies could be misunderstood. For example the bruising resulting from the practice of *cao gio* where a warm coin is rubbed briskly over a child's body to cure ills. Lack of supervision of children was another area of possible concern. This was attributed not to lack of care by the parents, but to incomplete adjustment of some families to drastic changes in their environment. In effect they needed to be educated to the dangers of their new settings.

Filipino-American respondents in this paper felt the dominant Anglo culture was over-concerned about sexual abuse and they allowed their young children, weather permitting, to roam naked in their homes. These Filipino respondents thought that seeing children as sexual beings was a very 'odd notion'.

With the Japanese-Americans there were fewer practices which might be misconstrued, although the heavy emphasis on spending free time on study, the value placed on humility in a child, and the intentional lack of praise might be considered emotional harm.

With the Blackfeet Indians there were a number of practices which caused concern. One practice which differed greatly from non-Indian child-rearing was the belief that children should not be guided but that they should learn by experience. As an example Gray and Cosgrove talked of a small boy sticking his finger into a fire in full view of a number of adults who watched, but who did nothing to restrain him. The watchers felt that if he got hurt he would then stay away from the fire. According to several Blackfeet respondents, this belief in allowing the children to learn from experience had been part of the Indian child-rearing philosophy for generations.

> Indians traditionally have relied on setting an example for their children, rather than punishing them. Unfortunately with the breakdown in families, increasing divorce, increasing drug and alcohol use, the parents are often not good examples. (Gray & Cosgrove, 1985, p. 395)

A similar picture emerged with their child-minding patterns. Traditionally young children would be cared for by the elders, but the young parents had not adjusted to the fact that the elders were no longer there as they were dying younger.

Summary

A number of facts emerge from these cultures in transition. Firstly, this analysis highlights the inherent dangers of ethnocentricity in child protection services in a dominant culture. Further abuse by the system can be caused if the meaning and origin of practices are not understood. These studies also give clues how minority cultures adapt within a dominant culture. In the Gray and Cosgrove study (1985) there were fewer practices which could been misconstrued amongst the Japanese-Americans. Gray and Cosgrove postulate that this greater acculturation may be because the Japanese had had the longest TIME in touch with the Anglo-American culture. They had also more CONTACT and were more DISPERSED. It may also be that the original Japanese culture had more in COMMON with the Anglo-American culture. The Vietnamese, who demonstrated more child-rearing practices which could be thought of as abusive, had, compared to the Japanese, been in contact with the Anglo-Americans for a shorter time, had less contact, were less dispersed. In addition, the original Vietnamese culture had less in common with the Anglo-American tradition. In other minority cultures, such as the Spanish-Americans, the acculturational process may be RESISTED when they see child-rearing practices in the dominant culture which they feel are inferior to their traditional practices and values. The Spanish-Americans saw maintaining discipline through severe physical discipline as preferable to the permissive parenting which they felt led to licentiousness, drug misuse and gang behaviour (Gray & Cosgrove, 1985).

THE NEED FOR CROSS-CULTURAL DEFINITIONS

This chapter has highlighted issues that are important in understanding cultural patterns of child-rearing and child abuse and the processes of cultural change. As the international community develops a broad consensus or 'social construction' about what exactly is 'good-enough parenting', and what is child maltreatment, and as communities share information and knowledge about child-rearing it is likely that many of the practices that at present lead to intergenerational patterns of maltreatment will change. Whether this will lead to a better deal for children will depend on what 'social constructs' come in their place. Those involved in child protection have a role to play. If they get it wrong, in time they may look back and discover that the measures undertaken in the name of protecting children were in fact more abusive than anything done by parents.

Despite the difficulties and dilemmas, universally acceptable broad defi- nitions of what constitutes child maltreatment are needed, but different societies will have to define their own priorities. In the final analysis, a judgement has to be made about what is in the best interests of a particu- lar child living in a particular society, at a particular time. These judge- ments will never be easy.

SUMMARY: CULTURAL MECHANISMS IN INTERGENERATIONAL CHILD MALTREATMENT

- Parents around the world are faced with a similar task in rearing children
- Cultural patterns of child-rearing are passed from generation to generation
- Culture compromises religion, different concepts of parenting, and values attached to particular children
- Culture exerts a powerful influence but its influence is not static
- Every society attempts to formulise what they feel is a proper concept of childhood
- The more distance in time, geography, class, the more different these social constructions will be
- Historically many children have suffered severe ill treatment
- 'Badness' is culturally constructed
- Parenting reflects the specific needs of a society
- Children around the world today suffer from a wide range of violence and exploitation
- The most common form of violence to children in all societies is physi- cal chastisement
- Some children are particularly vulnerable to abuse
- Networks have a protective role
- Children are particularly at risk at times of rapid social change
- Family violence is less common in societies characterised by coopera- tion and commitment, sharing and equality
- Many societies have denied the existence of abuse only to discover it
- Child-rearing methods of minority groups living in a dominant culture may be more likely to be labelled abusive
- There is a need for a greater consensus cross-culturally on what is or is not child abuse

5

PSYCHOLOGICAL MECHANISMS IN THE CYCLE OF ABUSE

The majority of individuals do not abuse their children . . . even when highly stressed by economic problems or repression, racial discrimination, or highly aversive behaviour of the children or partners. . . . Such observations under-score the role of the individual or psychological analysis as one operates in a larger sociocultural context. (O'Leary, 1993, p. 15)

The idea that people's experiences in childhood might be linked to their later functioning as parents is not an altogether unreasonable one, even though the processes involved in such links may reflect extra-familial influences or the structure of society, as well as the functioning of individual families. (Rutter, Quinton & Liddle, 1983, p. 60)

INTRODUCTION

Although the majority of families in highly stressed circumstances do not maltreat their children, the reality is that some do. Some may through a constellation of psychological factors be more at risk than others. Psychological analyses have repeatedly documented a number of intrafamilial variables that consistently predict child abuse. The focus of this chapter is to consider these analyses that support a psychological basis for inter-generational child maltreatment and in examining these studies to elicit factors which may help us to predict and prevent future maltreatment.

Child abuse threatens us all. There is an instinctive need to pathologise and marginalise the abuser. We want to believe that the family is a safe nurturant environment and that only 'sick' people perpetrate these terr-ible acts against innocents. The uncomfortable evidence is, however, that physical child abuse is a continuum of behaviour found in many parents, and that only about 10% of incidents are perpetrated by those who have conventional mental health problems (Steele & Pollock, 1968; Straus, 1979).

Steele and Pollock, in the 1960s, in forcing the general public to recognise the extent and tragedy of abuse, effectively challenged the stereotypes:

> If all the people we studied were gathered together they would not seem much different from a group picked up by stopping the first several dozen people one would meet in a downtown street. (Steele & Pollock, 1968, p. 106)

Since this influential study, there has been a massive research investment into the origins of family violence. Today, although an abusive incident can never be predicted, studies do seem to indicate that certain kinds of influences are quite frequently present and are associated with violent behaviour in parents. There are particular difficulties and dilemmas in attempting to predict child abuse. This will be discussed in greater detail in Chapter 10. Despite the difficulties and dilemmas, identification of those more likely to be at risk will assist in directing resources in order to mitigate the risks.

As we have seen, child protective agencies in many parts of the world are mandated by the societies they represent to try and ensure that child maltreatment tragedies do not occur. Throughout the 1970s most of these agencies were 'reactive'. Their legislative and protective powers only came into operation after a child had been significantly harmed. In a humane society, we would surely wish that children should be protected before they are hurt.

> It can be argued that the values and norms we embrace create a climate for child abuse. They produce the social structure that produces racism, poverty and other social ills that trigger abusive behaviour. The skeptic argues that to prevent child abuse we would have to change the assumptions that form the basis of our society. (Cohn, 1982, quoted in Roberts, 1988, p. 44)

Jacquie Roberts, who worked with Margaret Lynch in the UK at the Park Hospital in Oxford and who assessed and treated parents who had abused their children, argues:

> For those of us who are employed in the helping professions with the expressed purpose of preventing child abuse and neglect, such scepticism seems a luxury. We are charged with the responsibility to protect children in certain families from abuse. In order to do this job perhaps it is more practically helpful to ask what makes them vulnerable to child abuse. The concept of vulnerability allows for the possibility of change and gives dignity to a family who could otherwise receive the stigmatising label of 'potential abusers'. (Roberts, 1988, p. 44)

Although there are a few very dangerous families, most parents do not want to harm their children. They certainly do not want to live with the evidence that they have irrevocably damaged their child (Buchanan & Oliver, 1977). It therefore makes sense to try and identify families who may be in need of support before they hurt their child and before they get swallowed up in the child protection processes.

The task is not easy. A physical assault on a child can never be precisely predicted.

> It may be triggered off by a chance event as unpredictable as a television breaking down. Factors identified as 'predicting and predisposing' to abuse must therefore be balanced out by an understanding that for every case of child abuse there has been a complex process leading up to the injuries—a process that may have begun years or even generations before the child is harmed. (Roberts, 1988, p. 43)

ELICITING PREDISPOSING FACTORS

Prior to the 1970s the majority of models were linear or main-effect. According to the main-effect model developmental outcomes were the direct result of some specific pathogenic experience or process or of an inherent biochemical/biological dysfunction. Abusive incidents, it was thought, were inevitably brought about by personality characteristics in the parents which had been developed in response to their upbringing.

As we have seen, the psychiatric pathological model was popular in the 1970s. Basically the premise was that abusive parents had personality disorders which broadly meant they were unable to control their aggressive impulses. This rather limited view discouraged a focus on the social and cultural factors but fitted in well with the opinion then held by psychologists and psychiatrists that personality traits were determinant of a great deal of human behaviour.

The problem was that perpetrators of child abuse did not fit easily into the existing diagnostic categories. Steele and Pollock (1968), instead of trying to associate child abuse with a specific type of psychiatric disorder or a commonly accepted character type, identified a range of behaviour patterns which separated out the abusers in their study from the non-abusers. During five and a half years they studied 60 families in which significant abuse of infants or small children had occurred. Many of their cases came through the paediatric service, which may have encouraged a more middle-class bias to their sample. There was no control group. A criticism of this and other early studies, as we have seen, is that most factors predisposing families to abuse were derived from retrospective inquiries, and that many of the characteristics found in a sample of abusing parents may simply have illustrated the population from which the sample was drawn rather than differentiating abusers from non-abusers.

In Steele and Pollock's study, most of the abusing parents were in their twenties, and had a history of depression at some time in their lives. With few exceptions they had emotional problems of sufficient severity to be accepted for treatment should they have presented themselves at a clinic or a psychiatrist's office. More importantly, they noted that the parents expected and demanded a great deal from their infants and children, treating the child as someone much older. They remarked on the phenomenon of the 'role reversal' where the child took on the parenting of the parents, and the parents' 'sense of rightness' in justifying the highly disciplinary and physically aggressive treatment of their child. They also noted the isolation of the abusers, their lack of confidence, their identity confusion. The child could directly or indirectly contribute by being born 'unwanted' or by being difficult or 'unsatisfying'. Above all Steele and Pollock found that abusing parents had been treated as a child in the same way as they treated their children. Despite the methodological problems in their research, it is interesting that many of their observations have been supported by later studies. Research, however, was not able to support the low profile given to social factors. In Table 7 Roberts summarises the 'predisposing factors' elicited from the Oxford studies (Lynch, 1975, 1976; Lynch, Lindsay & Ounsted, 1975; Lynch, Roberts & Gordon, 1976; Lynch & Roberts, 1978). These studies advocated the 'critical path analysis' for understanding the process of abuse, and for helping professionals to identify the predisposing factors to abuse as a means of prevention (Lynch, 1976).

Table 7: Vulnerable parents and vulnerable children

VULNERABLE PARENTS	VULNERABLE CHILDREN
Unhappy childhood (abused themselves, with low self-esteem)	Born too soon (premature)
Early parenthood	Born sick or handicapped
Psychological problems	Born different
Bereaved parents	Born unwanted
Drug and alcohol abuse	
Ill health	
Poor marriage	
Diffuse social problems	
Social isolation	
Interactions between the parent and child	

Adapted from Roberts, J. (1988) in K. Browne, C. Davies & P. Stratton (Eds), *Early Prediction and Prevention of Child Abuse*, pp. 45–54. Reprinted by permission of John Wiley & Sons Ltd.

Murray Straus in 1979 in his interview study of 1146 families with a child aged 3 to 17, made a strong case for the role of social factors in the aetiology of abuse, but also recognised that there was an obvious need to include data on the psychological characteristics of the parents and the child.

> It is likely that certain combinations of factors are much more potent than either of the factors by themselves; and also much more potent than one might imagine by adding together the effects of each of the two factors. (Straus, 1979, p. 214)

His checklist (those who scored ten or more) identified a third of all the abusing families (Table 8). Murray Straus recognised that further work was necessary before abusing families could be predicted with more certainty. A risk list which predicts only 33% of abusing families is little improvement on the single factor 'history of abuse in parent'.

It is notable that Murray Straus highlighted the neglected area of pre-disposing characteristics of abusing *fathers*. In a retrospective study by Browne and Stevenson (1983), in 30% of the families the father was

Table 8: Characteristics included in child abuse checklist

CHARACTERISTICS ASSOCIATED WITH CHILD ABUSE

A: Important for child abuse by either parent
Was verbally aggressive to the child

B: Important for child abuse by father
Married less than 10 years
Wife full-time housewife
Husband was physically punished at age 13+ by mother
Lived in neighbourhood less than 2 years
Above average conflict between husband and wife
No participation in organised groups
Grew up in a family where mother hit father
Two or more children at home

C: important for child abuse by mother
Husband was physically violent to wife
Husband was dissatisfied with standard of living
Husband a manual worker
Husband was verbally aggressive to wife
Wife was physically punished at age 13+ by father
Wife age 30 or younger
Wife a manual worker

Reprinted from *Child Abuse and Neglect*, **3**, Straus, M. (1979), 'Family patterns and child abuse in a nationally representative sample', 213-225. With kind permission from Elsevier Science Ltd, The Boulevard, Langford Lane, Kidlington, OX5 1GB, UK.

suspected of physically abusing the child in comparison to 39% of families where the mother was considered responsible. Brown and Saqui later commented: 'Obviously more emphasis should be placed on father–child interaction in abusing families' (Browne & Saqi, 1988, p. 67).

Ecological Models and Studies

Belsky (1980), in extending a model by Garbarino (1977), and drawing on existing research findings, developed a more comprehensive model of child abuse risk factors. Central to his model was the concept of risk factors at different levels: the ontogenetic, micro-system, exo-system and macro-system. The model was further developed by Cicchetti and Rizley (1981). Here the difference was that there are not only 'vulnerability' factors and transient 'challengers' but also 'protective' factors and transient 'buffers' which protected families (Table 9).

The challenge of this model was the potential for change. Intergenerational transmission was best understood by examining the transmission of risk factors. Cross-generational transmission was operated by either increasing vulnerability or by decreasing protective factors. Intervention could reduce risk factors and increase buffer factors. Maltreatment was expressed only when potentiating factors overrode compensatory ones.

Having a high IQ, awareness of early abusive experiences, a resolve not to repeat the abuse, and a history of a positive attachment relationship with one caregiver were compensatory factors (Egeland & Jacobvitz, 1984; Hunter & Kilstrom, 1979). At other levels, having healthy children (Hunter & Kilstrom, 1979; Smith & Hanson, 1974), a supportive spouse (Egeland & Jacobvitz, 1984; Herrenkohl, Herrenkohl & Toedtler, 1983;

Table 9: Risk factors for child maltreatment: impact on probability of maltreatment

Enduring factors	Vulnerability factors enduring factors or conditions which increase risk	Protective factors enduring conditions or attributes which decrease risk
Transient factors	Challengers: transient but significant stresses	Buffers: transient conditions which act as buffers against transient increases in stress or challenge

From Cicchetti, D. & Rizley, R. (1989), in D. Cicchetti & Vicki Carlson (Eds), *Child Maltreatment*, p. 382. Reprinted with the permission of Cambridge University Press.

Quinton, Rutter & Liddle, 1984), good social supports (Hunter & Kils-trom, 1979) and few stressful life events (Egeland & Jacobvitz, 1984) were also supportive. Special talents (Cicchetti & Rizley, 1981) economic se-curity (Straus, 1979), religious affiliation (Helfer, 1984), positive school experiences (Rutter & Quinton, 1984), and/or good peer relationships (Freud & Dann, 1951) were also protective. Therapeutic interventions could also produce compensatory effects (Egeland & Jacobvitz, 1984).

Risk factors that could increase the likelihood of abuse occurring were a history of abuse, low self-esteem, low IQ and poor interpersonal skills. At the micro-system level, marital discord, children with behaviour problems, pre-mature or unhealthy children, being a single parent and poverty were factors that could increase risk. At the exo-system level, unemployment, isolation, and poor peer relations were negative indicators, and at the macro-system level an acceptance of corporal punishment, children viewed as possessions and economic depression also increased risk (Kaufman & Zigler, 1989).

The Work of Rutter and his Colleagues

The work of Kaufman and Zigler linked with findings from other re-searchers. Quinton, Rutter and Liddle (1984), for example, sought to un-pack the bidirectional effects of intergenerational transmission. Quinton, Rutter and Liddle noted that prediction was problematic. Early experi-ences could influence the quality of partnership relationships, but good partnership relationships could ameliorate the effects of childhood adver-sities. Prediction was further complicated in that it was not possible to predict the impact that a stressor, for example unemployment, might have on a particular person.

Rutter noted that experimental studies of rhesus monkeys reared in isola-tion (Harlow, 1961) provided the most convincing evidence that experi-ences in early life could directly impair parenting (Rutter, 1981). These monkeys, however, were reared under very extreme conditions. It could be argued that such distortions in rearing were never experienced by humans. A further question was why did some parents who had experienced severe disadvantage in their own childhoods *not* exhibit disorders in later parent-ing abilities? There was obviously a substantial recovery rate from severe disadvantage. This was supported by Harlow's studies on primates (Harlow & Suomi, 1971). Rutter did not doubt the empirical associations. It was the mechanisms involved in transmission which were in doubt. The quality of later parenting appeared to be affected by the whole integrated package, including a person's own emotional state, presence of other life stresses and the existence of satisfactions apart from parenting.

To test some of these hypotheses, Rutter and his team undertook two major studies. The first of these (Quinton & Rutter, 1984) was a retrospective study of 48 families with European-born parents who had had children admitted to residential care. The comparison group consisted of 47 families with a child of the same age but in which no child in the family had ever been taken into care. The different childhood experiences between the two groups was remarkable. A quarter of the mothers with children in care had been in care themselves compared to only 7% of the control group; three times as many had suffered harsh discipline; 44% had been separated themselves from one or both parents for at least a month as a result of family discord or rejection compared to 14% of the controls. A further finding was that although all manner of childhood adversities were more common in the families of the 'in care' group (61% had experienced four or more adversities) they were also surprisingly common in the comparison group (16%—four or more adversities). Overall two-fifths of the control families had experienced some sort of childhood adversity. The conclusion was that intergenerational continuities were stronger looking back but unlikely to be so strong looking forward.

A second study 'looking forward' (Quinton & Rutter, 1984), consisted of a follow-up into the early life of girls who in 1964 were in children's homes. The contrast group were mothers of the same age, never admitted into care but living in the same neighbourhood. Both groups were interviewed at length in their mid twenties. Again, the differences between the two groups were striking (Table 10).

Table 10: Pregnancy and parenting histories of women

	EX-CARE WOMEN (N = 81) (%)	COMPARISON GROUP (N = 41) (%)
Ever pregnant	72	43 (P = 0.01)
Pregnant by 19	42	5 (P = 0.001)
Had surviving child	60	36 (P = 0.02)
Of those with children	(*n* = 49)	(*n* = 15)
Without male partner	22	0 (Exact test P = 0.039)
Any children ever in care/ fostered	18	0 (Exact test P = 0.075)
Temporary or permanent breakdown in parenting	35	0 (Exact test P = 0.009)
Living with father of all children	61	100 (P = 0.02)

From Quinton, D., Rutter, M. & Liddle, C. (1984), in D. Cicchetti & Vicki Carlson (Eds) (1989), *Child Maltreatment*, p. 328. Reprinted with the permission of Cambridge University Press.

The researchers were concerned that findings on the breakdown in parenting could reflect, as well as their parenting abilities, the willingness of the parents to give up their children, and the willingness of the authorities to intervene. Accordingly, observation of parenting skills was undertaken by researchers blind to the status of the parents. Although there was substantial overlap between the groups, the mothers who had been brought up in institutions had more areas of difficulty in parenting.

These studies concluded: 'That institutional rearing, together with the parental deviance and family discord with which it was associated, significantly predisposed to poor parenting (in adult life)' (Quinton, Rutter & Liddle, 1984, p. 115). There was, however, a need to unpack the parcel further. The central interest was why did 25% of the mothers, despite their early institutional disadvantage, demonstrate good parenting skills?

The studies demonstrated that there were *mediating* and *ameliorating* factors. Positive relationships during the teenage years might not influence parenting ability but could influence social functioning. Better social functioning might delay early pregnancy, increase the overall quality of life and thereby reduce later social stressors when parenting. Where there was a discordant family atmosphere, the institutional mothers, on leaving care, were more likely to become pregnant at an early age and thereby increase the stressors on their lives. They noted that it was striking that one adversity led to another. No one bad experience was decisive but each one created a set of circumstances that made it more likely that another bad experience would occur. Less widespread or severe parenting difficulties were not associated with intergenerational continuity.

There was little that was unalterable. The choice of a supportive partner was an important factor in breaking the cycle. Positive school experiences could exert a powerful protective role. Those with multiple psychosocial problems suffered because they acted as if they could do nothing to change their situation. The experience of some form of success or accomplishment was important, not because it diluted the impact of unpleasant happenings, but because it served to enhance confidence and competence to deal with the hazards and challenges of everyday life. Increased self-esteem and self-efficacy helped these mothers to plan their lives to a better end.

In an important comment at the end of the study they noted that, for these women, their life lacked personal meaning or affection and perhaps the main damage came from what was LACKING in the institution rather than what was wrong with the child's own home. There was a particularly poor outcome for children admitted to a Children's Home in infancy and who remained there for the remainder of their upbringing:

Perhaps surprisingly this was the group with the worst parenting of all. The importance of this finding lies in its practical and theoretical implications. It will be appreciated that the children had been admitted to the institution to protect them from the damage of remaining with their own parents in a discordant, disruptive and malfunctioning family. Accordingly it is chastening to realise that this policy seems to have had such a devastatingly bad effect on the young people's functioning as parents. (Rutter, Quinton & Liddle, 1983, p. 95)

The Continuum of Aggressive Behaviours in Intimate Relationships

Rutter's work links up with others who were also trying to unpick the mechanisms that lead to the observed characteristics in abusing families. O'Leary (1993) noted that there was a continuum of aggressive behaviours in intimate relationships (Figure 3).

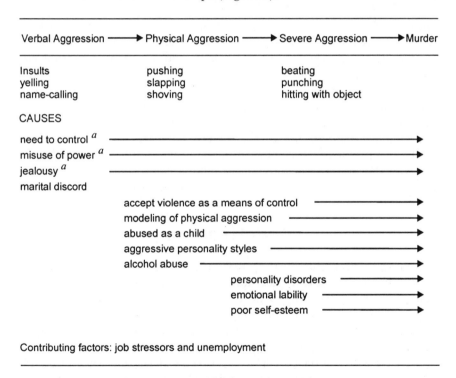

Figure 3: The continuum of aggressive behaviours in intimate relationships
[a] More relevant for males than females

From O'Leary, K. (1993) in R. Gelles & D. Loseke (Eds), *Current Controversies on Family Violence*, p. 20. Reprinted by permission of Sage Publications, Inc.

Wolfe (1987) suggested that a similar continuum of physical aggression applied to child abuse. Burgess called this 'a continuum of parenting behaviour' (Burgess, 1979). Using this idea, child abuse was seen as the 'degree to which a parent uses negative, inappropriate control strategies with his or her child' (Wolfe, 1987). Abusive parenting therefore resembled 'typical' parenting but differed in terms of degree.

Gelles (1993) argued against the concept of a continuum of aggression. Firstly, because there were discontinuities. Apparent continuities could reflect an increase in the reporting of violence. Child maltreatment needed to be seen within its social context. Gelles and Edfeldt (1986) compared the United States and Sweden. Physical punishment occurred less frequently in Sweden than in the United States and yet rates of severe violence towards children in the two countries did not differ. However, the law against physical punishment in Sweden may account for the fewer reports of physical punishment there.

Jaffe, Wolfe and Wilson (1990), and Fagan and Wexler (1987) in their work with delinquent populations, estimate that between 20% and 40% of families of chronically violent adolescents had experienced marital violence. In approximately 25% of these families the child had been hit with an object. Almost 40% of parents had been arrested. Lewis, Shanok, Pincus and Glaser (1979) note that 79% of violent adolescents had witnessed extreme violence between their parents whereas only 20% of the non-violent offenders did so. There were, however, a number of methodological problems with some of these studies. Often they relied upon retrospective accounts with a lack of comparison groups. They assist in unpicking the mechanisms but are not all encompassing.

Social Learning

The studies from Feshbach (1974, 1989), Hertzberger (1983), and Gelles and Straus (1979) connect with these ideas. They demonstrated that aggressive behaviours were transmitted by teaching the child that aggression was appropriate. Children observed and modelled their parents' aggressive behaviour and developed rules that supported it. Hertzberger (1983) speculated that abused children were most likely to form rules supporting abusive behaviour if the parents action was seen as normative; for example if the abuse was accompanied by rationalising verbalisations and if the abuse occurred during discipline following an actual wrongdoing. Hertzberger found some support for this hypothesis. The researchers asked college students to judge the abusive treatment of children described in case histories. They found that students who had been physically abused regarded the treatment received by the children in the stories as more appropriate than did the students who had not been abused. Furthermore, when students were given a description of the parent's abuse, the child was judged by the student to be more responsible for the parental discipline and the disciplinary act was rated less severe.

Cognitive Behavioural Studies

But what of the cognitive processes that may mediate the transmission? Cognitive behavioural models, in particular 'learned helplessness', built on social learning theory, but tried to elicit the cognitions behind the actions. Learned helplessness describes the process by which organisms learn that they cannot predict whether what they will do will result in a particular outcome (Seligman, 1975). Walker (1984) demonstrated that there were measurable changes in the perceptions of people who were exposed to repeated inescapable aversive stimulation. This links to Rutter's finding described earlier where mothers brought up in institutional care felt unable to change or control their lives. This learned sense of powerlessness could have intergenerational affects on parenting.

Crittenden and Ainsworth (1989) carried the ideas further. Neglecting mothers were expected to have models centring around the concept of help-lessness. They did not perceive others as having, or being able to give them, what they needed. Neither did they see themselves as effective in eliciting the help and support of others. The effect accompanying their relationships would be one of emptiness and depression. Crittenden and Ainsworth's main contribution, however, was in their studies on attachment.

Studies in Attachment

Attachment theory originates from Bowlby (1953, 1979, 1984) and the psychoanalytical tradition. There are also important links, as has already been mentioned, with the classic studies on primates by Harlow (1961). Although Rutter and others (Rutter, 1981; Sluckin, Herbert & Sluckin, 1983) have reassessed the earlier versions of attachment theory, it is an enduring concept in the aetiology of child maltreatment. Central to the concept is that the early caregiver–infant attachment relationship is the model for later relationships. Aetiological theory proposes that these species-characteristic patterns of behaviour have evolved because they function to promote species survival. Children can form attachments to primary caregivers, even when the quality of the relationship is poor, but from these attachments, the infant develops representational prototypes or, to use Bowlby's term, 'inner working models' of self and significant others. At an early age the child builds a cognitive model that best fits the reality experienced. As the child grows older new relationships are assimilated into existing models. These models are largely outside consciousness. They constitute a set of expectations about self and and how other people will relate.

Crittenden noted that knowing the effect of deleterious social conditions only allowed one to predict increased incidence of maltreatment. However, knowing the nature of family attachment relationships and the individuals associated might enable one to specify more precisely which families and/or individuals would be the most vulnerable to external stressors. Crittenden in 1984 was aware that although clinicians have long believed that an individual's style of child-rearing was based in part on his or her parents' style of parenting, studies had been criticised on the basis of having a pre-selected subject and using possibly inaccurately remembered and subjective data. Crittenden (1984) proposed to avoid these methodological difficulties by observing the parenting behaviour of siblings of abused children. The hypothesis was that maternal style would predict sibling style. In the study, 36 families with a maltreated infant between 6 and 11 months of age with a sibling between 2 and 10 years were recruited from welfare departments. Crittenden demonstrated that siblings as young as 2 years old were already displaying some of the salient aspects of their parents' pattern of child-rearing. Data suggested that the maternal style of child-rearing began to influence the child at a very young age and that most children were influenced to be similar to their parents.

Zeanah and Anders (1987) have noted that inner working models lead an individual to re-create experiences in line with his or her relationship theory. Sroufe (1983), in observing children in pre-school who were classified as either secure or anxiously attached in infancy, found support for this idea that children re-created relationships with their teachers that were consistent with their earlier relationships with their primary caregivers. However, a child who has been maltreated expects others to be rejecting, hostile and unavailable. A child who has been neglected (physically, emotionally or both) expects others to be unresponsive, unavailable, and not willing to meet his or her needs. Maltreated children bring these expectations to relationships and they respond to others in a fashion consistent with their expectations.

Zeanah and Zeanah (1989) argue that early patterns of relating and the development of inner working models have more far-reaching consequences than do specific adversities. It is not violence *per se* which is passed on from one generation to the next, but the ongoing theme of the caregiving relationship which is transmitted. Egeland's findings on the 'emotionally unresponsive' or 'psychologically unavailable parent' link in with these ideas (Egeland & Sroufe, 1981; Egeland, Sroufe & Erickson, 1983).

Erikson, Egeland and Pianta (1989) further postulate that from the attachment experience, maltreated children learn the role of both victim and victimiser. Crittenden (1985) examined the role of power and coercion seen in parent and child behaviour among maltreating families. She suggested that abused children would be expected to show submissive behaviour in the presence of a powerful caregiver and aggressive behaviour in the absence of this powerful person. This strategy may be protective for the child in the immediate situation but may be maladaptive in the long term. Avoidance of a caretaker may be reasonably adaptive in the short term, but may lead to subsequent cognitive or linguistic problems or problems in socio-emotional development (Schneider-Rosen, Brauwald, Carlson & Cicchetti, 1985).

Crittenden postulated (1985) that neglected children, on the other hand, would be expected to exhibit withdrawn behaviour. Erikson, Egeland and Pianta (1989) however, found in their study that neglected children were both withdrawn and aggressive. They note, however, that upon school entrance neglected children presented the most severe and varied problems and this may be because in the structured school environment these children found themselves without the social and organisational skills necessary to cope.

Erikson, Egeland and Pianta (1989) conclude from these studies that this does not mean children *cause* their own maltreatment or are responsible for eliciting appropriate care, but they are part of a system and behave in ways that influence interactions within that system.

Main and Goldwyn (1984) have shown there is a higher risk for abusive parenting when early abusive experiences are not remembered. They interviewed 30 women about their relationships with their mothers and then observed them interacting with their children in the Ainsworth Strange Situation (Ainsworth, Blehar, Waters & Wall, 1978). Women who remember their mothers as rejecting were more likely to reject their own children than those who reported positive parenting. The ratings of maternal rejection during childhood also were found to relate positively to the degree mothers idealised their own mothers. Non-abusive parents reported more detailed accounts of their own maltreatment and expressed more anger about these experiences than abusive parents.

Disattachment behaviour may also be activated by undue time or distance away from the attachment figure, and may lead lead him or her to form expectations regarding the nature of future interactions. In Main and Goldwyn's study (1984), attachment ratings were found to correlate significantly with the mother being avoided by her own infant following brief separations.

Carlson, Cicchetti, Barnett and Braunwald (1989) have demonstrated that maltreated infants are much more likely than comparison infants to be rated as insecurely attached to their caregivers and are particularly likely to demonstrate disorganised, disorientated attachment behaviour. Main and Hesse (1990) found that it was the introduction of fear and/or wariness in the attachment relationships which produces strong conflicting emotions in the child.

Attachment theory has been criticised for ignoring wider contextual issues, but Crittenden and Ainsworth (1989) feel it permits the integration of 'external', that is environmental conditions and events, with interpersonal conditions such as interlocking influences upon the development of attachment. Attachment is no longer seen as a developmental issue of the first year of life. It is recognised that attachment relationships develop. They continue to undergo transformations and reintegrations with subsequent accomplishments such as emerging autonomy and entrance into the adult world. As a result children are continually renegotiating the balance between being connected to one another and being independent and autonomous. Attachment is a lifespan developmental task (Crittenden & Ainsworth, 1989).

Bowlby (1979), Bretherton (1985) and Sroufe (1988) have all underscored that internal working models of relationships can change. The reworking of existing poor-quality models of attachment relationships would appear important for preventing the intergenerational transmission of child maltreatment. The establishment of unidealised reflections for their early experience would appear to be a prerequisite for the creation of future positive relationships (Cicchetti, 1989; Hunter & Kilstrom, 1979).

Crittenden and Ainsworth (1989) postulate that anxious (or insecure) attachment is a critical concept both to the origins of intergenerational child maltreatment *and* to the rehabilitation of families.

Studies in Self-esteem

Altemeier *et al.* (1986), in their large study of 1400 low-income women, compared the self-esteem of those who had been battered as children with that of those who had not. The findings indicated that low self-esteem placed them at risk for abusing their own children in turn (Table 11). Despite the rather pessimistic view of the abused parents' parenting potential, the study was unable to document that mothers who were abused as children did in fact later abuse and neglect their own offspring.

The cross-cultural research of Rohner and Rohner (1980) links in to studies both of self-esteem and of theories of attachment. They noted that rejected children all over the world, when compared to accepted children, tended to be more aggressive and hostile, dependent or 'defensively independent' according to the levels of rejection. These children had an impaired self-esteem and sense of self-inadequacy. They might also have been emotionally unstable or unresponsive. Rohner and Rohner (1980) concluded that as we tend to view ourselves as we imagine 'significant others' see us, if we have been rejected by the most 'significant other', that is the primary caregiver, we define ourselves as unworthy and inadequate human beings. Such children, so often seen when one is trying to arrange foster placements for chronically neglected children, have a desperate need for affection but lack the ability to respond appropriately when affection is given. Rohner and Rohner (1980) conclude that rejected children will be more likely to reject their own children than parents who were not so rejected.

Studies in Attribution Theory

Newberger and White (1989) took a different approach in assessing the parental *cognitive* processes that could lead to child maltreatment:

> A mother's capacity to foster the healthy development of her children may be influenced by her own upbringing . . . this capacity is also influenced by such characteristics as her own self-esteem, depression, the quality of the social and physical environment, knowledge of developmental norms, *and how she understand the child's needs*. (Newberger & White, 1989, p. 303)

Larrance and Twentyman had noted in 1983 that a person's perceptions were jointly influenced by a need to understand the environment objectively, and subjectively to serve their own needs to enhance or protect self-esteem. In general, research subjects tended to make positive attributions about their own behaviour.

Newberger and White (1989) noted that parents who maltreated their children were more likely to make negative attributions about their children's behaviour. They would, for example, attribute difficult behaviour to 'badness' rather than 'tiredness'.

Table 11: Self-esteem in battered and control women

	95 BATTERED (%)	832 NOT BATTERED (%)
Do you usually feel good or bad about yourself? Bad	21	9**
How would you describe yourself— usually successful or unsuccessful? Successful	38	52*
Does it spoil your day when someone criticises you or puts you down? Yes	36	33
Isolation of battered and control mothers		
Who do you talk to about your problems most of the time? No one available, don't want anyone	31	17**
If you need help do you have friends other than your parents who would help you? No	28	11**
Are you a friendly person who likes to be with people or would you rather keep to yourself? Keep to myself because I do not trust others	17	5**
What kind of relationship do you have with your baby's father? Separated	20	11**
Assessment of potential intergenerational transmission of child maltreatment in Battered and Control women		
How does it make you feel when you hear a screaming baby? Angry	11	3**
What is the best way for mothers to get their children to behave? Hit other than on hands, legs, buttocks	5.3	1.6*
Have you become so angry that you have lashed out and done things that you were sorry about? What did you do? Hit with hand or object other than on legs	41	17**

* p = 0.05
** p = 0.01 by Chi Squared Test

Reprinted from *Child Abuse and Neglect*, **10**, Altemeier, W., O'Connor, S., Sherrod, K. & Tucker, B. (1986), 319–330. With kind permission from Elsevier Science Ltd, The Boulevard, Langford Lane, Kidlington, OX5 1GB, UK.

How they reasoned appeared to be related to how they behaved as parents. Parents with especially troubled relationships with their children were frequently unable to perceive their children as having needs and rights of their own separate from those of the parent. (Newberger, 1980, p. 3)

In Newberger's initial study (Newberger, 1977, 1980) 51 families representing a broad cross-section of social and family backgrounds were interviewed. An analysis of the interviews revealed that parental levels of awareness could be grouped into the following hierarchy:

Level 1: Egoistic orientation: The parent understands the child as a projection of his or her own experience and the parental role is organized around parental wants and needs.

Level 2: Conventional orientation: The child is understood in terms of eternally derived . . . definitions and explanations of children. The parental role is organised around socially defined notions of correct practices and responsibilities.

Level 3: Subjective-individualistic orientation: The child is viewed as a unique individual who is understood through the parent–child relationship, rather than by external definitions of children. The parental role is organized around identifying and meeting the needs of this child rather than as the fulfilment of predetermined role obligations.

Level 4: Systems orientation: The parent understands the child as a complex and changing psychological self-system. The parent grows in the role . . . and recognises that the relationship and the role are built not on meeting the child's needs but also on finding a way of balancing one's own needs and the child's so that each can be responsibly met. (Newberger, 1977, pp. 12–13)

Further analyses of the parental awareness data (Newberger, 1980) also suggested that parental awareness was a developmental process that unfolded during childhood and continued to develop with parental experience and was responsive to intervention. In a study of 13 of the 16 children seven years later, this showed that parental development continued to unfold (Newberger & Cook, 1986).

Studies on the Role of Empathy in Child Abuse

Another approach was that of Feshbach's studies in empathy. Using a scale especially developed Feshbach and Caskey (1985), studied 336 participants, of which 219 were mothers and 117 were children. Of the mother–child pairs, 26 consisted of physically abused children and their abusing mothers, a further 25 mother–child pairs were non-abusing clients of child guidance clinics, and the remaining 66 pairs were obtained from day care centres and parent education classes. All the parents were administered the Parent/Partner Empathy Scale developed by the team. The abusing parents achieved a significantly lower empathy score than the control group, but their score was not significantly lower than the clinic group. From this work Feshbach highlighted the potential of empathy training both for abusive parents and for their children in order to break the cycle of abuser – abused – abuser (Feshbach, 1989).

Feshbach's work may link with that of Egeland, Jacobvitz and Sroufe (1988). This demonstrated that although parents might wish to change their patterns of child-rearing, many were not able to. It could be hypothesised that this was because such parents had never experienced empathy in their own lives. In their study parents who were abused as children were asked in interviews spanning a 12-month period, whether they would raise their children differently from the way they themselves were raised. All but four said yes, avowing not to repeat their maltreatment. Nevertheless a substantial number of caregivers abused as children did later maltreat their own children. Egeland, Jacobvitz and Sroufe's conclusion was that working models of oneself and others developed in the early years appear to play a prominent role in the quality of care provided for children in the next generation. High levels of anxiety could interfere with a mother's ability to be flexible in learning and using new approaches to child care. However, mothers who were severely abused as children but did not abuse their own children had a number of characteristics in common. These parents were characterised by having at least one parent (or foster parent) who provided some love and support, and by having more supportive partners. Following Feshbach's model it could be said that these parents had learnt empathy through experiencing models of empathetic care in their own lives.

Transactional Models

Although this model was developed some 20 years ago, the ideas are still relevant in understanding intergenerational patterns of child maltreatment. The transactional model developed by Sameroff and Chandler (1975) presents the environment and the child as exerting a dynamic mutual influence on each other. Thus if a child demonstrates deviant development across time it is assumed that the child has been involved in a CONTINUOUS maladaptive process. The continued manifestation of maladaptation depends on environmental support whereas the child's characteristics reciprocally determine the nature of the environment.

Child maltreatment is therefore an expression of an underlying dysfunction in the parent–child–environment system, rather than aberrant personality traits, environmental stress or deviant child characteristics.

FAMILY SYSTEMS

Trickett and Susman (1989) looked further into the family processes that lay behind intergenerational abusive parenting. They felt it was important to look beyond the parent–child dyad. Literature on *family systems* showed that a disturbed person might have an impact on multiple family systems, all of which might affect individuals within a family or the family as a whole (Margolin 1981). For instance, depression in a parent might affect his or her marital relationship which in turn could have a negative consequence. In families with parental psychopathology children had been shown to have more behaviour problems than those in families where there was no parental psychopathology (Rutter, 1971; Emery, 1982). The difficulty Trickett and Susman felt with such studies was that they failed to elucidate the causal mechanisms between the associations.

Trickett and Susman sought to establish whether:

(a) Do abusive and nonabusive families differ in the degree to which parents report themselves to be in agreement with the childrearing styles and values of their own parents using their own parents as sources of knowledge and support?
(b) Do abusive and nonabusive families differ in the degree to which mothers and fathers share childrearing values and perceptions of the psychological environment of the home?
(c) Is the development of abused and nonabused children related to the degree of perceived similarity and/or disagreement about children between the generations and/between parents? (Trickett & Susman, 1989, p. 284)

Their sample was 34 two-parent families elicited from protective agencies in Washington, DC with children aged between 4 and 11. Half of the children had been physically abused by one or both parents, and there was a long history of repeated incidents. Two thirds of the sample were white and one third black. The past history of the parents was self-reported.

They found that parental disagreement about child-rearing and the nature of the family environment was related to a higher incidence of behaviour problems especially in boys and they suggested that such a disagreement was another risk factor in the development of abused children. The study, although small, did demonstrate the importance of the broader family context in the processes of abuse.

Trickett and Susman (1989) also found that both groups of parents were equally likely to pass on what they had learnt about parenting from their own families. This was of particular consequence where it related to values and attitudes which sanctioned harsh punishment. To break the intergenerational cycle, these parents had to reject the attitudes and values of their own parents.

Other research has come to similar conclusions. Hunter and Kilstrom (1979) found that non-abusing parents were better able to give clear accounts of the abuse they had experienced as children. They also found that they had more social support, physically healthier babies and fewer ambivalent feelings about the child's birth. While growing up they were more likely to have reported a supportive relationship with at least one parent.

Egeland and Jacobvitz (1984) reflect these findings. Those who broke the cycle of abuse had a greater awareness of their history and fewer life stresses. The integration of the abusive experience into the mother's view of herself was typical of those who broke the cycle of abuse. They seemed to be aware of how their early experiences had affected their expectations regarding relationships (Pianta, Egeland & Erickson, 1989). Of those who did not break the cycle, some appeared to 'split off' the abusive experience and idealise their past. Others appeared to have difficulty in recalling childhood experiences and avoided talking about their parents. Egeland hypothesised that because they dissociated from their own experiences they did not associate the pain they had felt as children with the pain they inflicted on their own children.

WHO GETS ABUSED

Despite differing theoretical frameworks and methodologies, there is considerable consistency between the researchers on the factors seen in intergenerational child maltreatment. Where they differ, however, is in the theoretical explanations they give for the factors seen and this in turn affects the interventions recommended. Some of the most fruitful ideas have evolved from finding protective factors as well as vulnerabilities in families and from demonstrating that, despite the strong impact of early relationship experiences, change is always possible. Psychological vulnerabilities within families and their family systems may lead to a repetition of the cycle of abuse, but parenting is a developmental process which unfolds during rearing. Vulnerabilities may be ameliorated by specific interventions or by later chance experiences. Deleterious social conditions will increase the levels of maltreatment, but knowing the nature of family relationships and the individuals associated enables us to specify more precisely which families and/or individuals will be the most vulnerable to external stressors. The challenge for child protection practitioners is to create a climate of positive parenting, where vulnerable parents can ask for and receive help before they are labelled as abusive. But this is the subject of the third part of this book.

CRITIQUE OF EVIDENCE

There is still much we do not know. The research on protective and mediating factors is still in its infancy. Practitioners in child protection need to know more precisely how to evaluate various risk and compensatory factors found in abusing families, not only in the short term but also in the long term. The Life History Research, promoted by Rutter and others, and discussed in the next chapter, promises dividends. Inevitably, the more we learn the more complex the picture will become. 'How consistent is the pathway between childhood and adult life: is it straight and narrow, or full of detours and unexpected reversals?' (Robins & Rutter, 1990, p. xiii) A criticism of much current research is that many of the studies have originated in the USA and UK. A question we must ask is how far these findings are relevant in other societies? More cross-cultural psychological studies on intergenerational patterns of child maltreatments are urgently needed.

A further dilemma relates to the difficulties of finding effective methodologies to research in this difficult area. The more we learn, the more we worry about how far we can rely upon on research findings which may be based on faulty methodology.

There are also noticeable gaps in the research. An important one is the neglect of men. Over the years there has been an overconcentration on the role of the mother. Creighton (1988) found that only 52% of the children were living with both biological parents at the time of the incident of abuse and 22% were living with a mother and a father substitute. This figure is likely to have increased with the changing patterns of family life. Substitute fathers pose a greater risk to children than natural fathers. Oliver et al.'s 1974 study of severely physically abused children demonstrated that violent men often moved from family to family, posing major risks to the mothers' natural children.

Too much research is still focused on post-abuse families. Individual post-abuse interventions are costly. Those who come to the notice of the child protection agencies are only the tip of the iceberg (Audit Commission, 1994). The challenge for the future, among the many other challenges, is to find better ways to identify those at risk; to find better ways to mediate risk and stimulate protective mechanisms; and to find better ways to measure outcomes from preventive approaches. This is also the challenge in breaking the biological cycle of child maltreatment.

SUMMARY: PSYCHOLOGICAL MECHANISMS IN THE TRANSMISSION OF CHILD MALTREATMENT

- Most families in difficult circumstances do not maltreat their children
- The reality is that some do
- Some through a variety of psychological factors may be more at risk than others
- A number of intrafamilial variables have persistently been associated with child abuse
- Physical child abuse is a continuum of behaviour found in many parents
- There are a few very dangerous parents but most parents do not wish to harm their children
- Child protection agencies are mandated to prevent the tragedies if possible
- Early medical models 'pathologised' abusing parents
- Comprehensive risks lists can, at best, predict only a third of abusing parents
- Ecological models are better at indicating both risk and protective factors
- Rutter has shown that there are continuities and considerable discontinuities in parenting patterns
- Specific one-focus studies have helped in identifying mechanisms
- Among these are studies on cognitive behavioural states, attachment, self-esteem,attribution, and empathy
- Transactional and family systems models have also been helpful in identifying mechanisms
- Parents who recognise and reject the abuse in their own childhood are more likely to break patterns
- There are still considerable gaps in the literature, notably the neglect of the role of men

- Much of the research has originated from the West and *may* not be relevant in all societies
- Too much research has focused on post-abuse treatment of families and children. Too little on prevention

6

BIOLOGICAL FACTORS IN INTERGENERATIONAL CHILD MALTREATMENT

They are right who hold the soul as not independent of the body and yet as not in itself anything of the nature of the body. It is not body, but something belonging to body. It, therefore, resides in body and moreover, a particular soul to a particular body. They were wrong who sought to fit the soul into the body without regard to the nature and qualities of that body. (Aristotle, *De Anima*)

Our bodies are our gardens. (Shakespeare, *Othello* I.iii.323)

All the world's a stage,
And all the men and women merely players:
They have their exits and their entrances;
And one man in his time plays many parts,
His acts being seven ages. At first the infant . . .
(Shakespeare, *As You Like It*, II.vii.139)

In the final analysis, we are biological beings. Psychological selves cannot be separated from the nature and qualities of our bodies. These bodies are biologically influenced by the conditions in which they develop. Broad developmental patterns follow a predictable biological course, but events along the way can bring about biological changes for better or worse. Parent–child relationships are inextricably linked to these biological forces.

The biological cycle of child maltreatment relates to two realities. Some parents are biologically more vulnerable to the risk of abusing their children and some children are biologically more vulnerable to being abused (Rutter, 1989). Biological factors may relate to intergenerational patterns of disease and poor health care which mean, for example, more children are born damaged and more mothers have poor health. They may be related to inherited characteristics which lower the ability of the parent to parent and of the child to be reared effectively; or they may relate to factors present in the environment such as pollution, iodine deficiency, lead ingestion, drug and alcohol abuse. These cause biological changes in either the mother and/or the child. Pathways through life may be influenced both by biological risk and by protective factors. Biological factors in addition to psychological factors are therefore a potent force in the development of intergenerational child maltreatment.

In this chapter we will examine these four areas. In the past there may have been a reluctance to consider biological factors in child maltreatment, particularly where heredity was concerned. Today such a fatalistic view is misplaced (Rutter, Macdonald, Le Couteur, Harrington, Bolton & Bailey, 1990). Much can be done by environmental manipulation to lessen or even eradicate the risks. The task is to identify both risk and protective factors.

INTERGENERATIONAL PATTERNS OF POOR HEALTH AND DISEASE

The *Human Development Report* (1994) published by the United Nations states that the foundation of human development is the universalism of life claims. The purpose of national developmental programmes is to create an environment in which *all* people can expand their capabilities and opportunities for both present and future generations. No child should be doomed to a short life or a miserable one merely because that child happens to be born in the 'wrong class' or in the 'wrong country' or is of 'the wrong sex'. The challenge to the international community is illustrated by the Child Survival and Development indicators shown in Table 12. These figures may underestimate the reality. In developing countries in 1992, large numbers of people had no access to health services (UNDP, 1994), so it may be impossible to know, for example, the true numbers of pregnant women with anaemia or the numbers of low-birthweight babies. These crude figures also hide disparities between and within countries. It could be argued that in extreme conditions only the fittest survive. However, as we saw in Chapter 3, infant mortality figures also indicate those who survive in a debilitated state. For these children and mothers, parenting and being parented will be more difficult. When these children become parents they will be biologically disadvantaged because of the legacy from their own lack of health care.

We know for instance, that pregnancy and childbirth are more hazardous for disadvantaged mothers and yet even in industrialised countries, the obstetric care of disadvantaged mothers is worse (Power, Manor & Fox, 1991).

Table 12: Child survival and development (percentages)

Prenatal care	Pregnant women with anaemia	Low-birthweight babies	Maternal mortality (per 100 000 live births)	Infant mortality	Mortality under five
				(per 1000 live births)	
1988–90 (%)	1975–90 (%)	1985–90 (%)	1988	1992	1992
All developing countries					
62	52	16	420	69	100
Least developed					
50	44	18	730	112	160
Industrialised countries					
...	...	...	24	13	15
World					
...	...	...	290	60	90

From *Human Development Report* (1994), p. 151, by the United Nations Development Programme. Reprinted by permission of Oxford University Press.

Low-birthweight babies carry a far greater risk of short- and long-term
disabilities than children of normal weight (Donald, 1979). Around 95%
of these infants are born in developing countries (WHO, 1987) but there is
also a significant proportion of low-birthweight babies in industrial countries. Brain damage and other injuries at the time of birth may leave a
child handicapped for life. Elliott (1988) indicates that 'patchy' cognitive
deficits, for example a limited vocabulary and slowness of thought, may
relate to minimal brain dysfunction and decrease parents' ability to cope
adequately with family- and child-related problems, thereby increasing
the likelihood of abuse. Damage to the child's nervous system may contribute to cognitive and behavioural difficulties in the child such as impulsivity, attention disorders and learning difficulties, which could
increase that child's likelihood of being abused.

A body or brain that has suffered damage does not just display a deficit—
in some cases it may adapt or compensate for that abnormality. Whether
this is possible may depend on environmental factors. Malnutrition further compounds the initial disadvantage. Inadequate calorific intake and
protein deficiency in diet can seriously affect the physical growth and
eventual health of children. Birth defects and congenital abnormalities
arise from a multitude of causes both genetic and environmental, but
included in this list would be mother's ill-health and malnutrition. Poor

health and malnutrition in both the mother and the child is also related to a range of preventable diseases and infections.

Diseases that Affect the Ability of the Mother to Mother and of the Child to be Parented

In industrialised countries there is considerable evidence that those who abuse children have more health problems and physical handicaps than non-abusers (Conger, Burgess & Barrett, 1979; Milner, 1986). In extreme conditions parents may be so debilitated by disease that apathy and neglect of children are likely outcomes.

In undeveloped countries, diarrhoeal and respiratory tract infections are a major killer. Intestinal parasites may also lower family functioning. In a study in rural Egypt intestinal parasites were found in 77% of children under 5 who came from large families (Sherbini, Hamman, Omran, Torky & Fahmy, 1981). Other families suffer from the long-term consequences of diseases, such as tuberculosis, diphtheria, polio and measles, that are preventable through immunisation. The World Health Organisation estimates that 30% of expected deaths from pertussis have been prevented through immunisation, as have nearly 40% of expected cases of polio (Belsey & Royston, 1987) (Table 13).

These figures hide the growing concern about the re-emergence of diseases such as tuberculosis, diphtheria and malaria in areas where it was felt they were no longer a health factor. Of the estimated 15 million who

Table 13: World health profile

YEARS OF LIFE LOST to premature death (per 1000 people, 1990)	TB (per 100 000 people, 1990)	MALARIA (per 100 000 people exposed to M-infected environments, 1991)	AIDS (per 100 000 people, 1992)
All developing countries 49	176	240	5.7
Least developed 92	220	...	10.2
Industrial 13	...	...	7.8

From *Human Development Report*, (1994), p. 152, by the United Nations Development Programme. Reprinted by permission of Oxford University Press.

are infected with the HIV virus, 12.5 million live in developing countries—9 million in sub-Saharan Africa, 1.9 million in Latin America and 2 million in Asia. In the USA, AIDS is now the prime cause of death for men aged 25–44 but it is also the fourth most important cause for women of that age range. Future projections are alarming. By the year 2000 it is estimated that between 30 and 40 million people will be HIV-infected and 13 million of these will be women. By the turn of the century more than 9 million African children could have lost both their parents (UNDP, 1994). The only parenting these children will receive will be from sick and dying parents and who ever else is around to fill the gap after they have died.

INHERITED CHARACTERISTICS WHICH AFFECT THE ABILITY OF THE PARENT TO PARENT AND THE CHILD TO BE REARED EFFECTIVELY

There is a strong emotional resistance amongst many in the helping professions to acknowledging the role of heredity in perpetuating family patterns. The reasons for some of the factors have been considered in Chapter 2. Images of the holocaust are still close. There is also quite rightly a fear of labelling and stigmatisation. For other practitioners, heredity is something you cannot do anything about and therefore it is better to focus energies on environmental influences.

With the new research into genetics, these views are no longer tenable. In many cases it is 'the risk' that is inherited and this vulnerability can be increased or decreased by environmental manipulation. Prevention of distress or disease is a realistic possibility. A person may be born with an inherited tendency to heart disease but whether this develops into a debilitating condition could depend on the life style that he or she adopts. In paediatrics, phenylketonuria is a dramatic example. Cognitive problems associated with the autosomal recessive gene can be avoided if phenylalanine is eliminated from the diet. Similarly there is probably a genetic component in some types of alcoholism but for this to be manifest requires access to alcohol (Rutter *et al.*, 1990).

Plomin (1994a) notes that determinants of individual differences in parenting have received relatively little attention in the research literature. Genes influence parental personality, life events and the types of social support. Neuroticism and extroversion are two of the most pervasive and most highly heritable personality factors. These traits in parents contribute to genetic effects in the family environment system.

Considerable caution needs to be exercised in interpreting such research. Research is demonstrating that it is no longer a question of either 'nature' or 'nurture' (Plomin, 1994a). Typically in these studies, 'nature' refers to what is thought of as inheritance. Inheritance denotes DNA differences which are transmitted from generation to generation. Inheritance is not the same as DNA because DNA *interacts* with the environment.

Genetic influences also serve to shape the environments that people select for themselves (Scarr & McCartney, 1983). Given a choice, the extrovert chooses the sort of life style or 'niche' that fits the characteristics he or she has inherited and he/she is in turn shaped by this life style. Genetic factors play a role in the choice of friends, teachers, in the types of social support, in life events and in what accidents you have; in whether you are exposed to drugs and even in what you view on the television (Plomin, 1994a). In some cases genetic factors may render some people more susceptible to environmental hazards (Cadoret, 1982, 1985). There is growing evidence that these genetic influences *increase* over a child's developmental period.

The new research in molecular biology is also helping to unwrap the relationship between inferred and actual heritability. For instance in Huntington's chorea, an inherited condition causing early dementia, affective disorder may be an early sign of the disease but conduct disorder is more likely to be related to associated psycho-social problems in the family (Folstein, Franz, Jensen, Chase & Folstein, 1983). In some forms of inherited mental disability, there may be associated mental health problems which are not part of the syndrome but an illness brought about as the result of environmental factors.

The power of the techniques in molecular genetics promises a new age in which DNA variation among individuals can be studied directly (Wachs, 1992). But nothing is static: just as genes interact with the environment, genes interact with other genes. Genotypes, that is the genetic endowment of an individual, may be manifested in a range of different phenotypes, that is the constellation of traits that we see when we look at the individual. These traits may include behavioural, physiological and biochemical features (Goldsmith, 1991). Phenotypes are the result of the interplay between genetic and environmental factors.

It is unlikely that there are single genes for altruism and aggression. It is not possible to map complex behaviours on the genome in such a simple fashion. Our genetic endowment is like a design for functioning and a strategy for living which interplays with external things and events (Wachs, 1992).

It has been argued that a disorder with strong heritability points to the likelihood of an organistic base. There are a number of problems in an 'assumption of dysfunction' (Sonuga-Barke, 1994). For example in behaviour, different cultural patterns, as we saw in Chapter 4, may reinforce different norms which may appear dysfunctional in different cultural settings. Psychologically some apparently dysfunctional behaviour may have an important 'function' in terms of reward, for example criminality, and this may be the mechanism that passes the 'learnt' behaviour from generation to generation. If a disorder is strongly heritable it has also been thought that this disorder would also be strongly resistant to environmental change. This is not necessarily the case. Height is strongly heritable but there has been a marked increase in height due to improved nutrition since the turn of the century. Similarly improved family circumstances can lead to major gains in intellectual performance (Scarr, 1981; Schiff & Lewontin, 1986).

It is now realised that the research strategies that traditionally were used to separate 'nature' from 'nurture' have in themselves a number of problems which may lessen the validity of the findings from such studies (Plomin, 1994a). Samples that provided the opportunity to separate genetic and environmental influences were often atypical in important ways. Central to much of this research were the twin and adoptees studies. Twins, however, differ from singleton children in the extent of birth problems, rates of language and speech problems, and in patterns of parent–child interactions. An adoptees' background is unusual in that it led to an adoption.

Despite the caution in interpreting such research and attributing blame to either 'nature' or 'nurture', there is a growing interest generated from the findings. 'Genetic research has illuminated the role of environmental factors . . . [and demonstrated] how improved environmental conditions can raise levels of functioning even with characteristics with high heritability' (Rutter *et al.*, 1990). When considering inherited characteristics which inhibit the ability of the parent to parent or of the child to be parented, such research is highly pertinent, especially if the effects of such characteristics and disorders can be mitigated environmentally. To do this, however, it is necessary to identify heritability of personality traits and disorders and their links to child maltreatment.

Personality, Traits and Disorders

Because child maltreatment is so often accompanied by serious family difficulties and disturbance, it is not surprising that most attention has been focused on environmental risk factors. Within such children, however, there are a number of characteristics and disorders which place them at higher risk of abuse than children who do not have these characteristics and disorders.

Firstly, let us consider heritability of personality. Table 14, taken from the Emmanuel Miller Memorial Lecture of 1993 and published in Plomin (1994b), summarises heritabilities of behavioural dimensions and disorders seen in the major twin studies. This table is important because some of the characteristics identified could be linked to child maltreatment. There are highly consistent findings supporting the hypothesis that infants or children having difficult temperamental characteristics may be more reactive to environmental stress than children with less fraught temperaments (Wachs, 1992; Wachs & Gandour, 1983). Maternal anger can be magnified by such characteristics in a child (Crockenberg, 1987).

In the early 1970s, several studies suggested that there might be an important genetic component in the behavioural syndrome Attention-Deficit Hyperactivity Disorder (Safer, 1973; Morrison & Stewart, 1973; Cantwell, 1975). This disorder ranges from the pervasive type disorder, where the child never sits still no matter where he or she is, to school-

Table 14: Twin results for studies of behavioural dimensions and disorders

	IDENTICAL TWINS (%)	FRATERNAL TWINS (%)
Twin correlations		
Personality	0.50	0.20
*MMPI (Personality Questionnaire)	0.45	0.20
Childhood behavioural problems	0.80	0.60
Vocational interests	0.50	0.25
Social attitudes	0.65	0.50
IQ	0.85	0.60
Twin concordances		
Conduct disorder	0.85	0.70
Alcoholism—males	0.40	0.20
Alcoholism—females	0.30	0.25
Schizophrenia	0.40	0.10
Unipolar depression	0.45	0.20
Manic depression	0.65	0.20
Autism	0.65	0.10

Reprinted from *Journal of Child Psychology and Psychiatry*, **3**, Plomin, R. (1994): The Emmanuel Miller Memorial Lecture 1993—Genetic research and identification of environmental influence, no. 5, 821. With kind permission from Elsevier Science Ltd, The Boulevard, Langford Lane, Kidlington, OX5 1GB, UK.

based hyperactivity. All these children are harder and more exhausting children to rear, and as such are more likely than other children to suffer maltreatment. Today the genetic component is less certain, but it is felt that to a greater or lesser extent these children display the same underlying trait (Goodman & Stevenson, 1989). Hynd and Hooper note that it cannot be concluded on the basis of the present evidence that ALL children with ADHD have symptoms that reflect neurological dysfunction. However, the evidence from genetic, biochemical, neuro-behavioural and neuro-imaging studies indicates a neurological aetiology for the behavioural symptoms associated with ADHD in almost all children (Hynd & Hooper, 1992).

Knutson (1978) has suggested that abusers have a hyperactive trait. Wolfe et al. (1983) found that abusers had large increases in skin conductance and respiration rates in response to both stressful and non-stressful mother–child interactional scenes, Frodi and Lamb (1980) found abusers more reactive to a crying child. Crowe and Zeskind (1992) and Casanova et al. (1992) found greater and more prolonged physiological reactivity in high-risk (for abuse) parents compared with low-risk parents. To what extent these conditions have a biological basis is uncertain but these studies suggest certain temperamental traits may increase the risk that a child is abused or a carer becomes an abuser.

There is a body of data demonstrating a substantial genetic component for both criminality and anti-social personality disorder in adults (Coninger & Gottesmann, 1987; Rutter & Giller, 1983). In the Gottesmann (1985) twin study, the link was 51% in identical twins and 22% for non-identical twins. There is a weaker genetic effect in juvenile delinquency, possibly because most juvenile crime does not persist into adulthood. Criminality in adulthood, however, is virtually always preceded by juvenile offending (Farrington, 1987).

Graham and Stevenson's (1985) careful large-scale twin study of genetic influences on behavioural deviance raises an interesting issue. The heritability was higher in girls than in boys, suggesting a greater genetic component for emotional disturbance than conduct disorders. Conduct disorders are important because of the links with child abuse, juvenile delinquency and adult criminality.

Mental health problems in parents have been widely associated with higher rates of child maltreatment (Culbertson & Schellenbach, 1992). Motherhood, it is widely accepted, carries with it a considerable risk of depression (Brown, Brolchain, Harris & Harris, 1975; Brown & Harris, 1978), particularly where it is associated with disadvantage, poverty and social problems. Maternal depression is also associated with developmental delays in children (Richman, 1977; Rutter, 1980; Sheppard, 1994). There is a major (86%) genetic component in bipolar manic depression disorders but only 8% in unipolar depression (Rutter *et al.*, 1990). Weissmann , Merikangas, John, Wickramaratne, Kidd, Prusoff, Leckman & Pauls, (1986) have shown that relatives of probands who have had an early onset of major depression, carry an eightfold risk of developing a similar condition themselves at an early age.

Schizophrenia may present additional very serious risks, particularly where hallucinations and delusions are directed at the child. Walker, Downey and Berman (1989) found, for example, that for adolescent boys the combination of parental schizophrenia *plus* parental maltreatment resulted in significantly greater rates of aggressive delinquency than either schizophrenia or maltreatment taken in isolation. Surprisingly there were few if any significant findings for girls.

The incidence of schizophrenia amongst first degree relatives is between 3.2% and 15%. The concordance in monozygotic twins is about 40% or more. With this group, the expected concordance rate would be 100% for complete genetic determination. Holzman (1992) demonstrates that there might be a group of 'latent' schizophrenics—that is those who inherit the vulnerability but do not develop the full-blown disease. The importance of this finding is that 'protective' environmental factors may effectively divert the onset of schizophrenia.

Learning Disabilities (Mental Retardation) and Child Maltreatment

Low intelligence is associated with a range of other social problems such as poor housing and poverty. It is not surprising that children of parents with learning disabilities (in the USA this group is generally called mentally retarded), are at greater risk of abuse and neglect and are probably overrepresented in child care services (Levy, Perhats, Nash-Johnson, & Welter, 1992) and that there are intergenerational patterns in these links (Buchanan & Oliver, 1977; Oliver & Buchanan, 1979).

Parents with learning disabilities are not a heterogeneous group. Some parents despite their disability will parent effectively, others will need considerable support (McGraw & Sturmey, 1994). Additional problems, such as poor mental and physical health, overcrowding, marital discord, alcoholism and insufficient support, lower parenting thresholds but the effect may be more pronounced for the learning disabled than for those who are not learning disabled. Studies comparing parent–child interactions where the parent has mild learning disabilities demonstrate that they often show less affection, and are less able to stimulate and bond with their child than mothers who do not have learning disabilities (Crittenden & Bonvillian, 1984; Feldman, Towns, Betel, Case, Rincover & Rubino, 1986).

Although intelligence is highly heritable, the whole range of social factors has an important role in reducing/increasing potential. *Mental retardation* is the term used in the USA to define a population who fall at least 2 standard deviations below the mean on individually administered tests of intelligence. Within this conceptualisation all individuals with mental retardation fall between a range of 0 and 70 on standardised intelligence tests. The American Association of Mental Retardation requires that the retardation occur before the eighteenth birthday (Grossman, 1983). Historically, IQs below 50 are generally assumed to have an organistic base whereas those in the 50–70 range were felt to be biologically intact and the result of cultural familial patterns.

Post mortem and other research is now questioning this rigid divide. Jellinger (1972) after examining more than 1000 cases of institutionalised mental retardation found that more than 90% evidenced some degree of brain abnormality. There was a tendency for the worst cases of retardation to exhibit more severe brain abnormalities. Similarly Malamud (1964) in a sample of 1410 patients showed that in at least 97% there was evidence of neuropathology at autopsy. He concluded that brain pathology is present at all levels of mental retardation.

This is significant because the presence of a neurological disorder is associated with a higher rate of psychiatric impairment. Rutter, Graham & Yule, (1970) and Rutter, Tizard, Yule, Graham & Whitmore (1976) found a 30% to 40% rate of emotional disturbance in children with mental retardation compared with the general population, with the more severe forms of psychiatric disturbance being manifested with lower levels of intelligence.

Parents *without* learning disabilities (mental retardation) will need considerable support in parenting such children. Children with such disabilities carry a greater risk of being maltreated than children not so disabled (Buchanan & Oliver, 1977). Similarly parents *with* learning disabilities will need very considerable support in parenting. The risks may be greatest where both the child and the parent are similarly disabled. In addition, many parents with learning disabilities have multiple life-skill deficits (McGraw & Sturmey, 1994) which make the whole parenting task harder.

Alongside the risks there are also protective factors. When assessing parents with learning disabilities the challenge of the task, as in other cases of child welfare, is to balance the risk factors against the protective. By improving the quality of parenting of those who have learning disabilities, this could improve the abilities of the next generation and consequently improve the quality of their parenting.

It is possible to touch on only a few of the many known disorders which have a genetic component and which may limit the abilities of the parent to parent and of the child to be parented. In noting Plomin's figures in Table 14, we can also see that only occasionally does heritability account for more than 50% and this is in the most closely related (i.e. identical twins). In less close relationships the risks are considerably reduced. In all cases, protective factors may be important in determining outcomes. Protective factors may have a similar genetic loading, but can also be introduced into the environment. This is the challenge in breaking patterns of child maltreatment.

CROSS-CULTURAL ISSUES

The extent, however, to which one can generalise the findings from one area to another is repeatedly being questioned. Medical research is demonstrating marked differences in the prevalence of different diseases among different cultures. The suggestion is that some of these differences may be related to differences in the genetic pools.

Culture, as we have seen, consists of those patterns of learned behaviour, and their neural codes without which the demonstrated behaviour would not exist, which are passed on from generation to generation (Goldsmith, 1991). The assumption has always been that cultural differences reflect alternate phenotypic expressions of a common genetic heritage. There is, however, the possibility that there may be a relationship between genes and culture. For example, in some areas where dairy products are rarely consumed, this is related to a known difficulty within that culture to digest milk. It is quite possible that other behavioural differences, broadly equated as culture, may also be related to genetic variations.

For example, in a large cross-national study of child behaviour in Japan, China and Korea, in sharp contrast to findings in the West, no sex differences were found for neurotic behaviour (Matsuura, Okubo, Kojima, Takahashi, Wang, Shen & Lee, 1993). However, parents in Japan, China and Korea rated their children higher on somantic disorders than did parents in Aberdeen. In an interesting study of behaviour and emotional problems in 3 year olds of Asian parentage in Birmingham (Newth & Corbett, 1993), it was found that the prevalence of behavioural disorders was similar to white children but overall Asian children had significantly lower scores.

There are a number of cultural and sociological factors which would explain these differences. But just as evolutionary theory explains our physical adaptation to our environment, it is also probable that cross-cultural variations in behaviour may also be the result of similar processes.

The Theory of Parental Investment

Linked to these ideas are those of Richard Dawkins (1976), the Oxford biologist, on the fundamental significance of parental investment. As his theory goes, the task for both men and women, and indeed for all nature, is to reproduce their genes. In the mating process both parties are about obtaining the best partner to improve their genetic pool. A man cannot reproduce his genes without a woman. In this sense a woman is a 're-source to a man'. Once a woman is impregnated it is only acceptable to desert the woman if there is a reasonable chance that the woman will be successful in rearing the young without his help. From the woman's point of view, it generally helps if the man is around because by sharing the task, it increases the chances that the young will be reared successfully.

Raped women react very negatively to rape for sound evolutionary reasons; the act not only subjects them to physical harm but it also deprives them of choosing with whom they will mate. Quite simply rape is not in the interests of either the woman or her genes.

From the male perspective, access to resources and elevated social status in contemporary society are important factors in determining his reproductive success. It is argued that there is a biological basis for rape in that it is frequently performed by men whose prospects for increasing their reproductive fitness through orthodox means are poor (Goldsmith, 1991). The argument, however, does not totally hang together as rape is common amongst athletic teams and conquering armies.

Children, however, can be at a greater risk of maltreatment from step-parents than from their own. These ideas are supported to some extent by the studies of Daly and Wilson (1982, 1985, 1994). In the 1982 study Daly and Wilson tested the hypothesis that allegations of resemblance are motivated by the problem of uncertain paternity. With newborn babies, mothers alleged paternal resemblance, far more often than maternal resemblance, suggesting that mothers were endeavouring to promote paternity confidence. In their 1985 study Daly and Wilson explored the links between child abuse and children who were not living with both natural parents; 841 families were surveyed by telephone and this was combined with information on 99 child abuse victims, 93 runaways and 449 juvenile offenders. Results showed that both abuse and police apprehension were *least* likely for children living with two natural parents. Pre-schoolers living with one natural and one step-parent were 40 times more likely to become child abuse cases than like-aged children living with two natural parents. Although the risk of abuse was significantly higher with children living with a step-parent than those living with a single parent, the reverse was true for apprehension for criminal offences. Socio-economic and other risk factors for abuse differed little or not at all between the two groups. Daly and Wilson concluded in line with evolutionary theory that step-parents constitute a significant risk factor for child abuse.

Daly and Wilson's 1994 study, using Canadian and British homicide data, examined killings of children less than 5 years old by stepfathers compared to genetic fathers. A high proportion of stepfather homicides were related to excessive beatings, whereas with genetic fathers a substantial proportion of child homicides were accompanied by suicide and/or partner murder. Daly and Wilson concluded that such findings were predictable from an evolutionary model of parental motivation.

FACTORS WITHIN THE ENVIRONMENT WHICH BRING ABOUT BIOLOGICAL CHANGES TO THE PARENT OR INFANT

Human beings rely on a healthy environment in order to thrive. Many human beings in the world, however, knowingly or unknowingly, ingest or inhale substances that bring about biological changes within them and make the task of being parented or parenting more difficult.

Pollution

In industrialised countries, one of the major environmental threats is air pollution which can result in severe respiratory distress and other problems. Los Angeles produces 3400 tons of pollutants each year, and London 1200. Mexico City produces 5000 tons of air pollutants a year (UNDP, 1994). Although the character of environmental threats differs between industrialised and developing countries, the effects are similar (Figure 4).

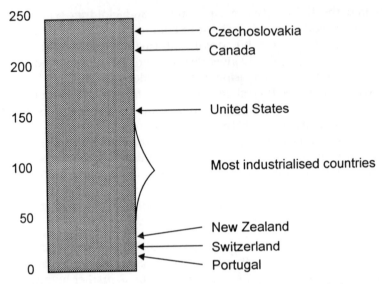

Figure 4: Pollution: kilograms of sulphur and nitrogen emissions
From *Human Development Report* (1994), p. 30, by the United Nations Development
Programme. Reprinted by permission of Oxford University Press

Many environmental threats are chronic and long-lasting. Bhopal and
Chernobyl are the most obvious environmental catastrophes which may
have intergenerational affects. Chernobyl produced radioactive fumes
which were then blown across Europe by the wind. It has been estimated
that in northern Britain for example, as many as 250 000 babies and young
children have been exposed to significantly higher levels of radiation than
is felt to be safe. One of the constituents of the Chernobyl fall-out was the
radioactive element iodine-131. This moves to the thyroid gland in the
neck and high doses could mean that those exposed are at greater risk of
thyroid cancer (UNDP, 1994).

Iodine Deficiency Disorder

Too little rather than too much iodine is a major cause of difficulties for
some families. For over 70 years it has been known that by adding minute
quantities of iodine to salt, the health problems of iodine deficiency can be
solved. The most visible consequence is the appearance of goitres around
the neck (Figure 5). The invisible results are more insidious. Hundreds of
millions are living their lives with reduced mental and physical capacity
caused by iodine deficiency. Most vulnerable are the very young. Children are stunted, listless, mentally retarded, or incapable of normal

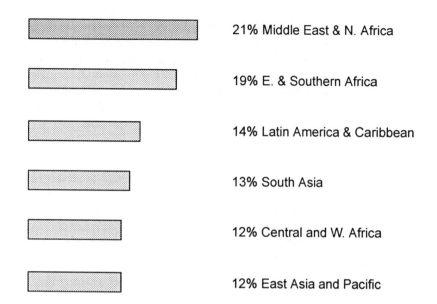

21% Middle East & N. Africa

19% E. & Southern Africa

14% Latin America & Caribbean

13% South Asia

12% Central and W. Africa

12% East Asia and Pacific

Figure 5: Iodine deficiency: percentage of school-age children with goitre
From UNICEF (1994), *The State of the World's Children*, p. 11. Reprinted by permission of Oxford University Press

speech, movement or hearing because they lack iodine which is the essential hormone that regulates normal growth and development (UNICEF, 1993). There is an obvious relationship between parenting ability and iodine deficiency. The solution is not expensive. Only a teaspoonful of iodine is required in a whole lifetime, but in many countries to effect this will require legislation, technology and the necessary control procedures (UNICEF, 1993).

Lead

In industrialised countries one of the most prominent campaigns in recent years involving children's health and the environment has been against the use of lead in petrol. Lead is a toxin which damages the nervous system. The consequences of acute lead poisoning include brain damage, stomach pains, anaemia, comas and ultimately death (Rosenbaum, 1993). Acute poisoning is rare but a wide variety of studies have linked lesser levels of lead to learning difficulties and behavioural problems in children including inability to concentrate, hyperactivity and aggression. Moore, Meredith and Goldberg (1977) in Glasgow, UK, found that water-lead concentrations in the maternal home during pregnancy were linked to high levels of mental retardation in the children. Needleman (1979) in a study of over 2000 school children in Massachusetts, USA, found that the higher the lead level in children's teeth the more likely they were to have low IQs and behavioural problems such as distractibility and impulsiveness. Fergusson, Horwood & Lynskey (1993) in a seven-year longitudinal study of 1265 New Zealand children found that early *mildly elevated* lead levels were associated with small but relatively *long-term deficits* in cognitive ability and attentional behaviours.

Children take in lead from a range of sources. They inhale air and dust containing it; they may suck their fingers and other objects which have been contaminated by it. Airborne lead comes mainly from motor vehicles but uncontrolled emissions from factories can also be responsible. In the UK and USA lead-free petrol has brought major benefits but there are still millions of British households where drinking water comes primarily from lead plumbing (Rosenbaum, 1993).

Polluted water the world over is, of course, the source of a wide range of debilitating diseases and conditions. Undoubtedly the situation in London has improved since Sydney Smith's time: 'He who drinks a tumbler of London water has literally in his stomach more animated beings than there are men, women and children on the face of the globe' (Sydney Smith, 1771–1845, in Rosenbaum, 1993, p. 7). Concern still remains, however, about the long-term consequences of newly identified microorganisms and pollutants such as nitrates (Rosenbaum, 1993), and there may be yet further links made with behavioural and other difficulties in children.

Drug and Alcohol Abuse

More directly related to child maltreatment are the concerns arising from the use and abuse of drugs and alcohol. As treatment programmes turned their attention on those who were chemically dependent, concerns were also expressed about the physical health of those children born and raised in addicted families (Hayes & Emshoff, 1993). The development of chemical dependence is influenced by genetic (Eskay & Linnoila, 1991), as well as psychosocial and environmental factors.

Parental substance abuse has repeatedly been linked to family violence and transgenerational transmission. Parental preoccupation with chemical use may also lead to neglect or emotional abuse (Edmondson, 1994).

Bays (1990) reports that in the United States there are approximately 10 million adult alcoholics, 500 000 heroin addicts and between 5 and 8 million regular cocaine users. Talbott (1991) suggests that of every 10 Americans, 2 are social users, 5 are drug and/or alcohol abusers, and 1 suffers directly from chemical dependence. It has been estimated that between 10% and 75% of chemically dependent people also have a primary psychiatric disorder (Hayes & Emshoff, 1993).

Black (1981) reports that 66% of the children raised in alcoholic homes are either physically maltreated or witness family violence and more than a quarter of the children are sexually abused. Violence and substance abuse share many common risk factors: individual, familial and environmental. There are a number of mechanisms involved.

(a) The risk factor may lead to substance abuse which in turn leads to violence
(b) The risk factor may lead to violence which in turn contributes to substance abuse
(c) The risk factors may independently manifest themselves as either substance abuse or family violence. (Hayes & Emshoff, 1993, p. 291)

Personality and behavioural correlates of substance abuse and violence overlap. Among these are hyperactivity (Garbarino, Guttman & Seeley, 1986) and 'difficult' temperament (Lerner & Vicary, 1984). Those from addicted families may be particularly at risk. Alcohol and drugs exacerbate any pre-existing mental health problems within the chemical user, including poor impulse control, bipolar disorder, low frustration tolerance and violent behaviours (Cicchetti & Olsen, 1990; Curtis, 1986).

The literature suggests that children of substance abusers have a specific temperamental vulnerability (Tarter, Alterman & Edwards, 1985). It may be that these children have less ability to recover from emotional distress and exhibit increased emotional lability. It may be that they have the same inherited traits that placed their parents at risk. While not all of their behaviour is violent, it is likely that these children are predisposed toward violent behaviour and thus perpetuate the familial cycles of both substance abuse and violence.

Sheridan (1995), in a study of 81 men and women serving prison sentences in two maximum security prisons, found generally high levels of parental substance abuse and abuse/neglect and relatively low levels of family competence. Analyses revealed significant direct and indirect relationships among parental substance abuse, family dynamics and exposure to both child and adult maltreatment. These four variables were significantly associated with the respondents' own substance abuse in later life, suggesting the potential for continuing the patterns in the next and subsequent generations (Figure 6).

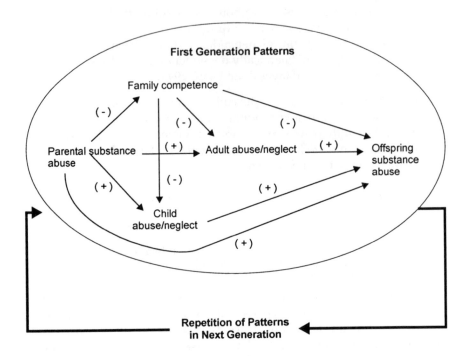

Figure 6: Proposed model of intergenerational substance abuse, family functioning and abuse/neglect

Reprinted from *Child Abuse and Neglect*, **19**, Sheridan, M., 'A proposed intergenerational model of substance abuse', 527, © 1995. With kind permission from
Elsevier Science Ltd, The Boulevard, Langford Lane, Kidlington, OX5 1GB, UK

Another area of concern has been the condition of infants born to chemically abusing mothers. These infants experience the consequences of their
parents' substance abuse while still in the womb. In the USA, as many as
93% of pregnant women in methodone treatment programmes also report
using cocaine and other drugs in addition to opiates (Bays, 1990). Chasnoff (1989) suggests that at least 11% of pregnant women in the USA are
using illegal drugs, and that more than 300 000 infants are born each year
to women using crack/cocaine.

The long list of potential perinatal effects from opiate, marijuana, phen-
cyclidine, alcohol and amphetamine abuse include spontaneous abortion,
sudden infant death syndrome, mental disabilities, birth defects, premature labour, foetal distress, growth retardation. As they grow, children
may demonstrate neurological deficits, learning disabilities, impulsivity
and antisocial behaviour (Hayes & Emshoff, 1993).

As one parent movingly wrote of his adopted foetal alcohol damaged child:

> I am a living, breathing encyclopaedia of what hasn't worked in curing or reversing the damage to one child prenatally exposed to too much alcohol. . . . Brain surgery has not worked. Anger hasn't worked. Patience hasn't worked. Love hasn't worked. (Dorris, 1992, p. 342)

The increasing number of infants born damaged as a result of chemical ingestion in pregnancy, is not of course, limited to the USA. The United States is the largest single market for drugs but narcotic drugs have become one of the biggest items of international trade. Many of the heaviest drug users are the poor and desperate. This underclass is not limited to industrialised countries. Pakistan, for example, is thought to have more than 1 million heroin users and Thailand has around 500 000 addicts (UNDP, 1994). Many of these will be pregnant mothers, ingesting substances which 'biologically' damage their children and affect their parenting abilities.

The challenge of prevention is both at an international level and at an individual level. With individuals who substance abuse, the hope is that improved early identification of risk and protective factors, combined with effective assessment and treatment strategies, will go some way to limit the damage to the next generation.

DEVELOPMENTAL PATHWAYS THROUGH LIFE

The emerging field of developmental psychopathology, or Life History Research, has begun to impact on a number of traditional fields. This discipline is challenging the three central principles that were felt to underpin biomedical models of psychopathology.

(1) The same entity will cause the same disorder in all affected individuals, whether they be children or adults.
(2) The same symptoms at different ages should be caused by the same entity.
(3) Specific disorders of children should lead to similar adult disorders. (Sameroff & Seifer, 1992, p. 53)

Not only is the disease model inadequate in explaining psychopathology, it is also inadequate in explaining many physiological processes. Developmental processes and modes of expression can vary depending on age, general health status and social context of individuals (Cassell, 1986). Rather than a focus on isolating 'markers' of specific biochemical or structural defects, the approach of developmental psychopathology is to use longitudinal studies to note the frequency with which childhood factors predict adult outcomes and to observe under what conditions the predicted links occur, and what prevents them from occurring (Robins & Rutter, 1992). The excitement generated from this research arises from the fact that it is demonstrating both continuities and discontinuities, and both risk and protective factors. In a study of the intergenerational transmission of child maltreatment, this research is important.

These studies have demonstrated the 'virtual necessity' of childhood behaviour problems to adult nonconformity, but they have also demonstrated that behaviour problems in children are by no means sufficient to create this outcome.

> Many difficult children become less difficult with age, and a minority of very difficult children become apparently normal adults. The natural histories of children who turn out to be normal adults despite the serious behavioural problems that generally predict adult difficulty are of great interest because they reveal environmental interventions or concurrent personality traits and skills that seem to counterbalance the bad prognosis associated with this behaviour. (Robins & Rutter, 1992, p. xiv)

Although Cicchetti would argue (1992) that the study of developmental psychopathology goes back to the early writings of Plato and Aristotle (Kaplan, 1967), and that more recently its foundations can be seen in the work of Freud, Werner and Goldstein (Cicchetti, 1992), the main source of recent data has been found in longitudinal studies.

In the United Kingdom there have been three large national birth surveys. The second of these was the National Child Development Study which has traced all children born in one week in March 1958—some 17 000 babies. The latest NCDS sweep traced some 12 000 respondents in 1991 when they were 33. Many had by then produced their own children. A vast number of papers on the physical, mental health and behavioural continuities amongst the respondents has originated from the NCDS study (Power, 1992). A recent paper by the author based on NCDS data (Cheung & Buchanan, forthcoming) has demonstrated the risk of depression in adulthood amongst children and young people who had been in public care. This risk was mitigated in adulthood by education and occupational status and, in the case of women, by marriage. The risk of depression in men who had been in care increased as they became older. The implication of this finding here, is that the care of a second generation could be affected by living with parents who are depressed, particularly if such children have some inherited vulnerability to depression themselves.

A study by Maughan and Pickles (1990) also using NCDS data focused on children who were born illegitimate but remained with their families as well as on another group of children who were adopted. In this study, they found relatively high levels of behavioural and adaptive problems in the illegitimate group which were not entirely explicable in terms of contemporary social disadvantage, whereas the adoptees appeared to have avoided this broad spectrum of risk. The picture was, however, less positive for men. These findings need to be viewed with caution as children born illegitimate in the 1950s in the UK were a particularly disadvantaged group.

In the USA the Berkeley Guidance Study from the University of California was initiated in 1928–1929. This involved every third birth in the City of Berkeley. Most of the 214 subjects in the original sample came from white Protestant, native-born families (Caspi, Elder & Herbener, 1990). Among papers originating from this have been those which demonstrated the links between intelligence, temper tantrums, education and occupational status in midlife, the life course of shy children, and the life course of dependent children.

They found for example that men who reacted with temper tantrums to frustration and adult authority as children encountered difficulties when they again faced frustration and controlling authority in adulthood, or when they found themselves immersed in life situations requiring management of interpersonal conflicts, such as in marriage. Whereas men who had an interactional style of dependency in childhood were able to transform their childhood dependency into a mature nurturant style in adulthood, which served them well in the intimate world of home and family. This has an obvious relevance to the prevention of child maltreatment.

The Chess and Thomas studies of 133 middle-class children from the New York Longitudinal Study (NYLS) have demonstrated interesting continuities and discontinuities in temperament from childhood to adulthood (Chess & Thomas, 1990). The dimensions followed up were, firstly, *difficult* temperament, where a child was slow to adapt, and where he/she had relatively negative mood, high intensity, irregularity and withdrawal. The second dimension was *easy* temperament, where a child carried the opposite characteristics, and the third dimension was the *slow-to-warm-up temperament* where there was a mixture of withdrawal, slow adaptability and mild intensity.

Their explanation for the continuities and discontinuities of temperament observed in adulthood was a theory they called *'the goodness-of-fit model'*. They asked why does one child show a smooth consistent course in his temperament and yet why does another show great variability over time?

Goodness-of-fit results when the environmental expectations, demands and opportunities are consistent with the individual temperament and other characteristics so that he can master them effectively. There is *poorness-of-fit* on the other hand when the environmental demands are excessive for the individual capacities, so that excessive stress and an unhealthy developmental course may be the result. (Chess & Thomas, 1990, p. 211)

Chess and Thomas argue that goodness-of-fit may promote consistency in temperament over time while in another child it will promote a change in one temperamental attribute or another. Dunn summarises the issues:

Do some children remain 'stable' in particular temperamental dimensions because they actively 'niche-pick' and seek particular kinds of environment? Do others remain stable because their parents consistently respond to and encourage certain styles of behaviour? (Dunn, 1986, p. 166)

The implication for the intergenerational transmission of child maltreatment is that patterns can be broken even when they relate to temperament and behaviour characteristics that may be biologically determined.

If . . . benevolent environments can be intentionally created for youngsters who would not encounter them naturally and if protective traits and skills can be taught or cultivated, they constitute the basis for interventions particularly likely to succeed. (Robins & Rutter, 1990, p. xiv)

SUMMARY: BIOLOGICAL MECHANISMS IN INTERGENERATIONAL CHILD MALTREATMENT

- Parents and children are biological beings
- Their psyche cannot be separated from the nature and quality of their bodies
- These bodies are biologically influenced by the conditions in which they develop
- Developmental patterns follow a predictable course
- Events along the way can bring biological changes
- Parent–child relationships are inextricably linked to these biological forces
- Some parents are biologically more vulnerable to the risk of abusing their children
- Some children are biologically more vulnerable to the risk of being abused
- Biological factors may relate to intergenerational patterns of disease and poor health

- They may relate to inherited characteristics which lower the ability of the parent to parent and of the child to be parented effectively
- They may relate to factors in the environment such as pollution, iodine deficiency, lead, and substance abuse
- Pathways through life may be influenced by biological risk *and* protective factors
- There is resistance to consideration of inherited characteristics
- These views are no longer tenable as much can be done to mitigate risk and enhance protective factors
- Personality traits and disorders may influence patterns of abuse
- Life History Research challenges biomedical models of psychopathology
- Patterns can be broken even when they relate to characteristics that may be biologically determined

III

APPROACHES TO INTERVENTION

7

PRINCIPLES IN
INTERVENTION

*Our challenge now is to be conscious of what we have learned, to monitor our
expanding knowledge base, and to continually pull in new insights, new
experiences which contribute to our ability to understand why abuse happens
and how it can be stopped. And then, our commitment must be to base our
policies and our program decisions and our budget allocations on that which
we have learned* (Ann Cohn, 1992, p. xv; Executive Director, National
Committee for Prevention of Child Abuse)

This chapter explores a possible set of principles that should govern
strategies to break the cycles of child maltreatment. In later chapters,
intervention strategies linked to these principles will focus on the separate cycles before coming together with a final overview. Before defining
a set of principles, Figure 7 summarises the mechanisms operating in the
four cycles which were identified in the previous chapters.

The 'H' approach outlines the four arms to a holistic overview. On one
side are the extrafamilial mechanisms operating in the socio-political
and cultural cycles. On the other side are the intrafamilial mechanisms
operating in the psychological and biological cycles. At the centre is the
symbol of the child and his/her children to act as a reminder that the
purpose of anything we do, however difficult it may be, must be to
promote the welfare of the child. The symbol to the left is intended to
indicate that the main force for change is in the socio-political and
cultural cycles and will come from social policy makers, legislators and
educators. As we will see later, this will be at international, national,
local and community levels, with those involved working in partnership
with each other and with families. On the right the symbol is intended
to indicate the diverse nature of the modern family. Not simply two
parents and one or two children, but a range of different relationships
which now and increasingly will constitute the family of the next
century.

Socio-political mechanisms

- It cannot be assumed that mechanisms of transmission involve family pathology
- The function of the family is altered by external forces
- Families need 'permitting circumstances' in order to parent effectively
- Social factors profoundly influence the effectiveness of the family and child-rearing
- Social policies have a direct bearing on the conditions under which child and family live
- Social policies in each country define, to some extent, notions of 'appropriate' parenting
- These notions of 'appropriate' parenting are often reflected in legislation
- Policies in each country reflect the availability of resources and define priorities
- Policies can have unintended consequences
- Families also suffer from lack of appropriate policies to support them in their parenting task
- Lack of policies can leave children unprotected
- Some policies directly result in conditions where families are unable to parent effectively
- Other policies directly lead to a child living in 'especially difficult circumstances'
- The international community indirectly fosters some of these circumstances
- Specific issues are: the role of poverty, discrimination, the role of women
- System abuse

Psychological mechanisms

- Most families in difficult circumstances do not maltreat their children
- The reality is that some do
- Some through a variety of psychological factors may be more at risk than others
- A number of intrafamilial variables are associated with child abuse
- Physical child abuse is a continuum of behaviour found in many parents
- There are a few dangerous parents but most parents do not want to harm their children
- Child protection agencies are mandated to prevent, if possible, the tragedies
- Early medical models 'pathologised' abusing parents
- Comprehensive risks lists can, at best, only predict a third of abusing parents
- Ecological models are better at indicating both risk and protective factors
- Rutter has shown that there are continuities and discontinuities in parenting patterns
- Specific one-focused studies have helped in identifying mechanisms
- Among these are studies on cognitive behavioural states, attachment, self-esteem, attribution, and empathy
- Transactional and family systems models have also been helpful in identifying mechanisms
- Parents who recognise and reject the abuse in their own childhood broke patterns
- There are still considerable gaps in the literature, notably the neglect of men
- Much of the research has originated from the West and may not be relevant elsewhere
- Too much research is focused on post-abuse families and children. Too little on prevention

Cultural mechanisms

- Parents around the world are faced with a similar task in rearing children
- Cultural patterns of child-rearing are passed from generation to generation
- Culture compromises religion, different concepts of parenting, and values attached to particular children
- Culture exerts a powerful influence but it is not static
- Every society attempts to formalise what they feel is a proper concept of childhood
- The more distance in time, geography, class, the more different these social constructions will be
- Historically children have been severely ill-treated
- 'Badness' is culturally constructed
- Cross-culturally there are taboos about children
- Parenting reflects the specific needs of a society
- Children around the world today suffer from a wide range of violence
- The most common in all societies is physical chastisement
- Some children are particularly vulnerable to abuse
- Networks have a protective role
- Children are particularly at risk at times of rapid social change
- Family violence is less common in societies characterised by cooperation and commitment, sharing and equality
- Many societies have denied the existence of abuse only to discover it
- Child-rearing methods of minority groups living in a dominant culture may be more likely to be labelled abusive

Biological mechanisms

- Parents and children are biological beings
- Psyche cannot be separated from the nature and quality of their bodies
- These bodies are biologically influenced by the conditions in which they develop
- Developmental patterns follow a predictable course
- Events along the way can bring biological changes
- Parent - child relationships are inextricably linked to these biological forces
- Some parents are biologically more vulnerable to the risk of abusing their children
- Some children are biologically more vulnerable to the risk of being abused
- Biological factors may relate to intergenerational patterns of disease and poor health
- They may relate to inherited characteristics which lower the ability of the parent to parent and of the child to be parented effectively
- They may relate to factors in the environment such as pollution, iodine deficiency, lead, substance abuse
- Pathways through life may be influenced by biological risk and protective factors
- There is resistance to consideration of inherited characteristics
- These views are no longer tenable as much can be done to mitigate risk and enhance protective factors
- Personality traits and disorders may influence patterns of abuse
- Life history research challenges biomedical models of psychopathology
- Patterns can be broken even when they relate to characteristics that may be biologically determined

Figure 7: Holistic overview of the mechanisms that can lead to intergenerational child maltreatment

PRINCIPLES IN INTERVENTION

The United Nations Convention on the Rights of the Child (1989) gives the framework which should govern strategies in attempting to meet these rights. An outline of these rights was given in Chapter 3. For the purposes of intervening in the cycles of child maltreatment, a further possible set of principles are outlined here. Some of these link to the UN Convention, others have been suggested by the preceding review of the literature. These principles can be adapted for interventions in all the cycles. These may need to be adapted to the different circumstances in different societies, but as far as possible the principles outlined here should have universal relevance in efforts in not only breaking, but also in *preventing* cycles of child maltreatment.

The first principle is that *children are best brought up within their own families*, and interventions at every level, international, national, state and community, need to create the circumstances where parents can parent more effectively. The second principle must be to ensure that *the child's rights to protection* take precedence over the rights of the family to non-interference in family life. In the extreme, and hopefully in few cases, this may mean separating children from their families through formal procedures. Child protection interventions need to be seen within *the wider context* of promoting the child's welfare both in the short term and in the long term. This also involves a recognition that not all child protection interventions may always be in the child's best interest. The third principle is that *a 'partnership' (a participation/empowerment approach)* with parents, with the child, with agencies and with communities should be the favoured strategy in preventive and protection programmes. This approach should take into consideration cultural factors and the child's right to a cultural identity. The fourth principle is that there should be a focus on *both risk and protective factors*, strengths and needs within families, children and communities. The fifth principle is that we need to establish *clear measure of outcomes* so that progress against objectives can be measured. In measuring outcomes, quantitative data and performance indicators may not be enough. In providing any service, clear channels of communication need to be established between those using the service and the providers. Without such feedback there is always a danger that evaluation does not measure what it is intended to measure (Buchanan, 1994; Buchanan, Barlow, Croucher, Hendron, Seal & Smith, 1995). Finally, the sixth principle should be that *intergenerational outcomes* should also be monitored.

Supporting Children within their Families

Central to breaking patterns of intergenerational patterns of child maltreatment are preventive approaches. Caplan (1964) has suggested the
terms *primary, secondary* and *tertiary* to indicate the possibilities of preventive efforts at different levels. In child protection literature this can mean
the following (Willis, Holden & Rosenberg, 1992).

Primary prevention is where efforts are made to target whole populations
in an effort to reduce the incidence of child maltreatment. In the UK, an
example of primary prevention would be the Health Visiting Service,
whereby trained nurses visit all mothers of newborn babies. A further
example would be the 'keep safe' programmes in school to help children
develop strategies against physical and sexual abuse. Non-targeted services are generally welcomed by families and children as they are non-
stigmatising. Chamberlin (1994) has argued that primary prevention in
the USA is the 'missing piece in child development legislation'.
Simeonsson (1994), also in the USA, suggests that in promoting the well-
being of children: 'In broadest terms, the implications of a primary
prevention agenda are to remove the risk factors, to capitalise on
protective factors, and to promote resilience' (Simeonsson, 1994, p. 297).

Secondary prevention focuses on pre-identification of target groups who may
be at risk. The purpose here is to reduce the overall prevalence of a disorder. An example here would be the identification of areas of high social
need (Buchanan *et al.*, 1995; Wulczyn, 1994; Noble & Smith, 1994) and the
allocation of resources to those areas. More specifically, secondary prevention has been used in maternity units to identify and support parents who
may later present with parenting difficulties (Olds & Henderson, 1989), or
early year schemes such as the High Perry Scope project in the USA which
offers structured, high-quality pre-school education to disadvantaged children (Berrueta-Clement, Schweinhard, Barnett, Epstein & Weikart, 1984).

Tertiary prevention is targeted at families with identified conditions. In
child protection circles this has come to mean services to prevent an
abused child being further abused.

> Basic to our understanding of child abuse is the recognition that it is a
> preventable phenomenon (Finkelhor & Korbin, 1988). A public health
> perspective in which approaches are conceptualised in terms of their prim-
> ary, secondary or tertiary prevention aims, provides a framework for the
> conceptualisation of services. (Huntington, Lima & Zipper, 1994, p. 171)

Hardiker, Exton and Barker (1991) would argue that levels of prevention
are inextricably linked to political forces and the choice of welfare models

operating within nation states. Under a *residual* model where the focus is on family responsibility there will be little effort at primary or secondary level. Under an *institutional* model, the main emphasis will be at secondary and other levels. *Developmental* and *radical* welfare models would operate at every level of prevention. The development of child welfare policies seen in different nation states in both the developed and developing world does not necessarily support such rigid divides, but the model does help to delineate the emphasis on what interventions may be possible under differing political regimes.

Categorisation of the preventive levels also defines how such preventive services are evaluated. If the aim of primary prevention is to limit the incidence of an infectious disease such as malaria, it is easy, as long as data are collected, to calculate the success of a programme. If the aim of a secondary programme is to improve the birth care of mothers at risk, statistics can produce hard data on maternal mortality. If the aim of a tertiary programme is to increase the lifespan of cancer patients, reliable information can also be obtained. In public health the clear divides between different levels of prevention have produced dramatic results. However, the multiple interacting factors in child maltreatment make it harder to elicit clear outcomes. Should, for instance, programmes to eliminate child maltreatment be evaluated in the short term, intermediately or, as is suggested by this book, in terms of reducing intergenerational patterns of abuse?

Chamberlin (1994) in the USA describes the 'River of Risk' metaphor used in international health programmes:

> Downstream state agencies are trying to rescue 'drowning' children (tertiary prevention) . . . Upstream (secondary prevention) . . . people are trying to ascertain whether children swimming in the river are 'at risk' for 'drowning' and should be rescued . . . still further upstream (primary prevention) children are jumping or falling into the river because of some combination of family and community dysfunction. . . . We are surprised to see that very little is being done either to teach children to swim or, more importantly, to keep them from falling into the river. (Chamberlin, 1994, pp. 36–37)

In child maltreatment, each preventive programme at each level in the river will need to establish its own objectives, and its own performance indicators. Hopefully, with clearer cross-cultural definitions of what is and what is not child maltreatment, and with more reliable and standardised tools, such evaluations will become more meaningful. Even with these, measuring the outcomes of preventive programmes in child maltreatment will remain an inexact science.

The important message from research is that programmes do not have to focus simply on reducing the levels of child abuse. There needs to be a wider vision of child well-being (Simeonsson 1994, Department of Health, *Messages from Research*, 1995). Indeed a single focus on child protection, as we have seen in Chapter 3, may be contra-indicated.

Albee (1992) has also pointed out that effective preventive programmes do not have to untangle the complex web of causation. We know, for example, that if parental stress is reduced and coping skills enhanced this will be likely to result in improved competence. If families can be helped to establish supportive networks this is likely to reduce the levels of child maltreatment. As we have seen, if the overall health of mothers and children is enhanced this can also raise the thresholds where children are abused.

The Child's Rights to Protection

Where a child cannot be brought up safely within its own family, protection procedures may need to be initiated. The extent to which these are available will vary from country to country and will involve different legislative approaches and procedures. Evidence from the US and UK, as we have seen, suggests that there may have been an overfocus on protection, or tertiary prevention, and an underfocus on family support—primary and secondary prevention. Research suggests, however, as outlined in Chapter 4, that in all societies there are extremes of parenting behaviour to children which is deemed unacceptable. As we will see, each society, together with the international consensus, will need to make judgements of what is unacceptable treatment of children.

In whatever society he or she lives, the child's welfare should be the paramount consideration. The United Nations Convention on the Rights of the Child, article 19, makes it clear that nation states have a responsibility to use all appropriate measures to protect children from all forms of child maltreatment while in the care of their parents, legal guardians and/or other person who is caring for them (UN, 1989). This clearly suggests that children's rights to protection override the rights of the parents to non-interference in family life. As outlined by Maclean and Kurczewski (1994) even in the developed countries of East and West Europe there can be a strong resistance to state intervention in family life.

In England and Wales, the Children Act 1989 tried to negotiate a delicate balance between the rights of the parents to non-interference into family life and the rights of the child to protection. An important judicial judgment preceded this Act. This has become known as the Gillick principle:

Parental rights are derived from parental duty and exist so long as they are needed for the protection of the person and the property of the child . . . parental right yields to the child's right to make his own decisions when he reaches a sufficient understanding and intelligence to be capable of making up his own mind on the matter requiring decision. (*Gillick* v. *West Norfolk and Wisbech Area Health Authority*, 1986)

The Children Act 1989 now responds to the difficult dilemma, by ensuring that parents keep what is known as 'parental responsibility', even when their child has been placed in public care by a court. In this case, however, they share 'parental responsibility' with the local authority.

Partnership–Participation–Empowerment

Partnership is a difficult concept and may not translate easily. It has links to the term 'participation' and also to the term 'empowerment', but it is not quite the same as either of these terms. In England and Wales, although the word did not appear in the Children Act 1989, it was a central concept in the many volumes of Guidance and Regulation which accompanied the Act.

Pugh, Aplin, De'Ath and Moxon (1987) define it as follows:

A working relationship that is characterised by a shared sense of purpose, mutual respect and the willingness to negotiate. This implies a sharing of information, responsibility, skills, decision making and accountability. (Pugh *et al.*, 1987, p. 5)

In the UK the idea arose from the work of Pugh & De'Ath (1985), who demonstrated that the confidence of parents was undermined by the increasing number of child care experts with whom they came into contact through their children. Parents were seen as falling into two camps: either they were 'good enough' and did not need help from the state, or they were 'deficient' and needed the local authority to take over parental rights. Spearheaded by the Partnership studies (De'Ath & Pugh, 1985–6; Pugh *et al.*, 1987) evidence grew that in centres where professionals 'worked with parents' rather than 'did things to them', more effective relationships between professionals and parents could be created, especially where these relationships were built on notions of partnership and mutual respect. It was noted that these relationships also benefited the child. At the same time, other groups were demonstrating that parent involvement and the use of written agreements could lead to more appropriate child care planning, better decisions and more parental cooperation (Aldgate, 1989).

In England and Wales, under the Children Act 1989, partnership is advocated as a recommended method of working with parents, with children, with families going through child protection procedures, with agencies and with parent self-help groups (Buchanan, 1994). Partnership has become a buzz word of the 1990s. There was concern that the Partnership Principle would become another unquestioned ideology: 'This nice-sounding term makes us feel good, perhaps even to the extent of being offered as a solution to all child-care difficulties' (Family Rights Group, 1991, p. 1). There was also concern that the 'Partnership Principle' would impede effective child protection. It was argued that there cannot be a true partnership when the state would always have the edge on power. Evidence now suggests that although working in partnership with families is difficult and not always achieved, especially in child protection cases (Thorburn, Lewis & Shemmings, 1995), the greater sharing of information, more openness, and the demonstration of greater respect, add up to a more effective method of promoting the welfare of children than non-participative approaches. In other areas of child welfare, partnership approaches are also producing dividends. Smalley (1994) has shown in her work as a paediatrician in Community Child Health in the UK, that she received better outcomes in terms of child health by recognising the expertise of parents, allowing them to keep their child's own health records, and working with them in partnership.

Similarly Faupel (1994) also in the UK, an educational psychologist, has found that by working in partnership with parents and their children who have special needs, more positive outcomes are possible. Other centres providing support services for families and children, especially those with special needs, also find the method of working helpful (Goodwin, 1994; Walton, 1994; Farmer & Blanchard, 1994). Internationally, as we will see in the following chapters, there are some powerful examples of the successful programmes which are based on an empowerment and participative approach.

The child's right to participate in decisions affecting his/her life is enshrined in the UN Convention as well as, in England and Wales, under the Children Act 1989. This should be in keeping with the child's 'age and understanding' (Children Act, 1989). It does NOT mean that the child's wishes should always rule the day. The child has the right to make his/her views *known*, and for these views to be incorporated in the decision-making process. This is a difficult and controversial area, and in some societies, as we have seen, may conflict with strongly held views on family rights. The reasoned approached, however, implied by the Gillick principle above, is that the child of sufficient age and intelligence may be *better able* to weigh up to reality his/her own situation and make more appropriate decisions.

Effective participation is a learning process, where the child is given opportunities to make everyday choices in order to learn about the consequences and the responsibilities inherent in making choices; is given information appropriate to his/her understanding; is given support to make views known. Hearing what children and young people say is also a learning process. There is growing evidence that if we want to improve children's well-being, and if we want young people to 'own' the decisions made, particularly with adolescents, there is greater need for this two-way communication (Cloke & Davies, 1995, Buchanan *et al.*, 1995, Wheal & Buchanan, 1994).

An Acknowledgement of Both Risk and Protective Factors, Strengths and Needs

Rutter (1989), as we have seen, has demonstrated that life pathways are characterised by continuities and discontinuities. The extent to which *risk* factors become predictive is related to the presence or absence of various *protective* factors, interacting with the environment. The identification of protective factors offers the possibility of manipulating the environment, even in cases of biological risk, to effect better outcomes. Enhancing protective factors and reducing risk factors is the task for all levels of prevention. In identifying these risk and protective factors, an acknowledgement of communities', families', carers' and children's expertise is central to the process

A linked approach is that of Barrowclough and Fleming (1986). In their case they were working with people who were elderly, but the principles expounded have wider applicability. This approach also links to the 'non-deficit' model now widely used in working with people with disabilities. Rather than focusing on what the person cannot do, there is a focus on what they can do—their *strengths* (Barrowclough & Fleming, 1986). Problems are then reframed as *needs*. Rather than 'John X is very difficult to manage because he is hyperactive', the focus changes to 'John X needs help to direct and contain his energies'. This reframing more easily suggests possible interventions. In a community context, this might be 'X area is a crime ridden-area, with many young offenders who are out of school'. This would be reframed as 'X area needs a programme to keep young people out of school occupied and to prevent them offending'. As with the identification of risk and protective factors, a strengths/needs approach is relevant at all levels of prevention.

The advantage of identifying *protective factors* and *strengths* within children and families, is that the protective factors can be used to mitigate the risk and the strengths can be used to meet the needs. Kaufman and Zigler

(1989) quote a case of a young girl who was rendered paraplegic. When fostered, she acquired an interest in computers and eventually developed expert skills. These skills considerably increased her self-esteem and took her to University. Put another way, it could be said that her interest in computers was a strength which went some way to meet her needs to develop greater self-esteem.

The identification of strengths within communities can be a powerful force for change. Interventions which focus exclusively on pathology will always be of limited value. We also need to believe that change is poss- ible. Working with protective factors, and the strengths of people, chil- dren and communities, while being realistic about risks and needs, will give us this hope.

The Need for Child Maltreatment to be Seen Within its Social Context and the Need to View the Overall Quality of Parenting Rather than Single Abusive Episodes

There is a need to identify children who may be at risk, as will be discussed in Chapter 10, but these risk and protective factors need to be seen in *their social context*. Even within families environments for different children will differ (Rutter, 1995). There is also a need for the abuse to be seen within the *developmental* context of the child (Kaufman & Zigler, 1992), and finally there is the need to view the *wider context of the parenting relationship*. It is not necessarily the abusive experiences that are transmitted intergenera- tionally but the *quality* of the parenting relationship (Kaufman & Zigler, 1989; Egeland & Jacobvitz 1984; Hunter & Kilstrom, 1979). Combinations of different kinds of abuse or abuse and neglect together tend to lead to poorer outcomes than isolated episodes of abuse (Gibbons *et al.*, 1995).

> Long-term problems occur when *the parenting style* fails to compensate for the inevitable deficiencies that become manifest in the course of 20 years or so it takes to bring up a child. During this period, occasional neglect, un- necessary or severe punishment or some form of family discord can be expected . . . If parenting is entirely negative, it will be damaging; if nega- tive events are interspersed with positive experiences, outcomes will be better . . . In families low on warmth and high on criticism, negative inci- dents accumulate as if to remind a child that he or she is unloved. (Depart- ment of Health, 1995, *Messages from Research*, p. 19)

In developing strategies to break cycles of child maltreatment there is therefore a need to help parents re-evaluate their overall *parenting style*.

There is considerable evidence that parents who broke the cycle of child maltreatment were better able to challenge and reject the maltreating experiences of their own lives (Egeland & Jacobvitz 1984; Hunter & Kilstrom, 1979; Kaufman & Zigler, 1989).

Measuring Outcomes

Measuring outcomes also gives the hope that change is possible. As we have already discussed, measuring outcomes of child protection is difficult and inexact. Hard definitions of what is being measured are also crucial. As we will see, data are now being routinely collected in most countries at various levels—international, national and local. The quality and reliability of the data, of course, vary from setting to setting. The increased availability of computer technology makes data collection an easier and more effective task.

The first challenge in data collection is to ensure that the factors that are being monitored are indeed the factors that indicate change. The most usual way is to identify a range of performance indicators that suggest that objectives are being met and these indicators are then monitored. A local authority, for example, may use as an indicator the number of young people it has in its care (Hutchinson, 1994). In the UK, with the concern about the outcomes for such children (Rowe & Lambert, 1973; Rowe, 1988), there is pressure from central government to reduce the numbers of children being admitted (Department of Health, 1994; Children Act Report, 1993). The local authority may feel that a reduction in the numbers of children being looked after in out-of-home care is a positive step. The dilemma is that such a single indicator tells us little about how well children are being protected and nothing about the outcomes for them after they leave care. In Hampshire Social Services, in the UK, for example, monitoring is a day-to-day statistical activity through their Client Record System; that is computer records are kept of those children and families needing services from them. The other side of their monitoring is 'evaluation'. This is a longer term process and seeks to ascertain how far their aims and objectives are being met. Central to this process is eliciting the views of the service users (Audit Commission, 1994; Buchanan et al., 1995). This can be done through a variety of methods. At one level is the Representations Procedure, commonly known as the Complaints Procedure, now mandatory under the Children Act 1989; at another level is informal feedback from community forums; at the third level is research into users' views. Feedback from users is important to ensure that indicators are measuring what they are intended to measure.

None of these strategies measures *outcomes* for individual children. In the UK, there is a useful initiative which has developed a set of Assessment and Action Records, known as the Looking After Children project (LAC) (Ward, 1995). These schedules, which act as practice tools, management tools and potentially research tools, monitor the progress of children who are being looked after in out-of-home care. They are also being developed for use with other children at risk. In addition, they being translated by academics and policy-makers for use in a number of countries, for example Canada, Romania, Belgium, offering the possibility of an international data base on children. The potential of these records will be discussed further in later chapters.

The Value of Intergenerational Data

From the perspective of this book, short-term outcomes are not enough. We need to know what happens in the long term; what happens to the next generation. Statistics from the United Nations, World Health, and other such organisations provide an overview of change year by year. Census data and other national surveys also give useful information. None of these, however, measure outcomes for *individuals* in the long term. In time through the LAC system in the UK there will be clearer outcome measures.

In the meantime, as we have mentioned, useful outcome indicators can be elicited from longitudinal studies. There are a number of useful longitudinal studies. The National Child Development Study in England, Scotland and Wales, is based on a nationally representative sample of all children who were born during one week in 1958. There have been five sweeps at different ages to collect data on those involved. The original sample were last monitored when they were aged 33 when many already had established families. This study now offers opportunities to consider the realities of intergenerational patterns. Understandably child maltreatment, as such, could not be considered in the longitudinal data collection, but data were collected about current and past relationships, behaviour patterns, parenting types and current attitudes. These data are revealing important insights into risk and protective factors which may be associated with intergenerational patterns of child maltreatment (Cheung & Buchanan, forthcoming).

The topic of measuring outcomes will be returned to in later chapters. The principle outlined here is that it is only by measuring outcomes that we will know whether our efforts are being effective. Ethically, there is always the danger that if we do not measure outcomes, we may be unaware when interventions are causing further harm. The overriding principle in intervening in the cycles of abuse, must be that we do no further harm.

SUMMARY: PRINCIPLES IN INTERVENTION

- Children are usually best brought up in their own families
- The child has rights to protection
- Protection is best effected by *partnership/participation* with parents and child
- Awareness of both risk *and protective* factors within the child's developmental context
- Identification of *both strengths and needs* in child and family and community
- The need for child maltreatment to be seen within its social and developmental context
- The need to view the overall quality of parenting rather than single abusive episodes
- The importance of outcome measurement
- The need for an awareness of intergenerational outcomes
- The overriding principle: Do no further harm

8

BREAKING SOCIO-POLITICAL CYCLES OF MALTREATMENT: HIGHLIGHTS FOR INTERVENTION

One of the greatest . . . lies and self-deceptions is the denial of collective social responsibility for the welfare of parents and their children . . . the greatest threat to child survival in the world today is the poverty of Third World mothers. The abusive and infanticidal acts of parents are often the end-products of abusive and infanticidal social structural and economic and political relations. (Scheper-Hughes, 1987, p. 24)

At least some of the child maltreatment that is observed, diagnosed, and treated is actually created, and those forms of institutionalised maltreatment reproduced in our social policies and enacted in our popular culture, remain below consciousness, and therefore unrecognized and untreated. If we are to avoid this tangle of absurdities, it is essential to un-mask the contradictions in our behaviour. At that time, and not before, we will be prepared to solve, rather than use, the problems of child abuse. (Scheper-Hughes, 1987, p. 354)

It is now more than 30 years since Kempe so dramatically 'rediscovered' child abuse. In the intervening time, particularly in the developed world, the main focus has been on tertiary preventive efforts after children have been abused. There has been a lesser focus on the social and political conditions that foster situations where millions of children generation after generation live out their lives in suboptimum conditions and are daily subjected to abusive treatment.

De Mause (1984) in an analysis of political speeches in the USA in the 1980s of the cuts that were proposed for Aid to Families with Dependent Children, school lunches, child care, and food programmes, noted that the sense of guilt, and the acceptance of responsibility for the wider community, seemed to be absent. As Western governments seek to unwind the welfare state, it could be argued that the guilt has been displaced onto the selected 'criminal' scapegoats so that righteous anger is spent in punishing these 'bad' individuals rather than providing jobs, health care and social welfare programmes. Scheper-Hughes and Stein (1987) add that reactions to child abuse have also been fuelled by anxieties about the changes in society with respect to sex roles, sexuality and family life.

In the mid 1990s, however, there appears to have been a re-evaluation of approaches to child maltreatment. As it becomes apparent that child abuse is not just the prerogative of the developed world, there is growing realisation that child protection legislation and tertiary preventive efforts alone will not solve the problem of intergenerational patterns of child abuse. At much the same time there is concern that the elaborate Child Protection policies developed in the West, although necessary to protect the few, may not be the most effective use of resources for helping the many families who need comprehensive family policies focused on support rather than controls (Hutchison, 1994; Thorburn, Lewis & Shemmings, 1995).

This chapter feeds into this new willingness to view the wider picture. The mechanisms involved in perpetuating intergenerational socio-political patterns of child maltreatment identified in Chapter 3 suggest the responsibility for breaking these cycles of abuse rests at different levels, international, national, and local. In this brief review it is only possible to touch on a a few of the central themes.

INTERVENTIONS AT THE INTERNATIONAL LEVEL

The necessary task of drawing attention to human needs has unfortunately given rise to the popular impression that the developing world is a state upon which no light falls and only tragedy is enacted. But the fact is that, for all the set-backs, more progress has been made in the last 50 years than in the previous 2000 . . . In the decades ahead, a clear opportunity exists to make the breakthrough against what might be called the last great obscenity—the needless malnutrition, disease, and illiteracy that still cast a shadow over the lives, and the futures, of the poorest quarter of the world's children. (UNICEF, 1993, preface)

In this book a central argument is that breaking cycles of child maltreatment is inextricably linked to improving the health of the caring parent. Parents, as we saw in Chapter 3, need 'permitting circumstances' in order to rear their children. A secondary theme in this book is that numbers of children in developed countries are needlessly brought up in suboptimum conditions and these conditions are also transmitted across the generations. 'Many poor countries are today closer to meeting the most basic needs of their peoples than other countries that are considerably wealthier' (UNICEF, 1994a, p. 19). On the international scene UNICEF has been a central pressure group. It has collated statistics, disseminated information, set targets and led an unremitting public relations exercise to persuade the richer countries that they have a responsibility to meet the minimum human needs of the poorest people.

Setting achievable goals has been important. In relation to the above quotation UNICEF in 1994 notes that eight of the poorest countries with per capita incomes below $1000 a year and a wide range of political systems have already reached the goal of reducing under-five mortality to 70 per 1000 births or less. Without such achievements, there is a danger that the sheer weight of the world's distress will lead to a feeling of hopelessness. Breaking patterns of intergenerational child maltreatment, as part of the bigger picture, is similarly vulnerable to inaction born from this sense of hopelessness. We need to believe that change is possible.

Figure 8, from a UNICEF publication gives hope. It demonstrates how little changes can lead to an upward spiral. At the pivot of this spiral is progress against what they call the 'PPE problems', Poverty, Population growth and Environmental stress. Prosperity and security improve women's health and make family planning more likely. Fewer and more widely spaced births improve the health of children and women. Better education is associated with more health knowledge and educated women are more likely to marry later and have fewer children.

The Upward Spiral gives the faith to George Albee's (1992) hope that every baby born anywhere in the world should be a full-term healthy 'planned for' and 'wanted' child, and this hope is equally important for the future well-being of children in poor countries as it is for children living in the slums of the developed world. The key is improving health, education and prosperity for women.

UNICEF (1994a) notes that the end of the cold war and the beginning of a fall in military expenditure together with a tentative movement to greater democratisation in many parts of the world augur well for improvements in the lives of the poorest people in the world. However, only 25% of all aid goes to the poorest countries who house 75% of the world's poor (UNICEF, 1994a).

Aid to developing countries is very vulnerable to the boom and bust of economic life. Sustained support and pressure are needed from a broad

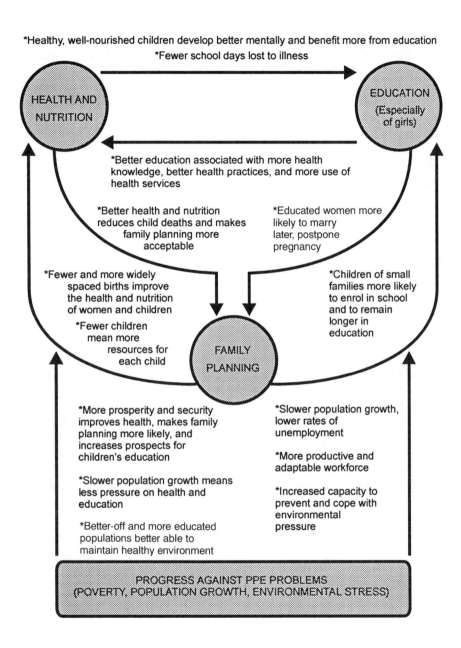

Figure 8: The upward spiral
From UNICEF (1994), *The State of the World's Children*, p. 49. Reprinted by permission of Oxford University Press

public, to ensure promises of aid become realities. We all have a responsibility to the community of the wider world. In doing so we will break the PPE cycle which contributes to intergenerational child maltreatment.

SPECIFIC INTERNATIONAL RESPONSIBILITIES

The international community also has a responsibility to monitor and intervene in specific areas where international action may be fostering situations which create the conditions that undermine the welfare of children.

Migration of Labour

The outcome for children where rural migrants can become part of the global labour pool is such an area. In Thailand, for example, Department of Labour statistics indicate that in 1989 alone, some 125 000 workers moved to the Middle East, or other Asian and European countries (Hiew, 1992). Hiew notes that entire villages in Thailand's northeastern region have only children, women and the old remaining, as the men have left to seek jobs. The men may be away from one to five years. This movement has widely been seen as nationally beneficial since remittances from overseas workers rank second in terms of national income (Singhanetra-Renard, Chaparnond, Tiyayon & Prabudhanitisarn, 1988). However, the international labour market has mixed benefits for children. The situation often ends with tragic results such as family discord, divorce or homicide and suicide and ultimately children can lose one or both parents. The international community needs the labour but it would appear that they could do more to assist families back home in coping with the situation.

Child Labour

International markets also work against children in encouraging the sale of goods which have been created by exploitative child labour. National figures of the extent of child labour may be suspect because this might be the result of children not being paid for their work (Hiew, 1992). Given the levels of unemployment and poverty in some of the areas, it would be impractical to eradicate child labour, but more pressure could be brought on the manufacturers to ensure that children have access to medical, educational and recreational facilities. The Nepali Government is taking such action in its carpet trade (UNICEF, 1994b), but presumably the international market could also do more by promoting only those goods which do not involve child exploitation.

Child Prostitution

International markets also have a role to play in fostering the tragedy of child prostitution. As we have seen, in some areas of the world, sexual exploitation of children linked to the tourist trade has reached monstrous proportions. The hard-hitting campaign by ECPAT, largely inspired and directed by Ron O'Grady from New Zealand, demonstrates what one small pressure group can do to influence world opinion. This international campaign has developed four main strategies:

(a) To lobby politicians so that they will enact laws which will protect children.
(b) To find ways to ensure that the law is enforced.
(c) To provide educational programmes for families and children in receiving countries and tourists from sending countries.
(d) To provide accurate information on the issue. (O'Grady, 1994b, p. 140)

As a result of the campaign, tourists violating children when on holiday are named and in some cases they can be prosecuted in their country of origin for the offence. Alongside the campaign to deter sexual tourism is a realistic programme to help children develop other means for earning their living. The risk of AIDS gives the international community a further incentive to limit such tourism.

Children in War Situations

Another important area of responsibility for the world community is for children in war situations. Around 25% of foreign assistance from the United States is for military assistance. Such assistance may bring peace but it may also bring war. UNICEF (1994a) highlights the international responsibility for children in war zones. Action is on two fronts. Firstly, development aid must include support for the strengthening of institutions of democracy (UNDP, 1994). Unless democracy takes root, violence, coup d'états, and wars take place and children are in the frontline. Secondly, the international community has a responsibility to respond to the child victims of war. The intense media interest in atrocities experienced by children, for instance the rape of girls as a systematic weapon of war in former Yugoslavia, and the growing knowledge of post-traumatic stress disorders, has given rise to a new commitment to alleviate some of the victimisation of children in war situations. The Declaration signed by the world's political leaders at the 1990 World Summit for Children specifically asked: 'That periods of tranquillity and special relief corridors be observed for the benefit of children, where war and violence are still taking place' (World Summit for Children 1990, UNICEF, 1994a, p. 4). Examples of small achievements are 'days of tranquillity' which allowed El Salvador's children to be immunised on several days each year during the civil war; national immunisation days in the Lebanon; and 'Corridors of peace' during the fighting in the Sudan.

More radical approaches, in areas of continuing conflict, are programmes to prepare children and young people to sustain the traumas (Schwebel, 1992; Breger, 1987). Breger has been working with child victims of the war in Bosnia. Klingman's (1978) work in Israel is seeking to 'psycho-immunize' children against the effects of trauma. Such expertise needs to be shared. Richman (1993) reminds us, however, that we need to look beyond Post Traumatic Stress Disorder, and alleviate the long-term secondary consequences of political conflict.

Landmines

UNICEF's campaign against landmines is another issue where international action may produce dividends. The accepted view is that the anti-personnel mine aims to tie up enemy resources in the evacuation and treatment of the wounded (UNICEF, 1994a). Mines have been laid in villages, fields, pathways and even outside houses. Decades after they have been laid landmines can still kill or injure, and children are particularly vulnerable. UNICEF is calling for a total ban on the production, use, stockpiling, sale and export of anti-personnel landmines. Countries which have agreed either to a moratorium or a total halt on exports include the United States, France, Belgium, Greece, South Africa, Israel, Germany and recently Italy which is the West's biggest manufacturer. UNICEF in 1994 noted that the UK was still opposing a blanket ban on landmines.

Approaches to Primary Prevention

The above examples illustrate how international organisations such as UNICEF and small campaigns such as ECPAT can bring international public pressure to bear to effect change. Where huge profits are made from labour, child prostitution, arms, and conflicts, the international community has both a responsibility and an effective power to elicit this change. Solutions mean taking note of both supply and demand, and developing realistic alternatives to local economic situations.

Solutions also involve the dissemination of information about the extent of particular problems, the effectiveness of schemes set up to tackle them and the progress made in achieving targets. Important to improving the lot of the world's children, is the belief that it is possible.

INTERVENTIONS AT THE NATIONAL LEVEL

The central task for government at the national level is to promote the individual well-being of its citizens and ensure the future well-being of the nation. In a democracy, voters make judgements about the effectiveness or otherwise of its elected governments in responding to this task. As we have seen, social policies of governments both directly and indirectly affect the institution traditionally held responsible for rearing the next generation . . . the family. Virginia Bottomley, who was Minister of Health in the UK, suggests we need to construct policies that are relevant, effective and reflect the realities of modern life. That is, policies which underpin rather than undermine families (Bottomley, 1994).

The Challenge of Family Change

The dilemma for politicians is that the 'the family' is undergoing tremendous changes. On the one hand, with the help of medical improvements, family size in underdeveloped countries is increasing, while on the other hand, in the West, family limitation is bringing about its own stresses (Hess, 1995). The paradox, as we have seen, is that the higher the level of prosperity the fewer children people have.

> Repeatedly the world has seen a dramatic drop in birth rates in countries where children have been saved from early and unnecessary death. In many countries a decline in unnecessary death of children has preceded an economic upturn, led to reduced family size, and improved lives. (Albee, 1992, p. 320)

In China there is concern that future generations will be destroyed by the weight of their own numbers before the coming of economic well-being. Surveys from Hong Kong, however, illustrate that with growing prosperity birth rates can drop dramatically. Between 1961 and 1981 fertility dropped from 5170 to 1289 per 1000 women (Lau, Lee, Wan & Wong, 1992). Such a drop also undoubtedly reflects greater availability and use of contraception, but it is family planning from individual choice. In this case limiting family size may also be related to uncertainties about the future (Lau *et al.*, 1992).

Linked to lower birth rates is the tendency for higher divorce rates. In Hong Kong the number of divorce cases has doubled from 1981 to 1991 from 24 261 to 53 485 with an increasing number of young people delaying marriage (Lau *et al.*, 1992). In the UK divorce rates although high are comparatively stable, having risen by 1% during the last decade (Mackay 1995). Divorce rates in the USA are the highest in the world, although stabilisation is expected in the 1990s (Brubaker & Kimberly, 1993). 'Accordingly, it seems likely that the increase over time in parental divorce and remarriage may well mean an increase in risk for the children involved' (Hess, 1995, p. 177). Politicians and policy-makers have the difficult task of monitoring the subtle changes and trying to implement policies that relate to the realities of their situation. One of the problems is that in many parts even of the developed world, there are no formalised national family policies (Kamerman & Kahn, 1989). In Britain, for example, there is no Ministry with overall responsibility for family policy, although recently the Minister for Health was given 'special responsibilities for the family'. The difficulty in the UK is that responsibilities for families are split across many ministries. The white paper on divorce law reform (Mackay, 1995) seeks to ensure a greater integration of government policies supporting marriage. The importance of this has been highlighted by research by Cockett and Tripp (1994) which shows the cost to children of family breakdown in terms of lower educational achievement, health problems and emotional distress. This research is controversial as it contradicts some of the earlier research (Cherlin, Furstenberg, Chase-Lansdale, Kiernan, Robins, Morrison & Teitler, 1991; Block, Block & Gjerde, 1986) which suggested that it was family conflict before and around the divorce, rather than the divorce itself, which had the deleterious effect on children (Rutter & Smith, 1995).

One of the difficulties about formulating family policy is the lack of knowledge, despite considerable statistical data, about current family patterns. Utting, Bright and Henricson (1994) note that there is an increasing interest in stepfamilies but remarkably little is known about them. Traditional stereotypes about what is or is not 'a family' may colour not only social policies but how the figures that inform the policies are added up. Do we know, for instance, how many children in Britain have moved between different parental cohabiting relationships? Presumably every time such a relationship breaks down, children are affected, but because the partners have not married precise information about what is happening to the children involved is difficult to monitor. If we are to create policies which support families we need to know more about the real families in which children live. As Wisendale in the USA states:

> Whatever policies we adopt in relation to families, it is imperative that they reflect an understanding of the growing diversity in family structure. We can no longer afford to live in the nineties and dream in the fifties . . . clearly the family is changing and policy makers are being called upon to respond accordingly. (Wisendale, 1993, p. 250)

In the USA, family policy has also been an elusive concept (Wisendale, 1993). Kamerman and Kahn (1989) note that the concept was first mentioned in the United States in the 1960s but its development has been slow and disjointed. This is partly because family law still remains predominately the responsibility of the individual states.

The increase in the rate of divorced and single-parent households led by females (expected to rise to 25% of households by the end of the century) and teen pregnancy, as well as a 75% participation of women in the labour force between the ages of 18–44 have inspired important initiatives at both state and federal level. In a recent survey of 42 states, Wisendale (1990) found that 28 had made a special effort to focus on the family during a legislative session within the previous two years. According to the National Conference of State Legislature (1989) states have chosen to focus on four policy areas. Firstly, work and family issues; secondly, child welfare; thirdly, family health policy; and fourthly, teen pregnancy. State legislature appears to have focused more on children and child welfare legislation than on the family as a whole. Much of this emphasis has been on passing stringent child abuse and neglect laws. Kamerman and Kahn (1989) would argue that all family policy initiatives should centre on how to do better by children rather than on what is wrong with families.

Programmes to Combat Poverty and Lack of Health Care in the US

In the US, several programmes have been designed to reduce the impact of poverty, including Aid to Families with Dependent Children (AFDC), supplementary Food Program for Women, Infants and Children (WIC), food stamps, school lunch and breakfast, and medical assistance. These programmes are not designed to prevent child maltreatment as such, but they provide important assistance to low-income families and thereby support the functioning of these families (Harrington & Dubowitz, 1993).

In addition there is the Head Start programme, in some areas, to provide intensive pre-school education for children living in poor families. Many of these programmes have been criticised for making the family the unit of eligibility, but only when poverty is the criterion employed (Wisendale, 1993). Harrington and Dubowitz (1993) indicate that in addition to providing increased benefits to more families, Federal programmes such as the Job Opportunities and Basic Skills Training Program need to be expanded to serve more families.

In the US a national child care bill was finally passed in the autumn of 1990. A $2.5 billion funding was argued for, much of which was to go towards expanding the Head Start programme. In the event they got $750 million and the Head Start programme was not expanded (Wisendale, 1993).

In the US, the lack of health care is critically linked to poverty. Evidence in 1993 suggested that almost 11 million children, or 16.9%, either had no health insurance or their insurance status was unknown. Low-income and minority families were the most likely to be uninsured. For example only 62% of children in African American families earning less than 200% of the Federal poverty level were insured (Harrington & Dubowitz, 1993). A number of recent reforms in the Medicaid programme may substantially expand the availability of health care to children in low-income families. Harrington and Dubowitz, however, argue that this is not enough. Universal health care for children and pregnant women should be a priority for the Federal Government.

CHILD MALTREATMENT AND THE LEGAL SYSTEM

Patricia Spakes (1985) in the USA argues that the role of the legislative and the Court is central to the formulation of family policies: 'The court may be old fashioned, it may be slow, and it may be inconsistent, but no attempt at designing a national family policy can ignore its role' (Spakes, 1985, p. 186). Levine, Ewing and Levine (1987) suggest that the law seeks to prevent or limit harm in a number of differing ways. Firstly, the law seeks to *deter* those committing crimes, by defining what is a crime and forewarning that such offences will be punishable. Secondly, the law together with its associated Regulations seeks *to limit harm* from negligent behaviour through civil and occasional criminal sanctions, by defining what behaviour is deemed negligent. Such penalties it is hoped will ensure more caution. Thirdly, the law gives *specific rights to specific groups*, for example children, in order to protect their status and vulnerability. Finally the law seeks to protect *individual rights*, for example, freedom from discrimination, freedom of speech (Reppucci & Aber, 1992).

As Jan Carter noted at the Royal Society of Medicine's Proceedings of the Conference on The Challenge of Child Abuse (White Franklin, 1977):

> There is a problem of whether child abuse is appropriately dealt with in the area of operation of the criminal law . . . The possible logical responses to the question (made to members of the general public) 'is child abuse a crime?' are as follows:
> 1: Yes, it is always a crime. 2: Yes, it is sometimes a crime. 3: Yes, it is rarely a crime. 4: No, it is never a crime. 5: It's an irrelevant question. 6: It depends what you mean by crime. (Carter, 1977, p. 201)

There are considerable consequences, as we saw in Chapter 3, in how child abuse is defined or 'constructed'.

Carter points out that within the framework of the legal code, child abuse is a crime if the courts say it is, and if it can be proved the act has taken place. The legal code assumes that the majority of people agree about the value of the legislation, and the legal code is based on the assumption that a rational person weighs up the advantages and disadvantages. It also assumes that the judiciary is competent in deciding what is and is not child abuse and what is damaging to a child.

'The innocency of the judiciary and at times the naivety of its ideas about family behaviour remain of deep concern to professional workers' (White Franklin, 1977, p. 276). Franklin expressed considerable concern about family rights and separating children from their families. 'The baby is saved from physical abuse or death, but condemned to emotional deprivation' (White Franklin, 1977, p. 277). It is notable that nearly 20 years later, although times have moved on and in particular the judiciary may now be more sensitive to, and informed about, the needs of children, many of the dilemmas remain.

In the last 30 years, the legal system has played a prominent role in child protection. In the USA child abuse reporting laws swept the nation in the late 1960s. Their goal was both to identify offenders and to deter potential abusers (Reppucci & Aber, 1992). Looking back over the 30-year period, most professionals would probably agree that child protection legislation, where it has existed, has increased awareness about what is and what is not child abuse and has limited, at least in public, physical chastisement of children. In this respect, legislation to protect children has had an important role. Finkelhor (1993) would suggest that the rise in the number of reported cases of child abuse—in the US from 669 000 to 2 163 000 between 1976 and 1987—is related to a greater awareness about the problem.

However, it can also be argued that many parents who have been wrong-fully accused have suffered as a result of child abuse reporting laws (Schultz, 1988). Legislation has to negotiate the difficult balancing act between protecting children and protecting the rights of the family. Evidence from the UK suggests it has not always achieved this balance (Butler Sloss, 1988).

In the USA, the controversy rages. On the one hand it is felt that over-reporting and underreporting are twin problems (Besharov, 1993).

> On the one hand, many abused and neglected children go unreported because they are afraid to come forward on their own or they are overlooked by informed professionals. The price is great: Failure to report exposes children to serious injury and even death. On the other hand, a large proportion of reports are dismissed after investigations find insufficient evidence upon which to proceed . . . These cases . . . divert resources from already understaffed agencies, thus limiting their ability to protect children in real danger. (Besharov, 1993, p. 257)

Besharov suggests that screening of potential abusers should be improved. Finkelhor, however, argues that the main problem is still underreporting, *not* overreporting. 'In spite of the dramatic increase in reporting, however, most researchers and clinicians believe that a large quantity of abuse is still not being counted on statistics' (Finkelhor, 1993, p. 273). Finkelhor (1993) quotes the National Incidence Study (Sedlak, 1991) which noted that the majority of serious abuse was not known to the Child Protection Agencies. Investigation is, of course, not the same as a criminal prosecution. The purpose of child abuse reporting laws is to identify children before they experience serious harm. The dilemma is that both in the US and UK investigation may not lead to the necessary supportive services (Finkelhor, 1993; Thorburn, Lewis & Shemmings, 1995).

Perhaps both sides of the controversy would agree that what is needed is better support services for those children identified as at risk and better resources for those who are not safe living with their families.

> If we have nothing to offer when abuse is reported, it is silly to argue about whether we are reporting too little or too much. And if we were truly offering help, rather than stigma, blame and punishment, what would there be to complain about? (Finkelhor, 1993, p. 285)

In the US, states are required under the National Adoption Assistance and Child Welfare Act of 1980 to exercise 'reasonable efforts' to prevent out-of-home care. This has led to a range of Family Preservation Services, for children and families *after* they have been identified through *substantiated* reports of having been abused and/or neglected. The Edna

McConnell Clark Foundation has been instrumental in promoting one model, the crisis intervention approach of the Homebuilders' programme in Washington, also called Intensive Family Preservation. Most family preservation services are short-term and provided in-home, with 24-hour availability and assistance with practical services (Pecora, Whittaker & Maluccio, 1992). Although initial evaluation studies showed very positive outcomes, more recent research points to rather mixed outcomes with regard to placement prevention (Barth & Berry, 1994). This may relate to the greater intensity of problems in families served, in particular substance abuse which is a major contributor to rising foster care caseloads (Besharov, 1989).

Barth and Berry (1994) note that the Directory of Family-based Services lists 131 intensive services in 37 states, of which more than one third of the total are in four states. Taken together the total number of families receiving these services is less than 30 000 each year out of the total 'substantiated reports' of roughly 1 000 000. In 1991 there were 224 000 new entries to foster care (Tatara, 1994) suggesting that family preservation services are still not available for the majority of families. Rzepnicki, Schuerman, Littel, Chak & Lopez (1994) note that as the emphasis changes from placement prevention to outcomes focusing on family and child well-being, the basis on which family preservation programmes are sold may have to change.

> While improvements (from family preservation programs) are desirable, program effects in this area are likely to be modest at best. Increasingly social problems that affect families' lives . . . require sweeping changes in social policy. (Rzepnicki *et al.*, 1994, p. 79)

In the US, despite a long history, parent support and education programmes have never been central to the education and human services. Powell (1993) feels this is a reflection of the US culture that assumes families should rely on their own resources in their child-rearing responsibilities. Evidence is now emerging of the effectiveness of family support services and early educational programmes which have led to a growing emphasis on the provision of family support as an integral part of efforts to alter a child's development course (Dunst & Trivette, 1988).

Policies towards Children and Families in Need in England and Wales

The Children Act 1989 in England and Wales was intended to indicate a major shift of policy from the child protection interventionist policies of the previous 20 years to policies to support the family. Central to the Children Act 1989 was the duty placed on local authorities to support families of children designated as 'in need'. A child in need was defined as:

(a) he is unlikely to achieve or maintain, or have the opportunity of achiev-
    ing or maintaining, a reasonable standard of health or development
    without the provision for him of services for a local authority, or
(b) his health or development is likely to be significantly impaired, or fur-
    ther impaired, without the provision for him of such services or
(c) he is disabled. (Children Act 1989, Section 17.10)

These children *did not* have to be be identified as abused or neglected before they received services. Local authorities were given a duty to provide a range of services to meet their needs. If a child met the criteria for being 'in need', his/her family was then also eligible for services.

Local authorities, perhaps anxious about opening the flood gates, have generally interpreted the legislation conservatively, and in practice there is still an overwhelming emphasis on giving priority to children for whom they already have some responsibility, with children at risk of abuse and neglect and those in out-of-home care ranked highest (Department of Health, 1994: Children Act Report 1993).

The recent Audit Commission Report 1994 in England and Wales on children's services (health and social services) underlines that we spend £2 billion on these each year. Because of the costs involved, the argument is whether children's services should be 'open' to all those families in need or should be 'targeted' to those most in need.

Virginia Bottomley, in the UK, when Minister of Health, argued that every family regardless of its shape or size needed help at times and that there should be no shame in not being able to cope. Many successful families today, she felt, owed their existence to the fact that they received help at a crucial time (Bottomley, 1994).

Despite the Minister's statement, and despite the emphasis on family support in the Children Act 1989, there is an underlying move in England and Wales towards more *residual* rather than *institutional* approaches in providing welfare. With targeting as advocated by the Report of the Audit Commission, social services will become increasingly residual. This tendency is increased by the devolvement of services away from the state either to voluntary agencies and/or joint partnerships in order to create a market in welfare, as in the US. The dilemma is that families in 'need' may be reluctant to approach the *residual* social services because of the stigma attached. This was vividly illustrated in a study of users' views (Buchanan *et al.*, 1995).

Measuring Outcomes

The reluctance of local authorities in England and Wales to move towards more family support may also be related to the lack of real evidence of its effectiveness. The lack of research evidence is illustrated by the fact that the two most commonly quoted studies in Britain are the Olds and Henderson (1989) study in the USA and the High Perry Scope Longitudinal study, also from the USA (Schweinhart & Weikart, 1993).

The Audit Commission Report (1994) highlighted how little we know about the 'outcomes' for children from all the money spent on them. In allocating resources to children and families, local politicians have to make difficult decisions about where best to place the money. A greater focus on outcomes will undoubtedly improve the knowledge that informs effective policy-making.

Tools, as we have mentioned, are being developed to monitor the outcomes for children in out-of-home care as well as for international use (Ward, 1995). These Assessment and Action records monitor seven domains in the child's life: health, education, identity, family and social relationships, social presentation, emotional and behavioural development, and self-care skills. They are completed by the child's carer and with the older groups, together with the child. The records are repeated at regular intervals, giving over time a long-term profile of that child. There are different records for different age bands, but in each age range the broad range of questions is comparable. The records can be computerised and made available as collated management statistics. Statistics can also be extracted from the records for the mandatory reporting to the Department of Health.

It is anticipated that these tools could also be used to monitor outcomes for children receiving family support services. The LAC tools may offer family support services in the UK, a way to demonstrate their effectiveness. Indeed the tools are being developed for use in Canada and Belgium for a similar purpose (Flynn, 1995; Kufeldt, 1995; Van Oost, 1995).

The Wider Scene

The development of policies to support children and families in developing countries reflects many of the dilemmas seen in more advanced countries. Firstly, there is a need for national policies and accurate information on which to base these policies. Secondly, there is a need to know that these policies reflect the realities of family structure and family needs in the societies in which they operate: 'Each country whether or not fully equipped with data and planning machinery should develop a national policy for its children and youth which should contain a statement of the major problems facing the young generation' (Obikeze, 1984). Thirdly, every society has to make decisions as to where it will place its resources and the relative balance between child protection and family support services.

In Australia an interesting initiative has been developed to separate child protection services from the wider responsibilities of preventing child abuse and neglect. Prevention has become a Federal responsibility with separate Federal funds.

> Until recently no comprehensive policy and practice framework for preventing child maltreatment existed in Australia. Much of the research, practice and resources concentrated on identifying and responding to existing cases. Over the past 2 years this has changed. A policy context for prevention separate from intervention and treatment has been established. Prevention as a concept has been refined and a model developed which focuses exclusively on preventing child abuse before it occurs. The target population is all people living in Australia. (Calvert, 1994, p. 268)

The programme is involved in a range of areas from publishing educational material, to television and radio broadcasts, to community programmes. Such separation of responsibilities and resources allows family support and family preservation a primary role rather than picking up left-over resources after child protection services have had their fill.

POLICY AND INTERVENTIONS AT THE LOCAL GOVERNMENT LEVEL

Different societies have different relationships between central government and local government. In the USA, as we have discussed, there is an element of Federal legislation but the individual states formulate and legislate most policies relating to children and families.

In the UK, historically there have developed a range of different authorities relating to health, education and welfare services which have different relationships and different methods of resourcing between central and local government. Although legislating policies is the responsibility of national government, implementing the policies within the national guidelines, particularly in the case of social welfare, is the responsibility of the locally elected politicians at the local authority level. This uneasy relationship between central and local government is reflected in how local authorities 'interpret' the legislation and decide on their priorities.

Despite these difficulties, the Department of Health in London has, in relation to the Children Act 1989, had some success in recent years in persuading local authorities to develop their services for children and families towards uniform standards. In implementing this change, the Department of Health has been involved in interdisciplinary training programmes, publishing guidelines, funding and disseminating research studies, and publishing indicators achieved in each local authority.

Because of the separate administration of health, education and social services, there was evidence that they were working independently of each other when in reality the research evidence demonstrated that children in 'need' crossed all territories. In November 1992, Circular LAC, 18 (DOH, 1992) advised local authorities to draw up plans for Children's Services which linked health, education and social service provision.

Central to these plans was the requirement to work together with a range of service providers to establish data on the needs of different groups of children in different localities and to elicit the views of consumers. Following completion of their plans, local authorities were advised that these plans should be published and available to the general public so that they would know what services they were entitled to and under what conditions. To some extent this will bring market forces to bear on what services local authorities offer. Although the market may not be paying directly for their services they have the power of their vote to pressurise local politicians. The dilemma remains, of course, to what extent it is a true market since families undergoing child protection investigations have no choice whether or not they are investigated, but by creating a more open service they may be freer to comment on how the processes may be made more effective (Buchanan *et al.*, 1995).

Other Studies

Studies in the USA have also demonstrated the benefits of effective data collection in identifying need. Between 1986 and 1989 in New York City the total number of children in placement increased from 18 793 to 47 145 (Wulczyn, 1994). They noted that admissions of babies had increased and these babies stayed in care longer, while the numbers of adolescents had declined. Maps of the area were constructed and infant placements plotted on these maps. Similarly maps of low-birthweight babies, births to teenagers, infant mortality and lack of prenatal care were also constructed from New York's Office of Public Health data. There was a close correlation between placement rates and birth outcome. This information led to renewed efforts to obtain prenatal support services for 'at risk' pregnant mothers in the identified areas.

Another example of the value of careful collation of local data has indicated the importance in India not only of identifying need, but also of monitoring longer term outcomes. Since the early 1970s, Ludhiana health authorities have been monitoring the reproductive and health status of the surrounding population. The monitoring is part of a decentralised, comprehensive basic health care programme that focuses on the welfare of mothers and children. It also includes a home-based educational programme. In 1983, analysis of this data revealed startling sex differentials in mortality between 7 and 36 months. Female deaths constituted 85% of the total. An intensive home visiting programme was set up which resulted in the reduction of female child deaths. However, longer term monitoring has indicated that although more girls are surviving, there has been a corresponding increase in the number of malnourished girls (Miller, 1987).

Interventions at the Community Level

The first strategy considered here is the role of Parent Education. Utting, Bright and Henricson (1994) note that we cannot assume that parents, living in a complex society, faced with a new child, instinctively know how to care for their child. Utting suggests that coherent strategies for parent education need to start when the parent-to-be is at school. In the UK, however, there is a lack of coherent education for parenthood. The National Curriculum does not include preparation for family life (Utting, Bright & Henricson, 1994).

In the US, although it is not central to family policy, there is a longer history of parent education programmes. The Federal government launched such efforts as the Comprehensive Child Development Program and Even Start (Powell, 1993) both of which are aimed at helping parents assist their children to reach their full potential. Further efforts are fuelled by the ideas of Mattox (1991) that *'parenting deficit'* in America is more pressing than *budget* or *trade deficits*.

Mass media, television and radio can play a useful role in parent education. In the US popular movies in recent years have explored dimensions of parenthood and a frequent topic is the difficulties of parenting in today's complex society (Powell, 1993). Television, radio and video courses can impinge on millions of homes. In the UK, the Open University has developed a range of courses on health education which includes parenting. The materials include booklets, videos and cassettes. They estimate that their course 'The Pre-School Child' reached 151 000 people, many of whom came from disadvantaged groups. Follow-up studies indicated that many of those who took part had gained a greater understanding about children, had improved skills, changed attitudes and higher self-esteem (Open University, 1992). Other approaches have also proved helpful in parent education. Exploring Parenthood is a professional-based organisation in the UK which combines a national helpline offering advice and counselling to parents (Utting, Bright & Henricson, 1994).

Another scheme in the UK is the Parent Network–Parent Link scheme. This scheme connects with the Parent Network movement in the US, notably Parent Effectiveness Training (PET), and the Systematic Training in Effective Parenting in Canada (STEP). The basic training course is known as Parent Link, 'a toolkit for parents'. The aim is to build up the self-esteem of parents while ensuring that they acknowledge and develop strategies for meeting their own needs. Parents are also encouraged to be specific when challenging 'unacceptable' behaviour in their children. Halpern and Weiss (1988) have evaluated a number of such programmes and have found that, provided parents persist with the skills they have learnt there are a range of benefits for their children, including lower rates of child abuse and neglect. Recently in the UK Parent Link has tried to make its approach more accessible to families on low incomes. In Exeter, UK, for example, a Parent Link Family Centre is based in a large council estate and offers post-natal care with mother and toddler groups and other activities as well as the parent training.

Family Centres, which under the Children Act 1989 in England and Wales became mandatory in every local authority, also offer a range of parent education and family support services. The debate rages as to what extent these should have 'open' access or should be referral-based: that is for families at risk of neglect or abuse (Smith, 1995). Smith demonstrates that families prefer the 'open' access model as they can feel stigmatised if it is known that their centre is referral-based. In the UK there is no uniform pattern of provision amongst Family Centres. Holman (1988, 1992) notes that as local authority services in England and Wales are increasingly focused towards child protection, Family Centres are less able to be involved in primary preventive work.

Many of these Family Centres were converted from local authority nurseries, and as such the professional training of the organisers was often based in nursery education. Recently the training of the professionals running such centres has been more orientated towards social work. The large national voluntary organisations such as NCH Action for Children, Save the Children Fund and Barnardos have now moved into the field, offering quality family support (Smith, 1995).

The Importance of Quality Day Care

Reliable day care for children is an essential component of support services for families. With the rise in the number of women working, calls for investment in child care have been justified on various social and economic grounds. Reliable day care is central to strategies for breaking cycles of socio-political child maltreatment. Mothers in Britain, especially lone parents, are often unable to undertake paid work because of the lack of accessible and affordable child care (Cohen, 1990; Bradshaw & Millar, 1991; Burghes, 1993). Finding ways to assist such mothers to escape the 'Welfare Trap' and enter the workforce is currently being debated in the UK.

In the US the new Federal Child Care and Development Block Grant will provide money for states to grant low- and moderate-income families increased access to affordable day care (Harrington & Dubowitz, 1993). It remains to be seen how many families will be eligible for such support.

In Sweden public provision and funding of day care for children, both pre-school and after school hours, has been a very significant development (Ginsburg, 1993). In 1967 in Sweden, children under seven with parents in paid employment were largely cared for privately, only 16% attended full-time or part-time nurseries. By 1987 53% were still cared for privately, but the other 47% were cared for by salaried childminders or municipal day care (Broberg & Hwang, 1991).

Around the world the provision of quality day care for children is a highly political issue. In Ireland, for example:

> The absence of child-care facilities coordinated well with the general tenor of state policy, which was firmly rooted in the belief that mothers belonged in the home and which reinforced traditional gender roles. (Pyle, 1990, p. 97)

In modern Hong Kong, despite an overall female labour force participation of 51% in 1986, with a much heavier concentration in the younger age groups (Lau *et al.*, 1992), there were only 1489 crèche places and 31 134 nursery places for an under-six-population of 600 000 (McLaughlin, 1993).

Hong Kong Chinese women are caught between the traditional Chinese values of having to care for their families and yet needing and wanting to work (Lau *et al.*, 1992). In 1991 there was a series of tragedies where children were left on their own (McLaughlin, 1993).

Holman (1988) quotes two important studies highlighting the significance of day care for supporting families under stress. In 1979 Devon Social Services Department reported that the three divisions with the highest rate of day care provision had a particularly low proportion of the child population in public care, whereas the opposite was the case in the two divisions with low provision. Similarly in Islington, the number of children received into their care dropped by 74% in eight years following the development of its day care and education facilities for under fives.

In Singapore, however, some sort of pre-school provision is experienced by 90% of children between the ages of 4 and 6 (Sharpe, 1994). Here the debate, as elsewhere, is about not the *quantity* but the *quality* of day care provision. In Singapore, when parents' aspirations stress both high standards of attainment and behaviour management, there is concern that teachers have moved to an academic style curriculum and strict behaviour control. Sharpe's study demonstrated that parents are less punitive than teachers. Others have demonstrated that the negative effects of caregivers' behaviour may have long-term consequences for the children involved (Holloway & Reichhart-Erikson, 1988).

In measuring the quality of day care in centres, many studies have made use of the Early Environment Rating Scale developed by Harms and Clifford (1980). This instrument has now been used outside the USA in New Zealand (Farquhar, 1989), England (Statham & Brophy, 1992) and in Sweden (Bjurek, Gustafsson, Kjulin & Karrby, 1994). Although some of the findings are inconsistent (Clarke-Stewart, 1987), this instrument has proved useful in measuring the overall quality of the educational environment in day centres and pre-school settings. The interpretation of the quality dimensions may, however, be influenced by national and educational philosophies concerning the aims and function of pre-schooling (Karrby & Giota, 1994).

CONCLUSIONS

This brief review has only been able to highlight some central themes which may be important in breaking socio-political patterns of child maltreatment. Firstly, interventions can be made at the international, national and local/state and community level. Secondly, improving the welfare of this generation and the next generation of children requires policies that look to the whole child and his/her family and which are effective in bringing about changes in health, family planning, education and social services. At the international level organisations large and small can pressurise for change and by publishing indicators can monitor and motivate that change. At the national level, legislation to protect children and reporting laws can have an important role in creating greater public awareness, but there is a need for policies which promote the welfare of children and families and these policies may need to be formally outlined.

At the local level strategies may need to be developed to ensure effective collaboration between health, education and social services. 'Although some families may be adequately served with programs that focus on one problem, such as substance abuse, many families require comprehensive services that address their multiple needs' (Harrington & Dubowitz, 1993, p. 277).

Consumers need to feed into the evaluation of services. Data need to be collected so that programmes for children and families can, as far as possible, support children who are in need *within* their families before they are abused, rather than by removing children from their families when they are no longer safe. Outcomes need to be measured both in the short term and the long so that services can be more effectively planned and 'wrong directions' redirected. Central to any strategy will be finding better ways to provide quality day care for children when mothers work.

SUMMARY: BREAKING SOCIO-POLITICAL CYCLES OF MALTREATMENT

Aim of Interventions. To Create Societies where 'Permitting Circumstances' for Parenting are Maximised

International

- Pressuring for change: the role of International organisations
- The power of international voluntary societies, e.g. ECPAT
- The consequences of maximising the upward spiral: progress against poverty, population growth and environmental stress
- Specific international responsibilities to campaign for change
- Monitoring international supply and demand leading to child maltreatment

- Dissemination of information
- Collection of data

National

- Policies that support the family
- Recognition of family change
- Combating poverty and improving health care
- Legislative frameworks that support families and protect children
- Child Protection procedures and reporting systems
- Policies to support children and families in specific need
- Measuring outcomes

Local government level

- Training
- Publishing guidelines
- Disseminating research
- Publishing indicators
- Linking health, education and social welfare services
- Identifying areas of special need

Community level

- Universal support services
- Specific programmes to educate for parents in parenting
- Family centres
- Quality day care

9

INTERVENTIONS IN THE CULTURAL CYCLE

Each child's right to grow up in, and belonging to, a community of kinship and meaning—i.e. a child's right to culture—as well as the right to live free from physical harm, neglect and the deprivation of necessities are all affirmed in the 1959 United Nations Declaration of the Rights of the Child, 1959 . . . It is unfortunate as well as contradictory for child protective workers to deny a child's right to culture in the name of acting in his or her 'best interest'. (Hughes, 1987, p. 387)

One must be cognizant of the viewpoint of members of the cultural group in question, termed the emic *perspective as well as an outsider, or* etic *perspective. . . . An understanding of both* emic *and* etic *perspectives is a necessity in sorting out the impact of the cultural and social context in which behaviour, including child abuse and neglect, takes on meaning.* (Korbin, 1980, p. 4)

This chapter explores some of the difficulties and dilemmas in intervening in the cultural cycle of child maltreatment. Central to the discussion is the idea that interventions have to be seen within their cultural context— the *emic* approach—but there is also a need for some international definition about what is and is not child maltreatment—the *etic* approach. In coming to these decisions, responsibility, as in the case of breaking sociopolitical cycles, lies at different levels, international, national and local.

The Difficulties and Dilemmas

The strategies for saving children and the 'Health for all by the year 2000' being waged by UNICEF and the World Health Organisation are not without their critics (Cassidy, 1987; Scheper-Hughes, 1987). The 'Image of Unlimited Good' expressed in absolute goals such as 'the eradication of hunger', and the moral and humanitarian reasons used to justify such approaches, fly in the face of the reality of many families in the underdeveloped world. To them the world contains only a finite amount of 'good'—that is in terms of resources, energy and goodwill, and one person's gain is necessarily another's loss (Foster, 1965). With modern low-cost life-saving technology a 'child survival revolution' is possible:

> This kind of salvage mentality is, however, counter-intuitive to the thinking and practices of many Third World parents, who may perceive some of their babies as 'wanting to die' and other babies as better off had they never been born. (Scheper-Hughes, 1987, p. 21)

From the child maltreatment perspective, the dilemma is when such a mother 'allows' her child to die, is this neglect? In developing countries where parents daily struggle for the essentials of living, most would be reluctant to attribute blame to such a mother for 'permitting' her child's death. But how well does this argument carry in the developed world, where an inner city mother isolated from the support of her traditional cultural context 'permits' her unwanted baby to die? Who is to blame, who is responsible?

Dinnage (1978) would argue:

> Children are weak; and the weak get hurt; and where there is hurting there are also lies, hypocrisy, rationalisations, the claim that the victim is not really human or is being hurt for his own good. (Dinnage, 1978, p. 38)

If, however, we are to intervene effectively, we need to see the wider picture. Traditional child care practices need to be evaluated according to both indigenous as well as Western standards of benefit and detriment before being labelled as neglectful or abusive. Such practices often require careful study before the potential benefit both short-term and long-term to the individual and the family becomes obvious.

INTERVENTIONS AT THE INTERNATIONAL LEVEL

The first decision to be made is whether to call the parental behaviours observed 'normal' or 'abnormal'. Cassidy (1987) outlines two world positions which are relevant to our discussion. Firstly there is the *Activist* position where it is felt that something can and should be done, and secondly there is the *Adaptor* position which would suggest that many parenting behaviours in the world are not desirable but that the world is not ideal. Some interventions may in the long term be more harmful than beneficial. Greater good comes from helping families to adapt their parenting behaviour to their situations. Cassidy (1987, p. 297) considers the implications of this framework in considering toddler malnutrition (Figure 9).

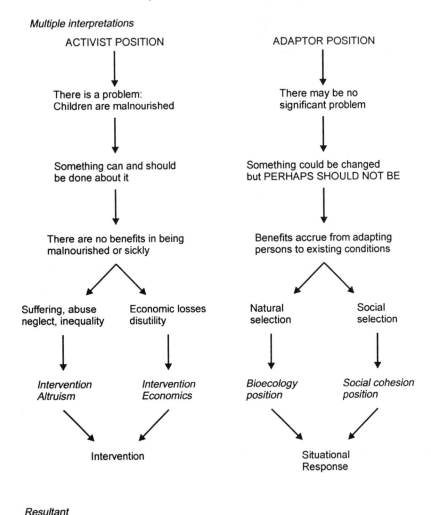

Universal observations: Toddler period is attended by fretfulness and crying, frequent sickness: children often die

Multiple interpretations

ACTIVIST POSITION

There is a problem: Children are malnourished

Something can and should be done about it

There are no benefits in being malnourished or sickly

Suffering, abuse neglect, inequality   Economic losses disutility

Intervention Altruism   *Intervention Economics*

Intervention

ADAPTOR POSITION

There may be no significant problem

Something could be changed but PERHAPS SHOULD NOT BE

Benefits accrue from adapting persons to existing conditions

Natural selection   Social selection

Bioecology position   *Social cohesion position*

Situational Response

Resultant policy recommendations

Figure 9: Four world views relevant to understanding development intervention to alleviate toddler malnutrition

From Cassidy, C. (1987), in N. Scheper-Hughes (Ed.), *Child Survival*, Reidel Publishing Co., p. 297. Reprinted by permission of Kluwer Academic Publishers

Cassidy would argue that neither the activitist position nor the adaptor position is effective because they ignore the social context of the children's lives and suggest changes that are better *in the interveners' own eyes*. In effect they were wanting to do good but defining good from only one perspective. She suggests a more helpful approach is to see the validity of both positions but in addition help families and communities to engage in true communication to redesign their own cultures. Central to this idea is that change is more likely to happen by the social valuing of people. There are 'no quick fixes' where the human factor is involved. Social change by a slow process of education may need to permeate the generations.

Towards an International Definition of Child Maltreatment

In this book we have argued that intergenerational patterns of child maltreatment are inextricably linked to the wider harms that befall children, and that progress in combating these harms generally will in the end go a long way to break the patterns of abuse. Finkelhor and Korbin (1988) would suggest, however, that child maltreatment is only one harm among many that befall children, and that those involved with children need to document the existence of what is child maltreatment in their own countries as a first step in combating the specific problem. As we have seen, cross-cultural beliefs about parenting behaviours indicate wide variability. The dilemma is whether cultural considerations should override all judgements about what is humane treatment of children.

The work of Finkelhor and Korbin (Korbin, 1980, 1981, 1987, 1991; Finkelhor & Korbin, 1988) and of ISPCAN, the International Society for the Prevention of Child Abuse and Neglect, has moved towards a consensus that while child maltreatment must firstly be seen in its cultural context, we must also strive to establish cross-cultural definitions of child maltreatment for both research and action. Rather than comparing statistics based on different national definitions which will have doubtful validity, global comparable measures are needed to elicit the factors that promote or prevent child maltreatment cross-culturally. Minturn and Lambert (1964) note that the starting point is to establish factors which have explanatory powers both within and between societies.

The following definition has been devised by Finkelhor and Korbin: 'Child abuse is the portion of harm to children that results from human action that is proscribed, proximate and preventable' (Finkelhor & Korbin, 1988, p. 4). Finkelhor and Korbin (1988) expand each section of their definition. They argue that *'results from'* indicates a focus that separates child maltreatment from other harms to children. To note that a child died is not enough to make a decision about whether such a death was the result of child abuse. There is a need to know why that child died. *'Human action'* excludes children who may be harmed from natural causes. They recognise that separating out children who may have been harmed by a combination of natural and human causes is difficult but the main focus should be on human action. *'Proscribed'* suggests that there is some harmful intent behind the action. The action deviates from legal codes or social expectations and it is this which renders it child abuse. *'Proximate'* is intended to indicate that child abuse is only where the action is closely related in time and space. We would argue that this short-term criterion may be less helpful in breaking intergenerational patterns of child maltreatment. The final element of their definition focuses on *'preventable'*. Here it is suggested that some alternate course of human action is possible within the resources of a particular society.

Finkelhor and Korbin also consider what they call the dimensions of child abuse (Figure 10). The first dimension mentioned implies that the human act must have the intention of inflicting harm or injury on the child. The second dimension focuses on whether the act is socially sanctioned or socially censured by the community in which it happens. For example, scarification may be acceptable in some societies but unacceptable in others. The third dimension is perhaps the most challenging. This seeks to draw together an international consensus about whether specific acts can be called abusive. This also links to scientific knowledge about child development. The fourth dimension considers whether the act is the result of societal or individual actions. Finkelhor and Korbin feel that societal acts are less likely to be considered abuse than individual acts. The potential for disagreement here is evident. The fifth dimension seeks to elicit whether children are the sole victims or joint victims with other members of their society and finally the sixth dimension tries to establish the extent of personhood endowed within the child. This links to the debates about abortion and infanticide.

The dimensions illustrate the tremendous complexities in coming to an international definition. These difficulties are further illustrated in coming to a consensus about different types of abuse. Broadly speaking, Finkelhor and Korbin (1988) use definitions currently in use in the developed world for physical abuse, physical neglect, sexual abuse emotional or psychological abuse, and neglect but modify their overall definitions by limiting them to human acts which are proscribed, proximate and preventable in the society where they occur.

Most clearly child abuse		Less clearly child abuse
Intentional acts	I	Unintentional acts
Acts that are socially censured in locale where they occur	II	Acts that have some degree of social approval in locale where they occur
Acts whose abusiveness is a matter of international consensus	III	Acts whose abusiveness is a matter of international disagreement
Acts perpetrated by individuals	IV	Acts perpetrated by organisations, governments, and society
Harms suffered solely by children as a group	V	Harms experienced by children together with others
Acts against children who are clearly endowed with personhood	VI	Acts against children who are not yet socially endowed with personhood

Figure 10: Dimensions influencing whether a harm is child harm
Reprinted from *Child Abuse and Neglect*, **19**, Finkelhor, D. & Korbin, J., 'Child abuse as an international issue', 3–23, © (1995). With kind permission from Elsevier Science Ltd, The Boulevard, Langford Lane, Kidlington, OX5 1GB, UK

Finkelhor and Korbin's definition is removed from Gil's (1981) broad-based definition used in this book and outlined in Chapter 1. It could be argued that in an international context, and given the work of UNICEF, there was no need to replicate their work but simply to supplement it with a specific focus on child maltreatment. With a narrow focus, it would be easier for nations to enact Child Protection legislation, the very presence of which would increase citizen awareness.

Strategies for Implementing Change

Finkelhor and Korbin (1988) suggested that three types of child abuse should be the focus of the campaign to prevent child maltreatment. Firstly physical abuse, secondly selective neglect, and thirdly sexual abuse.

In sustaining the campaign they felt there was need for an *international data base* about the scope and distribution of types of child abuse. They note, for example, it would be helpful if the World Health Organisation differentiated between infant deaths due to accidents and those due to inflicted injuries. If an international protocol could be established, this would give evidence which could then be used to monitor achievements. This protocol would need to have information from each country on what types of abuse were reported, estimates of the scope and distributions, children who are vulnerable and successes in interventions. The second strategy suggested is that of international awareness building.

Finkelhor and Korbin's paper written in 1988 concludes:

> This particular moment is a formative one in the development of international child abuse initiatives, and calls for both urgency and caution, mobilisation and reflection . . . Some action is inevitable. It is important that this action reflect the best ideas of the world community, the ideas most likely to succeed in alleviating these threats to children's health, development and survival. (Finkelhor & Korbin, 1988, p. 19)

Time has moved on since this original paper. The final sessions at the tenth International Congress organised by ISPCAN in Kuala Lumpur in Malaysia focused on 'Prevention'. The conference was a vivid reminder that a narrow focus on child abuse, and establishing elaborate medical and legal procedures while increasing awareness, would only go a small way in helping the large numbers of children who were maltreated. A wider ecological framework is needed to prevent intergenerational patterns of child maltreatment from recurring.

In both the developed and the developing world, action against child maltreatment often threatens entrenched political, religious, and economic interests. These too need to be challenged at an international level. The following debate about parental battering is a good example.

The Debate about Smacking

As we have seen, physical punishment of children is the most common form of culturally and legally condoned violence and it is practised to a greater or lesser extent in most societies. We have also seen that there is a relationship between the amount of physical violence culturally condoned and serious child maltreatment, and such physical chastisement can have long-term effects on the development and self-esteem of children.

Peter Newell of EPOCH-WORLDWIDE (End Physical Punishment of Children) (1992) and the Radda Barnen organisation would argue that physical punishment of children violates children's rights to physical integrity and human dignity upheld in the UN Convention on the Rights of the Child.

The central approach of EPOCH-WORLDWIDE is to campaign for legislation in all countries that prohibits physical punishment of children; to document the experiences of those countries which have initiated legislation; to disseminate knowledge amongst professionals involved with children about the consequences on individual children of physical punishment; to link this with the ratification of the UN convention and to ask governments to develop comprehensive plans to counter beating, slapping and smacking of children in administrative, social and educational actions as well as legislation. An important international seminar in London in 1992 brought together experts from 22 countries in Europe and was attended by observers from USA, Canada and Israel (EPOCH-WORLDWIDE, 1992).

However, despite a very powerful campaign, the strong evidence and reasonableness of the arguments, progress has been slow. Public action against physical punishment of children is seen as interference into family privacy. It is argued that when such treatment of children is so widespread it is unrealistic to enact laws against physical chastisement of children when it is known that such laws will be violated. Perhaps more important is the fear that parents in all societies need to 'control' children in order for those children to conform to the rules of that society.

The enactment of the legislation in Sweden came with a publication which crucially reflected the fears of parents 'Can you bring up children successfully without smacking and spanking?' (Sverne, 1992). The related worry was that large numbers of children would be separated from their families and removed into the public care.

The Swedish experience has proved otherwise. Research by Haeuser (1992) demonstrates that in 1981, soon after the enactment of the anti-punishment legislation, there was concern that parenting was becoming 'permissive' and that behaviour of children in public and private was beyond the levels of tolerance in other countries. 'I had to question the need for a ban on physical punishment in a milieu of permissive child rearing. A society that makes few demands of its children has little reason to punish them' (Haeuser, 1992, p. 113). However, by 1988 a dramatic change in child-rearing had occurred in Sweden. There seemed to be three reasons for the change. Firstly, child development experts were telling parents that the permissive approach did not work; secondly, Sweden had moved to a more conservative stance during the period, and thirdly, perhaps crucially, parents had found alternatives to physical punishment.

The message seems to be that legislation may have heralded the change but the associated educational programmes which demonstrated non-violent methods of child-rearing was more powerful. The child-rearing methods now used by Swedish families include time-put, rewards, denial of privileges, verbal conflict and direct eye contact, maybe in the context of holding their arms while a message is delivered. Linked to this is a campaign for child-proofing the home and fully paid parental leave from employment after a new baby.

Although the international campaign has been important in raising the challenge, national legislation has to reflect the broad consensus of the population it serves. The experience in Hong Kong, a Chinese society in transition, illustrates some of the dilemmas. In Hong Kong much of the societal abuse that children suffer elsewhere has been eradicated. O'Brian and Lau (1995), through an analysis of policy documents and practice records, examined the traditional Chinese parent–child relationships, the status of parental authority and corporal punishment, and the changes in current Hong Kong Life. Although remarkable tolerance serves to protect the young child from abuse, Chinese parents have very definite views on the discipline and education of the older child. Education of children over six is characterised by strict discipline and filiality. O'Brian and Lau note *The Family Instructions of Yen* which suggests that beating is an important part of discipline and the education of the child. The need for absolute obedience in the child is accentuated by the important of *'face'* or *'lien'*. Judgements are made about entire families rather than individuals.

Failure to bring up a child properly brings disgrace on the family and the ancestors of that family. Amongst younger more educated people, however, parents are beginning to use reasoning rather than excessive discipline (Cheung, Chau & Larn, 1986). Considerable discussions are in progress in Hong Kong about what is appropriate discipline:

> However, experience from other countries ahead of Hong Kong in child protection procedures suggests that questions of definition are not easily resolved. As professionals and concerned members of society, we all abhor the abuse of children. At the same time, we are reluctant to devastate families by our interventions . . . We have to be sensitive to cultural norms but at the same time push for some currently condoned behaviour to become unacceptable in the societies we serve. (O'Brian & Lau, 1995, p. 45)

The Role of the Media and the Export of Violent Entertainment

At the international and national level, as we have seen, the media have been very powerful instruments in changing attitudes. They have highlighted the extremes of violence against children and indirectly initiated national campaigns to protect children. The media, however, provide a twin-edged sword. Much more insidious has been the role of the media in perpetuating models of violence, particularly through television.

Abbott (1992), in describing a primary prevention programme conducted in New Zealand, noted that many of the most violent films shown had originated in the USA. In effect, television gives a window on the world. The 'cultural products' of one society can be disseminated and in some cases can undermine for the worse the national heritage of the receiving societies.

Television, for better or worse, is a powerful educator. In New Zealand (Abbott, 1992), they found that by the time children left school they had spent more time watching television than they had in school. More than 3000 published research reports have examined ways in which watching television influences behaviour and attitudes. The consensus amongst the research community is that there is a definite link between viewing television violence and aggressive behaviours in children. Laboratory and field studies have now established the most harmful kinds of depiction (Belson, 1978; Comstock, 1976; Doherty, 1990; Hargrave, 1993). There are four issues: firstly, where there is a reward or lack of punishment for the 'bad guy'; secondly, where violence is presented as justified; thirdly, where identification with the perpetrator is encouraged; and finally, where the violence is portrayed realistically. The findings suggest that children are most vulnerable between the ages of 8–10. Longitudinal studies show that effects persist into adulthood and women who have watched heavy doses of violent films in their childhood are more likely to use physical punishment on their children. Work by Leonard Eron and his collaborators in Poland, Finland, Australia, the Netherlands and Israel (Eron & Huesmann, 1987) has produced some of the soundest research methodologically. A study by Allerton (1995) demonstrates that children become increasingly sophisticated in their viewing and regulate what they see by switching off or changing channels. Problems arise when they cannot differentiate fact from fiction and this is when their normal protective mechanisms are not available. The issue is: can regulation be left to children?

National bodies such as the British Broadcasting Standards Council have an advisory role in deciding what is shown. In the UK there is a 'watershed' after 9 o'clock when more adult films can be shown. It is arguable how effective this is, when large numbers of children in the West have their own TV sets in their bedrooms.

Many socialist countries have very low levels of television violence (Haines, 1983), but market forces act against local controls. The International Coalition Against Violent Entertainment (1990) noted that US distributors had signed contracts with Eastern European counterparts that will result in an influx of some of the most violent television films that have been made in the Western world. The campaign in New Zealand is interesting because it has been successful in reversing the trends in the amount of violence that is shown on television (Abbott, 1992). The growing availability of satellite and computer technology, however, increasingly suggests that it is in the interests of the international community to come together to further regulate the trade in violent entertainment.

NATIONAL

Obikeze (1984) noted that so much prominence in Western literature is given to physical punishment that the impression is inadvertently given that child abuse is synonymous with child beating. As we have seen, children around the world suffer from many forms of violence. The task at the national level is not only to create policies and enact legislation which create a framework to support families and protect children, but also to do this within a framework which reflects both an *etic* and an *emic* position.

A further task at the national level is to become informed about disadvantaged groups within their broader society and ensure that their families receive support in their parenting task and their children receive protection under the law. Such interventions break into both the socio-political and cultural cycles of child maltreatment. An example in this area is the work of Grace Smallwood, in Australia. In her presentation to the tenth International Conference on Child Abuse and Neglect in 1994 she quoted Edith Carter:

> Rape and child abuse in the Aboriginal community are surrounded in silence, survivors are silenced by fear. A minority of rapes and child sexual abuse are formally reported. The majority of child sexual abuse is happening within immediate and extended families. The silence seems to be perpetuated by at least two things. The first is Aboriginal culture surviving within a white world. The second is Aboriginal perception of, and relationship to the white welfare, legal and justice systems. (Edith Carter quoted by Grace Smallwood, 1994, p. 15)

This raises important issues. Whether we are talking about, for example, the Aboriginals in Australia, the Black population in the USA and UK, or Gypsies in Eastern Europe (Buchanan & Sluckin, 1995), minority groups around the world need to feel that national policies and legislation will support them and build on their cultural strengths, rather than undermine their effectiveness.

Grace Smallwood estimates that one in every six or seven Aboriginal children were taken from their families this century while the figure for white children was about one in 300. Bebbington and Miles (1988) in the UK have demonstrated that one of the factors leading to a high risk of being admitted to public care was being of mixed parentage. Such 'child rescue' policies do not naturally lead to confidence and compliance with child protection procedures. Barn (1990) has demonstrated that in the UK, practitioners tended to carry out little preventive work with Black families and they approached them with a distinct amount of negativity.

National policies also need to establish systems of positive ethnic monitoring. Without such systems it cannot be established whether minority groups are indeed treated 'equally under the law' and whether they receive the services to which they may be entitled under the law. Such systems also highlight the need for ethnically more sensitive services.

Setting Up Ethnically Sensitive Systems

The Australian approach to child protection in Non-English-Speaking Background communities (NESBs) in New South Wales is a useful model on how to develop such services. Their report 'Culture—No Excuse' (NSW

Child Protection Council, 1995) was the first in Australia to document the views and aspirations of members of ethnic communities on the subject of child abuse and child protection. The study examined the following areas.

Child protection in a multicultural society

The starting point was the setting up of an Ethnic Affairs Commission in 1977. In 1983 all government departments were required to prepare Ethnic Affairs Policy Statements each year detailing strategies used in overcoming barriers to access by NESBs. These statements were designed to inform NESBs of their rights to services and rights to services which were appropriate to their needs. The second stage was focused on agreeing a cross-cultural definition of child abuse.

Data collection

Ethnic Affairs Policy Statements (EAPS) were then required to document the use of services by NESBs. This proved more difficult to implement as the different organisations involved, such as Community Services, Public Prosecutions, School Education, and Health and Housing had developed different recording systems. Accordingly it was recommended that all government agencies should collect uniform statistics on: the child's first language; the language spoken at home; the country of birth of both parent and child; the religion of parent and child. It was further recommended that The National Child Protection Council should collate the statistics.

Community consultation

It was noted that people from NESB communities did not have access to high-level committees for policy-making and implementation. If they were involved it was more token participation: 'We talk and talk. We voice our opinions and needs. I feel we go round and round talking but at the end of the day no-one listens' (Blacktown resident quote in NSW, 1995, p. 12). For more effective information exchange, strategies involved the use of reference groups to provide more broadly based representation of NESB views; the representation of NESB workers on Child Protection Area Committees and a commitment from the State Child Protection Council that Area Committees would reflect the composition of the local community.

Identification of child abuse in NESB communities

Four issues were considered under this heading: the effect of migration on children and families; the plight of refugee children held in federal

Detention Centres; barriers to identifying and reporting abuse; and the influence of common myths and perceptions.

Casework and practice issues

In this section key issues identified were: the lack of understanding among non-government organisations on the role of community services and child protection; the need for training to assist workers to resolve the conflict between the interests of the child and the NESB community; the need for support services to assist all members of NESB communities in identifying and reporting abuse; and the need to clarify the interpreters' role.

Counselling and support

Here it is was noted that the Western concept of counselling was unfamiliar to many cultures; there was a lack of adequate support for vulnerable groups and a need to provide acceptable forms of community-based support and links between community-based support and child protection agencies.

The two last sections of the report focused on worker training and strategies for providing resources in rural areas (NSW, 1995). The report has been detailed at length because it helps to identify the practical steps that are needed in setting up ethnically sensitive services.

Other Examples of the Development of Ethnically Sensitive Services

Another good example of working under the law with the strengths of a minority culture is the system of Family Group Conferences in New Zealand (Wilcox, Smith, Moore, Hewitt, Allan, Walker, Ropatam, Monu & Featherstone, 1991). Here, as required by the national legislation, the wider family of a child who has been identified as at risk of significant harm are brought together by an independent coordinator and then allowed to deliberate in private and decide on a plan for care and protection for that child. This builds on the strong Maori family tradition. As a result 'stranger placements' of children have been reduced by more than 60% and up to 90% in some areas. Family Group Conferences are now also being developed in the UK (Buchanan, 1994).

Chang (1993) has shown that a more effective deployment and use of resources is made when data force policy-makers, service providers, and community members to engage in collaborative processes of joint planning and decision-making.

INTERVENTIONS AT THE COMMUNITY LEVEL

It is perhaps at the community level where the greatest opportunity for improving the welfare of children is present. Most children are educated within their community and most parents meet within the community in providing for their families and meeting health needs. The community is a powerful force in reinforcing cultural norms or initiating change. This presupposes that there is an identifiable community and in inner-city areas and areas undergoing rapid socio-economic change this may not be so. In which case, initiating community involvement and developing a sense of community may be a necessary starting point.

Chang (1993) refers to two types of community processes: those focused on *empowerment* and those involved in *betterment*. Collaborative empowerment begins with the community and betterment is instigated by large institutions. Of the two processes, collaborative *empowerment* is more likely to produce ownership of the goals and to enhance the community's capacity for self-determination (Chang 1993). Communities are experts in their own cultural identity, and realistic about what can and should be changed and what the priorities should be.

Empowerment literally means the giving of power. As Arnstein said in 1969:

> Participation without redistribution of power is an empty and frustrating process for the powerless. It allows the policy-holders to claim that all sides were considered but makes it possible for only some of those sides to benefit. It maintains the status quo. (Arnstein, 1969, quoted in Family Rights Group, 1991, p. 5)

Arnstein further elaborates on what he called a 'ladder of participation'. The first step is *manipulation*. This is where a community is encouraged to do or say what those in power deem best. The second step is *decoration*, where members of a community take part in consultation but are not given sufficient information to discuss the issues. The third stage is *tokenism*, where community members are encouraged to think about the issues but have little or no choice about the scope of the ideas they can express. The fourth stage is *assigned but informed*, where those in power decide on a project. The community are informed but have little or no power to initiate change. The fifth stage is *consulted and informed* where projects are designed and run by those in power but the community are consulted and opinions taken seriously. The sixth stage is *community initiated but with shared decision-making*. The seventh stage is *community initiated and directed* with professionals available to assist. The final stage is where *the community initiate action and share decisions* with professionals. Arnstein argues that the first five levels are non-participation or degrees of tokenism. Total participation and/or empowerment is an ideal. To what extent it is possible can be questioned.

Around the world there are many examples of various levels of community participation. Ryklief (1994) from South Africa, a society in transition, reports on two centres serving West Cape which focus on the empowerment of parents linked to parent education and support. Thanki (1994) notes that many local authorities in the UK have begun to consult communities through convening 'open' neighbourhood forums. Swarup and Hayden (1994) discuss a research programme in Hampshire, UK, which consulted minority and ethnic community leaders about the need for children and families' services. They found, however, that lack of appreciation for religious, cultural and language difficulties limited the extent of effective consultation.

Chang (1993) notes that the main barrier to community empowerment is that the professionals, or those in charge, are often not of the same ethnic or class background as the families they serve. In these cases the divide created by cultural, language and information gaps can be especially difficult to bridge.

Community Programmes

In Sri Lanka, however, the Janasaviya Women's Health Programme involved community leaders as health workers. These health workers, who underwent some training, met families, 'sat on the doorstep or under a kohomba tree shade' and chatted about health issues. They claim the results were dramatic in achieving a greater awareness and practice of basic health as well as establishing a new-found solidarity amongst women and families (Sirivardana, 1992).

The work of Gray (1983) in the USA demonstrates how community programmes can use a range of approaches to involve minority communities. The value of Gray's work is that all the projects were carefully and realistically evaluated. The first project, known as The Blackfeet Child Abuse Prevention project, involved 6700 residents of an Indian reservation experiencing considerable social disadvantage. The project used presentations, an outreach programme and home visits, pamphlets, posters, and a guidance manual for service providers. Although this programme in-creased awareness, evaluation suggested that it was not sufficiently well focused.

A second programme by Gray used a mini television series to access 102 low-income 'high risk' parents. The aim was to provide knowledge and skills and to encourage appropriate attitudes to child-rearing. Here too, evaluation demonstrated inconclusive results. A third programme for 70 disadvantaged Hispanic women used an education curriculum to enable parents to help children overcome problems in child-rearing. This pro-duced significant post-test differences between the treatment sample and the control groups.

A fourth project used a street theatre to promote attitude change in child-rearing styles in 'hard to reach' parents. Here some significant results were obtained but results were often more significant for the general public audiences rather than for the 'hard to reach' groups. The focus of a fifth project was on Pan Asian Parental Education. Typical participants were non-working Vietnamese, Samoan, Japanese or Filipino mothers. The pro-gramme involved discussion groups that met over 5–8 weeks. Evaluation demonstrated that participants from most ethnic groups showed an im-provement in their knowledge about child development and child abuse law. A final project by Gray (1983) recruited 800 from a total of 7000 low socio-economic status black population in inner-city Atlanta. Education workshops, parenting skills groups, direct work as well as publicity and interagency work were used. Evaluation suggested that the majority of participants rated the parent training as 'good' and 'very relevant'. Par-ticularly useful was the link established between providers and users.

An issue highlighted by Powell (1993) in the US, as we have argued in this chapter, is that effective programmes have to be responsive to parent and community characteristics. Human service programmes do not lend themselves to mass production. In the US, he feels this lesson has been harder to learn because of the notion that programmes are 'treatments' which can be exported, like medicine, to any population in any area. Ideas may be exported, but effective programmes have to be tailored by those who are involved (Powell, 1993).

In this brief review, it has only been possible to highlight a few of the many community initiatives that seek to break into cultural patterns of child-rearing. The final example does not involve child-rearing as such but it is a project which effectively involved a whole community.

The Healthy Cities Project was initiated by the World Health Organisa-tion (Stark, 1992). Stark notes that in traditional medicine the professional is 'the expert' who cures the problems of the sick person. In contrast, the concept of empowerment adopted by the project in Munich was designed to enhance the strength of the community to control their own lives. In 1987 the Healthy Cities Project set up the Munich Self-Help Resource Center. The first stage was to network citizen groups who then became the organising force. They agreed a goal of health promotion for children and youth and established six task forces to initiate action. These groups designed their own health and health promotion needs and processes for their areas. The project appears to be achieving its goal of making Munich a healthier and more promising place for the city's children.

Stark notes that community participation is a fragile, challenging and necessarily unpredictable process. He notes that:

> Perhaps the first and most important task for professionals, if they want to adopt an empowerment perspective in their work, is to learn to ask questions, not give answers, to develop a sensitivity for strengths in people and settings. (Stark, 1992, p. 175)

By asking questions, we may improve our skills in working with communities, and better understand the world as they see it. Using their energies and expertise to improve conditions for children is a better strategy for breaking intergenerational patterns of child maltreatment than trying to impose a model of child-rearing from outside.

SUMMARY: INTERVENTIONS IN THE CULTURAL CYCLE

Aim: To Find a Balance between the *Emic* and the *Etic* Perspective

International

- Towards an international definition of child abuse
- The development of an international data base
- Disseminating information about child maltreatment
- Limiting the export of violent entertainment

National

- Defining child abuse within an *emic* and *etic* perspective
- Setting up ethnically sensitive services
- Establishing frameworks of community consultation
- Identification of levels of abuse in ethnic communities

- Parental education and child development awareness
- Building on the strengths of ethnic groups

Community

- Community participation and empowerment
- Establishing community programmes
- Learning to ask questions

10

INTERVENTIONS IN THE INTRAFAMILIAL CYCLES: PSYCHOLOGICAL AND BIOLOGICAL

> *It might be expected that as living conditions have improved over the course of this century, [psychosocial disorders] would have become progressively less frequent. The evidence . . . firmly contradicts that commonly held assumption . . . Against expectation, psychosocial disorders have shown no such fall in frequency, and indeed the evidence indicates that many have become substantially more prevalent.* (Smith & Rutter, 1995, p. 763)

> *Except in a few cases where the decision is clear cut, as a society we have to decide which of the several million potentially harmful situations that occur each year require intervention . . . the research evidence suggests that the need of the child and the family is more important than the abuse, or to put it another way, the general family context is more important than any abusive event within it. This message applies when defining maltreatment, designing interventions or assessing outcomes.* (Department of Health, 1995: Child Protection—*Messages from Research*)

The first quotation illustrates the central paradox. Although we have argued that to break the intergenerational cycles of abuse, the central strategy is to improve the health and well-being of mothers and children, the dilemma remains that this is only a partial solution. Rutter and Smith's recent book, *Psychological Disorders in Young People* (1995), demonstrates that such disorders, many of them closely related to child maltreatment, are on the increase despite global indicators that physical health is improving. It could be argued that improvements in health have struck unevenly across the socio-economic scales and that the poor are still at greater risk, but Rutter and Smith's book convincingly argues that we need to look beyond extrafamilial factors.

The crux is a return to intrafamilial factors: 'There is a wealth of evidence from biology, medicine and social sciences that there are major individual differences in people's susceptibility or vulnerability to almost every type of environmental risk' (Caprara & Rutter, 1995, p. 37). This does not negate extrafamilial factors. Rather it reinforces the mechanisms because almost all adversities are likely to have the greatest effect on those most vulnerable from pre-existing dispositions or characteristics. This was described by Elder and Caspi (1990) as the 'Accentuation Principle'.

Nature and nurture, as we have seen, interlock: vulnerability may be biologically determined, for example an individual's metabolic capacity to handle cholesterol, but it is environmentally determined by early feeding patterns, and there may be indirect chain reactions involved in the causal processes (Caprara & Van Heck, 1992; Elder, 1991; Endler & Parker, 1992; Magnusson, 1988, 1990; Rutter & Rutter, 1993).

Stresses brought about by rapidly changing social circumstances, such as unemployment, divorce, or changing patterns of family life, are also likely to have the greatest deleterious effect on the most vulnerable groups.

In this chapter, interventions in the psychological and biological cycle are discussed together. The task is to *identify* those who need protective interventions, *to assess* their needs; to make decisions on what type or packages of *interventions* meet these needs, and to be aware of the *likely outcomes* from these interventions. In identifying cases, there is a need to define both risk and protective factors so that 'buffers' can be set in place to offset the risks. One of the first tasks is to identify the context and the thresholds for intervention.

IDENTIFICATION: THE CONTEXT

As we have seen, it is difficult to define abuse and there are no absolute criteria on which to rely. Quite apart from cross-cultural and international considerations, there are wide differences in the numbers of children defined as abused in geographically similar areas. For example in the UK, the number of children placed on the child protection register in Gloucestershire in 1992 was 0.8 per 1000 whereas the figure was 5.4 in East Sussex. In two similarly disadvantaged inner-city boroughs in London, the rate was 10 per 1000 in Southwark and only 4.4 in Tower Hamlets. Gibbons, Conroy and Bell (1995) explain two sets of factors which explain the difference; firstly, differences in socio-demographic facts such as unemployment and births to single parents and secondly, factors associated with the way child protection procedures are operated in different areas. Among the factors which increase the number of children who are placed on a child protection register are lack of specialised child protection social workers, and shortage of family support services. In effect children are labelled as abused or having a high risk of abuse by social workers *in the context of their own agencies* (Department of Health, 1995). In some cases in England and Wales, children may be brought to case conference as a short cut to obtaining resources for that family (Thorburn, Lewis & Shemmings, 1995), although in theory, in England and Wales, this should not be necessary under the provisions to provide services for children in need under the Children Act 1989 (Children Act 1989, Section 17).

A second more general issue highlighted by the Department of Health *Messages from Research* (1995), as well as by Finkelhor (1990) is that those who come to the notice of child protection agencies are only a small proportion of those who have been abused. In the UK, there are 11 million children. With a rate of child abuse suggested as 5% (Kaufman & Zigler, 1992), this would indicate that more than half a million of children are abused each year. In England and Wales, under section 47 of the Children Act 1989, local authorities have a duty to investigate concerns where a child has suffered or is likely to suffer 'significant harm'. Gibbons, Conroy and Bell (1995) have suggested that out of the 11 million children in England, only 160 000 are referred under section 47. Of these, around 120 000 are visited in the home. In 80 000 of these cases no further investigation is undertaken while Emergency Protection Orders to remove the child to a safe place are taken out on 1500. Some 40 000 cases go to child protection conference following which in 11 000 cases there is no further investigation. In England and Wales there are 24 500 additions to the register each year; 3000 enter public care through the courts; 3000 are accommodated voluntarily and a further 3000 are retained in the process (Department of Health, 1995).

In the United States, where identification of child abuse has been more sophisticated, the US National Research Council (1993) notes that 1.7 million reports are made affecting 2.7 million children. This would indicate a referral rate of three times that in the UK (Department of Health, 1995). The context in which child protection agencies operate is therefore important in defining what parental behaviour is labelled abusive and what the thresholds are for intervention. The threshold will define the amount of abuse that there is at any one time in society. Child Protection has been likened to a fishing net:

> Problems may arise if the mesh of the net is too narrow or too wide. If we have a system in which it is so tight that not a single case of abuse is missed

then it is almost certain that innocent people will be wrongly accused. If the mesh is too loose some cases of abuse will be missed, but it is unlikely that innocent families will be disrupted. It is for society to choose in which direction we should lean and thereby potentially err. (Clayden, 1988, p. 836)

The Thresholds

In the UK, it is not society but professionals working in child protection who make these decisions on behalf of any given society.

Professionals see parenting behaviour on a continuum but they have the additional duty to decide whether to intervene and, if so, how. To do this they must draw a threshold; this involves deciding both the point beyond which a behaviour (or parenting style) can be considered maltreatment and the point beyond which it becomes necessary for the state to take action. Hence, decisions about what is abusive are closely tied to decisions about whether the state should intervene. Child protection professionals make many of these decisions on behalf of society. (Department of Health, Child Protection: *Messages from Research*, 1995)

In the States, with mandatory reporting laws, the citizen (in many states) and/or professional are mandated to report the case. In reporting the incident to the Child Protection Agency, they are effectively, if the report is 'substantiated' defining the person responsible for the child's care as an abuser. In recent years some 60% of these reports have turned out to be unfounded (Besharov, 1990). In New York State less than 1% of the child abuse allegations presented with serious physical injuries. The most frequent allegations related to 'lack of supervision' (Barth, Berrick & Gilbert, 1994). Many would argue (for example Barth, Berrick & Gilbert, 1994), that such parenting behaviour should not be labelled child abuse.

In England and Wales, the social worker taking the referral has to decide which route to direct the case. In deciding the route the case is effectively labelled as child abuse or a family support case. If it is felt to be child protection, that is the child 'has suffered, or is likely to suffer significant harm', this becomes what is known as a section 47 referral and will proceed along a child protection route with a possible multi-disciplinary case conference, possible registration on the Child Protection Register, and if very significant risk is present possible legal intervention. There is no requirement, however, to work with the family after investigation if the child is not registered, or to provide services. On the other hand, if the case is felt not to be a child protection referral, the social worker has the option to consider the child as 'in need' under section 17 of the Children Act 1989, which may or may not lead to family support services.

The crux of the professional's anxiety is which route to take. If the child protection route is not taken, there could be serious repercussions if that child were subsequently seriously maltreated. The British media are always happy to capitalise on such incidents. Such pressure has led to large numbers of children unnecessarily going through the procedures with the resultant stigma and distress (Thorburn, Lewis & Shemmings, 1995).

In both the US and the UK, it could be argued that the task of Child Protection agencies, and in the UK Child Protection procedures, is to identify that small number of children who may be in life-threatening situations and protect them accordingly. At present in both the US and the UK most cases involving child protection agencies or actions are not an immediate life or death matter. They are more about children living with an insidious and ongoing pattern of physical chastisement, and/or neglect, and/or emotional abuse and/or 'lack of supervision'.

The main task for social services is to intervene to promote the welfare of these much larger numbers of children whose future health and development may be at risk through such parenting patterns. The effects of such patterns on the child in the long term can be *far more pronounced* than the occasional abusive incident.

In England and Wales, the Department of Health (1995), in summarising the messages from 20 research studies, suggest that in defining thresholds, it may not be helpful to focus exclusively on the abusive incident. In most cases, it is important, as has been argued in this book, to understand the wider *context of the maltreatment* reported and the likely effects for that child. The challenge of the task is to develop child protection and child welfare legislation and procedures that promote the overall well-being of the child.

The Need for, yet Controversies about, Risk Lists

A possible solution is to develop risk lists at the primary level of prevention to identify those children and families whose standards of *parenting* may fall below acceptable standards. Kaufman and Zigler (1989) would argue that efforts to develop risk lists to identify families who may need services should be abandoned because of their inherent unreliability. In times of scarce resources, however, it makes sense to identify those who have greater needs and to target resources to those who may benefit most, despite the unreliability of current methods and possible risk of stigmatisation. It may be that we have yet to find the most effective way of doing this.

Browne and Stevenson's work (1983) is an example of some of the difficulties inherent in developing risk lists. Their starting point was a retrospective study with health visitors and professional colleagues on 124 families using a 13-item checklist of risk factors present in parent or child around the birth. Abusing families (n = 62) were identified as those where a case conference had been called for a child under five.

The factors outlined in Table 15 were identified. Most of the risk factors exhibited a significant difference between the later abusing and non-abusing families. Overall a good predictor was the Health Visitor's perception of the parent–child interaction. 'Was the parent indifferent, intolerant or overanxious towards the child?' In this, it could be said that the Health Visitor was processing a number of different risk and protective factors and comparing these against a baseline of experience of other families on her patch.

Table 15: Relative importance of screening characteristics for child abuse, as determined by stepwise discriminant function analysis

	ABUSING FAMILIES (n = 62) (%)	NON-ABUSING FAMILIES (n = 124) (%)
1. Parent indifferent, intolerant or overanxious towards child	83.9*	21.8*
2. History of family violence	51.6*	5.6*
3. Socio-economic problems such as unemployment	85.5*	34.7*
4. Infant premature, low birthweight	24.2*	3.2*
5. Parent abused or neglected as child	43.5*	6.5*
6. Step-parent or co-habitee present	35.5*	4.8*
7. Single or separated parent	38.7*	8.1*
8. Mother less than 21 years old at the time of birth	40.7*	23.4*
9. History of mental illness, drug or alcohol problem	61.3*	21.8*
10. Infant separated from mother for longer than 24 hours post-delivery	17.7*	5.6*
11. Infant mentally or physically disabled	1.6	0.8
12. Less than 18 months between birth of children	22.6	15.3
13. Infant never breast-fed	46.8	40.3

Adapted from Browne, K. & Saqi, S. (1988). In K. Browne, C. Davies & P. Stratton (Eds), *Early Prediction and Prevention of Child Abuse*, p. 68. Reprinted by permission of John Wiley & Sons Ltd.

* *Significant difference p. < 0.05*

In making use of their checklist Browne and Saqi (1988) used the discriminant function analysis to weight each risk factor, rather than simply adding the number of factors together. Their findings indicated a later detection rate of 82% of abusers compared to 12% false alarms. This suggests it would be necessary to separate out the 33 true risk cases and the 1195 false alarms. Even if a more lengthy assessment took place on the high-risk families, this would still miss the 7 cases in the families defined as low risk. Figure 11 suggests what would happen if such an approach were applied to all births in a given area.

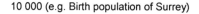

10 000 (e.g. Birth population of Surrey)

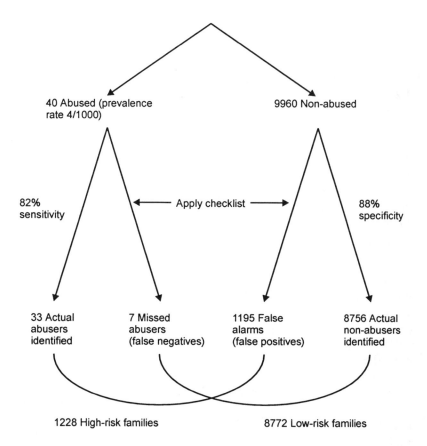

Figure 11: The effects of screening a population for child abuse
From Browne, K. & Saqui, S. (1988), in K. Browne, C. Davies & P. Stratton (Eds), *Early Prediction and Prevention of Child Abuse*, p. 71. Reprinted by permission of John Wiley & Sons Ltd

Browne and Saqi also used their method of risk identification in a prospective study of 83 families. They found that a significant number of families labelled low risk at birth went on to become high risk.

The above illustration demonstrates that when a significant percentage of the population can be falsely labelled as abusing, there are dilemmas in using such risk lists. Kaufman and Zigler (1992) note that given the low base rate for abusing even if screening processes could correctly label abusers 95% of the time, false labelling would still occur in around half of all the identified cases. Murphy, Orkow and Nicola (1985) and Straus (1979) have also developed comprehensive risk lists but these too demonstrate similar unreliability.

Although, as we have seen, there is a range of other information available to assist in screening of parent–child relationships, these are often limited by their single focus. For example, O'Leary considered the continuum of aggressive behaviours in intimate relationships (O'Leary, 1993); Zeanah and Zeanah (1989) considered the ongoing theme of caregiving relationships. Egeland's findings on the 'emotionally unresponsive' or 'psychological unavailable parent' are relevant; studies on attachment indicate vital clues (Pianta, Egeland & Erickson, 1989; Crittenden & Ainsworth, 1989); Altemeier et al.'s (1986) studies on self-esteem, Newberger and White's (1989) study on attribution and Feshbach's (1989) studies on empathy delve into the cognitive processing of parent–child relationships. Ideas from viewing the wider family system come from Trickett and Susman's (1989) work.

One of the difficulties is that child maltreatment needs to be seen within the wider ecological context of psychosocial *risk* and *protective* factors both inside and outside the family. A promising approach for identifying risk comes from criminological studies on victimisation, revictimisation and offender–victim relationships. Petrie and Garner (1990) suggest that because it is common for violent offenders to have had a previous relationship with a victim, and because such offences are usually concentrated in time and location, at least some forms of violence may be preventable. Those repeatedly victimised are amongst the most vulnerable and disadvantaged members of the community (Walton, 1995). In cases of domestic violence, after the first incident 35% of households suffered a second incident within five weeks, and after the second incident 45% of households suffered a third within five weeks (Moreley & Mullender, 1994). In such families, therefore, the risk can be calculated. Some police forces have responded to this by issuing alarms or vodaphones to victims for a limited period after the reported offence (Walton, 1995).

For those involved in protecting families and children in whatever capacity, there is a need for simple methods to identify those who may be at risk. In the US, when it comes to predicting child maltreatment *per se* promising findings have been reported concerning the predictive efficacy of the Family Stress Checklist (Murphy, Orkow & Nicola, 1985) and a parent attitude measure (Avison, Turner & Noh, 1986). On the other hand predictions of child maltreatment based on parent–child interactions (Starr, 1988) or self-report data (Bolton, Charlton, Gal, Laner & Shunway, 1985) have been significant. Tools focused specifically on neglect have also proved ineffective (Drotar, 1992). Predictions have generally demonstrated adequate sensitivity, that is the ability to identify correctly neglected children, but low specificity, that is the ability to identify correctly children who will *not* be victims (Brams & Courcy, 1985). This reinforces the view that widespread screening instruments used at the primary level of prevention may not be warranted. However, there are now some promising objective instruments which may identify families with special needs for preventive services (Avison, Turner & Noh, 1986; Murphy, Orkow & Nicola, 1985).

Measures such as the Child Abuse Potential Inventory (CAP; Milner, 1986), for example may be useful as a pre-post measure to gauge treatment effectiveness, as *part* of a more in-depth process. Despite impressive reliability and concurrent validity tests, the use of CAP frequently results in some misclassification both of confirmed abusers and of non-abusive controls (Kaufman, Johnson, Cohn & McCleery, 1992).

Browne and Saqi (1987) used a parental report behaviour checklist to assess high risk and low risk for abusing families. In Browne and Saqi's study, significantly more high-risk families had negative perceptions of their child's behaviour than low-risk families. The low-risk families had the most positive views.

Behavioural checklists, because of the tendency for abusing families to attribute their child's behaviour negatively, together with Family Problem Checklists to consider the wider ecological framework, may have a useful and easily administered role in assessing complex parent–child relationships and in identifying those in need of services and for measuring pre- and post-intervention outcomes. Buchanan *et al.* (1995), in a study of 89 families in contact with social services, found significant improvements in children's Rutter 'A', Health and Behavioural Checklist scores after social service intervention. A third of these were children who had been through child protection procedures. These measures were linked with others, such as a reduction in family stress as measured by the Gibbons, Thorpe and Wilkinson (1990) Family Problem

Checklist and simple statements by parents on how they perceived their and their child's current situation. If these scales do in fact indicate change, they may be useful tools. The scales are non-threatening, and are much easier to administer than the more complex instruments currently available.

Recently the Rutter 'A', Health and Behaviour Checklist has been developed by Quinton in the UK for the LAC scheme mentioned earlier, for measuring outcomes in looked-after children (Ward, 1995). These ongoing measurements, which are taken at regular periods, can therefore plot outcomes over a long period. Quinton's behavioural scales incorporated in this scheme may have wider applicability, but further work needs to be undertaken to assess their reliability. Potentially they will demonstrate both risk and protective factors. Carers are asked to reply to a series of statements to elicit whether the statement describes behaviour which is 'definitely like the child', 'quite like the child' , 'a bit like the child' or 'not at all like the child'.

RISK AND PROTECTIVE FACTORS

Risk and protective factors *are not absolute or static*; nor are they all good and all bad. They interact with the environment. On the whole single stressful experiences that occur in isolation are less damaging than cumulative stresses (Rutter, 1979; Kolvin, Miller, Scott, Gatzanis & Fleeting, 1990; Emery, 1982). *Timing of the experiences* may also be important. At particular moments, a child may be developmentally more protected or developmentally more vulnerable to adversities (Rutter, 1995). *The cumulative effect of risk factors* may be greatest where they set off a chain reaction, as we saw in the analysis of the Pathways in Chapter 6. Individuals also may have biological personal traits that may make them more or less likely to respond positively or negatively to personal adversities. *Compensatory experiences,* such as a good relationship with a significant other may increase 'resilience' to cope with psychosocial stresses (Jenkins & Smith, 1990). Compensatory experiences do not necessarily have to be present at the time of risk. *Early or later protective experiences* may compensate for the cumulative effects of the risk factors. Stacey, Dearden, Pill and Robinson (1970) have shown that children coped better with hospital separation if they had previous good 'separation' experiences, for instance by staying overnight with friends or relatives and Quinton, Rutter and Liddle's (1984) study of institutionally reared children found that in later life good partnership relationships could be compensatory for the early adverse experiences. *An early life free from life's adversities may in itself be a risk factor,* because the young person may never develop the necessary coping mechanisms and confidence to deal with later life stresses (Seligman, 1975; Hennesy & Levine, 1979). Risk and protective factors need to be seen in their *psychosocial context.*

Linked into this idea is that risk and protective factors have to be seen in *the context of how that person cognitively processes the experiences.* Rutter (1995) discusses the concept of 'shared and non-shared' environments. There are two interrelated issues here. Influences can impinge differently on different children in the same family, because the environment for different children *within* a family can feel very different, for example if a child is 'scape-goated'. Linked to this is the important idea that *perceived disparities* are important. People compare themselves to others in their setting. In comparison to living conditions in Hong Kong, very few if anyone in the UK experiences such levels of overcrowding. Adversities are seen in relation to the setting in which the person lives. Thus they may suffer psychologically even although in absolute terms their situation is improving.

Similarly increased academic stress at school may be viewed as a positive challenge to be met or it may be seen as an overwhelming burden. *Status* from doing a demanding but necessary job may compensate for the physical and psychological risks of the work (Bourne, Rose & Mason, 1967).

Risk and protective factors therefore have to be seen within the social context of the person, the timing and number of adversities, direct and indirect chain reactions, and the way the person cognitively processes the experiences.

THE CHALLENGES OF ASSESSMENT

The effective identification of risk and protective factors is central to the assessment process. Kaufman and Zigler (1992) consider this interaction as well as interactions with extrafamilial cycles of abuse in their adaption of Belsky's ecological model (1980). This model, as indicated earlier, can be related to the four cycles in this book. Ontogenetic and Micro-system factors are intrafamilial, that is they relate to the Psychological and Bio-logical cycles operating within the family, Exo-system and Macro-system factors are extrafamilial, that is they relate to Socio-political and Cultural cycles operating outside the family (Table 16). Kaufman and Zigler (1992) suggest that the Belsky framework can be used at primary, secondary and tertiary levels of prevention.

Table 16: The causes of child maltreatment

INTRAFAMILIAL (Psychological and Biological)		EXTRAFAMILIAL (Socio-political and Cultural)	
Ontogenetic factors	Micro-system factors	Exo-system factors	Macro-system factors
Risk Factors			
History of abuse Alcohol abuse Stressful experiences Low IQ Psychiatric and physical illness	Marital discord Single parenthood Premature or unhealthy child	Inadequate health care facilities Social isolation Unsafe neighbourhood	Economic recession Cultural acceptance of corporal punishment View of children as possessions
Protective Factors			
History of a positive relationship with at least one caregiver Good interpersonal skills High IQ	Supportive spouse Economic security Grandmother or other adult in home to assist with child	Good community social and health services Affordable quality day care Strong informal social supports Respite care facilities	Economic prosperity Culture opposed to violence Culture opposed to the use of corporal punishment

Adapted from Kaufman, J. & Zigler, E. (1992). In Willis, D., Holden, E. & Rosenberg, M., *Prevention of Child Maltreatment*, p. 270. Reprinted by permission of John Wiley & Sons, Inc.

Assessment in the Intergenerational Cycle of Abuse

The ecological framework is useful, as mentioned in Chapter 3, in assessing intergenerational continuities (Kaufman and Zigler, 1989). In addition to the factors outlined there is considerable research evidence, as we have seen in Chapter 5, which supports the idea that parents who broke the cycle were able to recognise, be angry about and reject their early parenting experiences and to make positive plans to effect a better quality of parenting for their own children (Egeland & Jacobvitz, 1984; Hunter & Kilstrom, 1979; Main & Goldwyn, 1984; Rutter & Quinton, 1984). Helping parents to face up to the realities of their own past presents particular challenges. Assessments are made more complex by the need for many who have been maltreated to idealise their past (Oliver, 1993). Contemporaneous records, if available, may be a better indicator of early parenting than self-reported adult recollections.

Hunter and Kilstrom (1979) also found that parents who broke the cycle had more social supports, physically healthy babies, few ambivalent feelings about their child, were less likely to have been abused by both parents and more likely to have supportive relationships with at least one parent as they grew up. Similarly Egeland and Jacobvitz (1984) found that such parents had one parent who provided support; they were currently in a supportive relationship; they 'had fewer life stressful events' and they too were aware of their history of abusive parenting. Kaufman and Zigler (1989) note that feeling unloved and unwanted by one's parents was a much stronger predictor for having a child reported as abused, than a history of being abused. Quinton, Rutter and Liddle (1984) found, as indicated by Rutter above, that compensatory and risk factors can have bidirectional effects. Early experiences can influence the quality of the partnership relationship, and a good partnership relationship can ameliorate the effects of childhood adversities.

Parents who have been abused may have to learn a *new parenting style* (Feshbach, 1974; Hetzberger, 1983; Gelles & Straus, 1979), develop a different attachment behaviour with their child (Crittenden, 1984), and develop new inner working models (Zeanah & Anders, 1987) about their relationships. In order to do this the development of a positive self-esteem will be important (Altemeier *et al.*, 1986) and such parents will need to learn how to attribute positively normal, naughty behaviour seen in their children (Newberger & White, 1989). Central to this process will be the development of empathy (Feshbach & Caskey, 1985).

The strong message from these studies is that very little is unalterable. Belsky and Vondra (1989) talk about 'parenting—a buffered system'. Because parenting is multiply determined, the parenting system is normally 'buffered' against failure from one part of the system by compensatory factors in other parts. Multiple adversities or multiple vulnerability factors, as we have seen, threaten the system. The challenge in assessing families where the parenting system is at risk is to find the appropriate artificial 'buffers', not only to support the parents to discover what 'buffers' can be set in place to compensate those children who are currently being maltreated.

CHILDREN WHO MAY NEVER BE SAFE WITHIN THEIR FAMILIES

'The reality for those who work in the field of child abuse is that some families cannot be treated or rehabilitated sufficiently to offer a safe enough environment in which children can live' (Jones, 1987, p. 409). Jones argues that helping parents understand that it is not safe for their child to live with them could in some cases be seen as therapeutic, and in some cases objective decisions will have to be made to identify these families. On a basis of clinical experience, Jones identified some of the reasons why families cannot be made safe enough for children.

(1) There are some families who simply will not change. They do not intend or want to change.
(2) Some parents persistently deny abusive behaviour in the face of clear evidence to the contrary.
(3) Some families cannot change in spite of a will to do so. There may be a subgroup here of families who are willing to change but resources to help them are not available.
(4) Some parents can change, but not 'in time' for their child's development needs. For example, a 6-month-old baby's abusive parent, who after two years becomes less impulsive and dangerous, but in the meantime whose baby has developed a strong attachment to a surrogate parent.
(5) Similarly, other parents may change in time for their next child but not for the index one.
(6) Finally there is the category of untreatable parents who fail to respond to one treatment approach but who may be amenable to another agency or approach. (Jones, 1987, p. 410)

Jones's paper is controversial in that it faces up to the reality of the inadequacies of services for abusive parents; that, for example, professionals may not be able to motivate parents to change; that specific resources needed may not be available; that treatment for parents may not move quickly enough for the developmental needs of their child; that the approach currently available may not be the most appropriate one. Decisions to separate a child from his/her family have to be made in which the child's interests are paramount and these decisions have to be made within the context of what services are available. In a review of studies, mostly relating to physical abuse and neglect between 1979 and 1985, Jones notes that between 60% and 16% of children are reabused. He indicates that selection may play a part in the differences seen between these rates but that despite the differences in methodology there is evidence that the more intensive programmes, particularly those that have an outreach programme, produce better results. The reality however, in any given area, is that such programmes may not be available.

From a review of studies, Jones identifies the characteristics which may be associated with a failure to rehabilitate a child safely within his/her family. He suggests that the following factors should not be seen as definitive but rather should help professionals working with the family to be alert to the potential difficulties.

Firstly, there are parental factors associated with untreatability. Among these are a *parental history of severe child abuse*, a denial of abusive behaviour, severe personality disorder and learning disabilities in the parents associated with a personality disorder. Secondly, there are *characteristics of the parenting behaviour* which are associated with poor outcomes. This may be where the parent is unable to see the child's needs as separate or different from their own and/or there is a lack of empathy for the victimised child. Thirdly, there are *certain types of severe abuse* which indicate poorer outcomes, for example, fractures, scalds and burns, Munchausen by proxy, non-accidental poisoning and severe failure to thrive. Fourthly, where the child lives with *a perpetrator who has committed a number of violent acts*—the greater the number of such acts, the greater the risk to the child. Finally, there is the professional response. *Better outcomes are where professionals are able to establish a helping relationship* with the family concerned together with an effective outreach component.

In the US, in particular, concerns for the safety of the child may be in relation to carer substance abuse. Recent sharp rises in the number of children exposed to drugs before birth have largely been held responsible for the growth in the number of children in foster care (Feig, 1990). Feig (1990) showed there was a 167% increase in referrals of drug-exposed babies to child welfare services between 1986 and 1989. Such were the concerns that out of every hundred drug-exposed infants referred to the Child Protection Services, more than a quarter were placed directly in family foster care, in relatives' homes or in another out-of-home placement. These children can be particularly difficult to rear because of their drug exposure, and many of them are never, or cannot for reasons of safety be, reunited with their families (Barth, 1994).

Jones suggested that when decisions are being made on the children who may never be able to return home, there should be a time-limit on programmes aimed at trying to keep the family together; for example where a child is under 3 this should be 12 months; where a child is over 3 this should be 18 months. In Kempe's words:

> We should stress that when we say a family is untreatable, we do not mean that the parents do not deserve treatment. What we mean is that the child should not be used as the instrument of treatment . . . there must be a more civilised way (Kempe & Kempe, 1978, pp. 128–131)

STRATEGIES FOR INTERVENTION

Strategies for intervention are as diverse as the aetiological reasons for child maltreatment. In assessing cases of child maltreatment and deciding on strategies for intervention, it is useful to know to what extent different strategies have been empirically tested. The task is to match the strengths and needs of individual cases with programmes that have demonstrable effectiveness. Strategies for intervention may be made up of individual programmes—a programme focusing on one aspect of the child maltreatment; or 'packages of care', that is a range of different interventions matched to the identified needs of a case within available resources. Since, however, the causes of child maltreatment are not independent, interventions that focus on one aetiological cause may lead to improvements in other areas. Nonetheless, Kaufman and Zigler would agree that the best intervention programmes are multi-faceted (Kaufman & Zigler, 1992). Kaufman and Zigler give a useful overview of the possibilities in programming, research and policy from a US perspective (Table 17). They link this to the Ecological framework described above.

Some of the programmes highlighted in Table 17 cover more than one level. For instance the Olds and Henderson (1989) home visiting programme for identified high-risk mothers had three components. Firstly, parent awareness about infant and child development was enhanced by a parent education programme. Secondly, efforts were made to widen informal networks of support, and thirdly, other members of the family with health and human service needs were linked to the appropriate services. Kaufman and Zigler conclude:

> The effectiveness of the home-visitation program was enhanced by: the use of multiple, ecologically sensitive prevention strategies; the coordination of program services with existing community services; and the provision of continuous, long-term assistance. (Kaufman & Zigler, 1992, p. 275)

The last sentence is critical, with interventions designed to break the long-term cycle of maltreatment. There was a period when it was felt that short-term interventions would miraculously improve the parenting skills both in this generation and the next. Although this may be true in a few cases, the reality is that many families will need long-term support which is adaptable enough to respond to the differing development needs of a child at different times, and the differing parental needs that emerge from changing circumstances.

The Importance of the Developmental Approach

The developmental approach implies that the parenting task has to be responsive to the characteristics and needs of the child at different times. Particular deficits in aspects of parenting can be more or less critical at

Table 17: The prevention of child maltreatment: programming, research and policy

INTRAFAMILIAL (Psychological & Biological)		EXTRAFAMILIAL (Socio-political & Cultural)	
Ontogenetic	Micro-system	Exo-system	Macro-system
Psychotherapeutic interventions for abusive parents (e.g. Galston, 1975)	Maritial counselling (Lutzker *et al.*, 1984)	Development of community, social and health services (Cohn, 1982)	Campaign to increase public awareness (Cohn, 1982)
Treatment programmes for abused children (Connor, 1987)	Home safety training (Lutzker *et al.*, 1984)	Crisis Hotlines (Johnston, 1976)	Formation of NCCAN grants for research
Alcohol and drug rehabilitation (Lutzker, Welsch & Rice, 1984)	Health visitors (Olds & Henderson, 1989)	Training professionals to identify abuse (Loadman & Vaughn 1986)	Establishment of a National Commission on Child Abuse and Neglect
Stress management skills training (Egan, 1983)	Enhancement of parent–child contact and interactions (O'Connor, Vietze, Sherrod, Sandler & Altemeier, 1980)	Location of foster adoptive homes (Rosenstein, 1978)	Require States to adopt procedures for the prevention, treatment and identification of maltreatment (Child Abuse Prevention Treatment Act, 1974)
Job search assistance (Lutzker *et al.*, 1984)	Parent aids programmes (Adnopez, Nagler & Sinanaglu, 1987)	Facilitate informal community supports (Pancoast, 1980)	Legislative efforts to combat poverty (Albee, 1980)
	Education for parenthood programmes (Zigler, 1980)	Establish family planning centres (Cohn, 1982)	Establish laws against corporal punishment in the schools (Zigler, 1980)
	Parenting skills training (Wolfe & Harlon, 1984)	Establish coordinating agency for child maltreatment services (Shay, 1980)	Research incidence maltreatment and effectiveness of prevention & treatments (Ross & Zigler, 1980)
		Parents Anonymous groups (Lieber, 1983)	
		Respite child care facilities (Cohn, 1981)	

Adapted from Kaufman, J. & Zigler, E. (1992). In Willis, D., Holden. E. & Rosenberg, M., *Prevention of Child Maltreatment*, p. 274. Reprinted by permission of John Wiley & Sons, Inc.

some periods in the child's development than at others. In addition, although many parents may need long-term support, some parents may have particular difficulties in meeting the developmental needs of children at different developmental stages. Intervention strategies need to link to the developmental context of the child. Aber and Zigler (1981) have proposed a *developmental definition* of child protection. For instance under US reporting laws, if a child is left alone without supervision this would become more or less a reason for a 'substantiated' report, depending on the child's age and competence (Aber & Zigler, 1981).

At the infant stage, the critical parenting task is to respond emphatically to the infant and to provide a stable and predictable environment which promotes the infant's development of trust (Erikson, 1968). As the child moves into toddlerhood, the striving for greater independence, the child's increased mobility and the characteristic negativism of this age can produce particular challenges for the parent (Culbertson & Schellenbach, 1992). At the infant and toddler stage health services and home visitation programmes may be helpful both in identifying families who may be in difficulties and in providing programmes to support them in place.

School-age children present different challenges. Rosenberg and Sonkin (1992) note that what is seen in school is often the product of how the family have coped with earlier transitions in the life cycle. There is a need for parents to approach children consistently on discipline, attitudes to school work, and relationships with peers. Stresses in the wider ecological system may interfere with the parents' ability to meet the child's development needs at this stage. The American Humane Association (1987) study of child maltreatment noted that while 31% of all children in the United States are aged between 6 and 11, 33% of all reports of child maltreatment fall into this age range. Schools play a major role in identifying these children and initiating programmes. Prevention is two-pronged: firstly, helping the parents overcome some of the difficulties impinging on their lives. In the UK, Education Welfare Officers are often involved in this role. Secondly, the task is to help the child to cope within his/her environment. Often children present in school with behavioural difficulties which if not treated can develop into a cycle of school failure. In the UK, the School Psychological Service has an important part to play (Faupel, 1994). In Wiltshire in the UK, health visitors are now employed in pre-school classes initiating behavioural programmes with children and their parents (Buchanan *et al.*, 1995).

The task of being a parent to an adolescent substantially differs from earlier parent–child relationships. Contrary to the stereotype view that adolescence is a time of turmoil and crisis, there is a low incidence of parental rejection and relationship difficulties at this time (Rutter, Graham, Chadwick & Yule, 1976). Around 20%, however, do experience serious turmoil as they grow up (Garbarino, 1993). In the United States. the National Incidence Study indicated that adolescents, who represent 38% of the population account for some 47% of known child maltreatment but they are less likely to be reported to Child Maltreatment Agencies than younger children. Adolescent maltreatment, apart from sexual abuse, tends to be linked with problematic acting-out behaviour in the teenager associated with difficulties within the family. Garbarino (1993) indicates that there are three types of families that appear to experience difficulties at this age. Firstly, there are the long-term multi-problem families where the adolescent difficulties are part of a long-term continuum in parenting difficulties. Secondly, there are the adolescent-onset of parenting difficulties. Thirdly, there is the parenting style in dealing with the adolescent. On the one hand, there is the 'authoritarian' parent who is characterised by paternalistic, harsh and rigid styles of child-rearing. On the other hand, there is the 'overindulgent' parent who overcompensates for emotional disadvantage.

In England and Wales, the Children Act 1989 has been criticised for over-responding to the rights of the adolescent child (Buchanan et al., 1995). Under the Act, an adolescent, unhappy in his/her home situation, can ask to be accommodated by the local authority. Listening to young people who may be experiencing physical or sexual abuse in the family can be important in preventing acts of deliberate self-harm, running away and delinquency (Buchanan et al., 1993). Buchanan et al. (1995), however, found that some parents of adolescents felt undermined by the powers given to their children under the Children Act 1989. Recently, the local authority which took part in this study has taken greater care in assessing the young people's difficulties. Where relationship problems appear short term and related to the adolescent period, it is now counselling parents and the young person, and providing safe after-school and holiday activities to try to divert entry into public care. This authority has a very low rate of adolescents in out-of-home care. Although the parents were often asking for their children to be accommodated, social workers consciously worked with families to resolve difficulties within the family without separating the young person. The research demonstrated that six months later, many of the families and young people had come to some sort of resolution of their difficulties without the young person being admitted to public care. This is a relevant finding. However, successful intervention depends on a careful assessment of the difficulties presented (Buchanan et al., 1995).

INTERVENTION PROGRAMMES

Gough (1993) has undertaken a useful review of international literature on child protection interventions. An essential component of this review was to assess to what extent interventions were empirically based. In talking about these programmes we need to remember the earlier discussion, highlighting that in the US, *Family Preservation Programmes* are those that follow a substantiated child abuse and neglect report and where there is a high risk of out-of-home care. Family Support Services there are located *outside* the child protection agencies. In the UK both types are combined under social services.

One of the areas considered by Gough (1993) was the use of *volunteers and parents' aides*. There were seven studies considered: Baker, Grant, Squires, Johnson and Offermann, (1981: parent aides); Barth (1989: parent/child enrichment); Cox, Puckering, Pound, Mills and Owen (1990: Newpin befriending); Gibbons and Thorpe (1989: Home Start volunteers); Miller, Fein, Howe, Gaudio, and Bishop (1984: time-limited parent aides); Rosenstein (1978: telephone and home counselling); Van der Eyken (1982: Home Start volunteers).

These studies all used volunteers and parent-aides to develop the parents' own abilities to cope. All the studies reported improvements and were positively valued by both users and workers. Gough notes that the lack of independent measures, particularly in relation to the children, made it difficult to assess whether there were actual improvements in behaviour and functioning. Such schemes had considerable benefits in that they were low cost; they focused on enablement rather than treatment; they were less stigmatising. Gough's conclusion was that:

> Parent-aides and volunteers have the potential of offering an extremely useful preventive service. Despite the lack of clear cut data the research here provides better evidence of success, than many other areas of child abuse intervention. (Gough, 1993, p. 79)

Another area considered by Gough was the use of *adult and child groups*. This is a cost-effective method of reaching many clients at the same time. Interactions within the group can also provide a powerful learning medium as well as providing mutual support. All the studies considered involved working with identified abusive families or those felt to be at high risk of child maltreatment. The groups had a variety of aims and a variety of techniques were used—social activities and mutual support, education, behavioural training and psychotherapy.

Seventeen studies were included in Gough's review. Among the more recent were those by Armstrong (1981), Armstrong and Fraley (1985: counselling, family, school, peer support); Howlett, Lunan and Symons (1985: behavioural training groups); Resnick (1985: weekly groups on parenting skills for disadvantaged parents); Roth (1985: Parents Anonymous); Scaife and Frith (1988: Behaviour management course); Schellenbach and Guerney (1987: parenting course for high- and low-risk parents); Schinke, Schilling and Barth (1986: problem-solving groups for adolescent mothers); Telleen. Herzog and Kilbrane (1989: mother support group, parent education in urban deprived area).

The majority of the studies reported improvements. In particular they increased the self-esteem of parents and improved their perceptions of their children's behaviour. There was insufficient research evidence to distinguish which strategy, for which parents, under what circumstances, was the most effective. Groups, however, obviously have great potential and may be more acceptable than one-to-one work, but there is a need for better evaluation (Gough, 1993).

In the UK, parental groups are a common form of intervention in Family Centres. In the United States there are also a number of special programmes for families. These are listed under National Resource Center on Family Based Services (1986). In the United States there are further studies focusing on family preservation (Nelson, Landsman & Deutelbaum, 1990; Whittaker, Kinney, Tracy & Booth, 1990; Wells & Biegal, 1991). Family preservation services in the US, as we have mentioned, only respond *after* the child has been identified as abused or neglected. In the UK, in theory, services for children *in need* are available wherever the child's health and development may be at risk. There does not need to be evidence of abuse or neglect.

In Gough's review, behavioural child abuse interventions record the most impressive results. In the UK, Herbert (1981), Hudson and Macdonald (1986) and Sluckin (1981) were early pioneers in demonstrating the effectiveness of such programmes for social workers when working with children and families. Conger, Lahey and Smith (1981) outlined the main focus of behavioural studies in working with families where child abuse was an issue. Gough (1993) summarised these as follows:

(1) To teach parents methods of child control that do not require physical punishment.
(2) To reduce their adverse reactions to the children's behaviour.
(3) To teach child development so that parents can be more realistic in their expectations of their children.
(4) To encourage positive rather than negative family interactions. (Gough, 1993)

The findings from all the studies reviewed by Gough were encouraging, although it seemed easier to reduce negative interactions than to increase positive ones. Motivation of the parents involved was important as there was a high attrition rate in some of the studies. Attendance at a course did not necessarily mean the parents were motivated to change, especially where they had been directed to the programme by a court. Many parents are resistant to the idea that they lack parenting skills, but court direction may, however, allow the parent to appreciate the potential benefits of such a service. Programmes usually lasted between one month and six months with weekly or biweekly meetings. Many of the studies involved single cases or very small numbers. Among the larger studies reviewed were Nicol, Smith, Kay, Hall, Barlow and Williams (1988: focused behavioural case work with 38 physically abusing parents); Reid, Taplin and Lorber (1981: social interactional training, a meta-analysis of 27 children with conduct disorder); Smith and Rachman (1984: social interaction treatment of 16 physically abusing parents); Szykula and Fleischman (1985: child management training of 24 child protection cases); Whiteman, Fanshel and Grundy (1987: cognitive behavioural training, abuse/anger control with 55 cases); and Wolfe, Edwards, Manion and Koverola (1988) on child management training with 30 cases referred by the child protection services.

The conclusion was that behavioural interventions can be very effective, but to date the techniques are not used as widely as they could be. Stevenson (1987) suggests that behavioural programmes could be more widely used by health visitors.

The clear focus of interventions means that behavioural programmes are better able to demonstrate their effectiveness. With some families behavioural interventions, however, may need to be integrated with interventions focused on the child's and family's needs in the wider ecological framework.

Ijzendoorn, Juffer and Duyvesteyn (1995) have undertaken another useful review on the effects of attachment-based interventions on maternal sensitivity and infant security in breaking the intergenerational cycle of insecure attachment. Twelve studies were included in a quantitative meta-analysis. The intervention studies had a common goal—to enhance the quality of infant–mother attachment relationship. In this case short-term preventive interventions were found to be more effective than longer more intensive and therapeutic interventions. Results showed that interventions were more effective in changing parental sensitivity than in changing children's attachment insecurity. Concern was also expressed as to how far such changes in the parental behaviour would generalise into later relationships, particularly as their child developed and demanded different types of attachment behaviour from their parent. This links into the ideas expressed earlier about the need to see child maltreatment interventions within the developmental context of the child.

In the studies reviewed a range of strategies were used. The Egeland and Erickson study (1993), for example, was a multi-service package addressing not only child–parent relationships, but financial, insurance, housing and other practical issues. Ijzendoorn, Juffer and Duyvesteyn note that:

> When urgent 'survival' needs dominate the intervention, it may well be at the cost of the effectiveness at the level of maternal sensitivity. And even if the broad-band approach is effective in changing attachment relationships it will be difficult to trace back this effect to specific facets of the program. (Ijzendoorn, Juffer & Duyvesteyn, 1995, p. 242)

EVALUATING OUTCOMES

Parenting is not a single focused activity and the *process* of the intervention and the interactions within the family system may be as important as the actual stated interventions (Department of Health, 1995). The purpose of all interventions is to improve the outcomes for children in both this generation and the next. Even with carefully controlled experimental studies and increased sophistication of statistical techniques, we may never know precisely which factors have brought about the changes. Perhaps we need to monitor children's overall outcomes both in the short term and the long term by using, as we have discussed, tools that measure a child developmental progress over periods of time. Hopefully this will give us clues about the effectiveness of our 'packages of care', but discovering which particular elements within the packages have brought about the changes may remain elusive. These ideas are reinforced by Gough's summary of factors influencing effective interventions and the Department of Health (1995), *Messages from Research*.

Issues in Evaluating Outcomes

It is useful to summarise some of the main issues in evaluating outcomes. These findings are based on Gough (1993). Overall, because of methodological weaknesses in the studies he reviewed, to date there is very little hard evidence of effectiveness. However, clues can be elicited from the studies on mechanisms which influence effectiveness. Acceptability of services to clients crucially influences the extent to which services are taken up and their outcomes. Positive outcomes for parents may not be the same as positive outcomes for children. Outcomes for children need to be measured as well. Research generally reports positive outcomes, but it is less good at reporting negative outcomes or possible disadvantages of programmes. In a resource-limited world, it is important to be aware of the relationships between costs and benefits of the services provided. Most children who are abused, or who are in danger of being abused, do not have access to the kinds of programmes described above. Many of the strategies discussed above, however, could well be adapted for wider use. In the real world, however, as we will see in the case summary in Chapter 11, social workers make use of a range of interventions that happen to be available in their area and 'best fit' the needs of their clients.

Intervening to Effect a Better Quality of Life for the Abused Child

In the families described by Jones (1987) above, legal procedures may need to be initiated to effect the immediate and longer term protection of the child. Recently in the UK, the Department of Health has published, as we have described, a review of 20 studies which give an objective and realistic overview of child protection services in the UK (Department of Health, 1995). Such research is useful because we need to be sure that in the UK and elsewhere, overall outcomes from the many procedures and strategies used do indeed improve the welfare of children. Interventions in child abuse programmes, as Gough (1993) has pointed out, are not just what happens in the treatment programme. Outcomes are also related to *the process* of what happens once a case is in the child protection system. At the very least we need to be sure that the system does not further abuse children.

Firstly, better outcomes for children are generally associated with greater parental involvement in the child protection process. Thorburn, Lewis and Shemmings' (1995) study in the UK of 220 child protection cases set out to examine the consequences of participation from several viewpoints. In general just over half of the families felt they had participated in the child protection process and just under half felt they had not. An early observation was the need for parents to have a written as well as a verbal agreement about the specifics of their child protection process. Even in cases of severe difficulties, it was possible to achieve 'participation', but in these cases, the crucial factors were the attitudes, skill and efforts of the social workers. Such workers needed to be supported by agency policies and procedures which encouraged creativity.

Secondly, the Department of Health's 1995 studies considered the effectiveness of the child protection process in dealing with 'heavy end' referrals. Although a few heavy end cases were missed or ignored, most cases were identified. Researchers' main concerns were:

Interventions were often limited in scope because of their restrictive emphasis on abuse. Non-abusing parents' requests for psychiatric help were overlooked, non-resident parents were rarely engaged, the needs of siblings were ignored and children were placed in foster and residential homes where further maltreatment occurred. (Department of Health, 1995, *Child Protection—Messages from Research*, p. 43)

The Gibbons *et al.* study (1995) of physically abused children demonstrated, as we have discussed, that overall children who were legally protected by a care or other order did *not* do significantly better than similar children who were not so protected. Nor did those who were removed from abusing families and placed in new or permanent long-term families have significantly better outcomes. Apparently this still held for those who were placed in new families early in their lives. These findings illustrate the difficulties in ensuring a better quality of life for a child by moving him/her to an apparently non-abusing family.

Thirdly, the Department of Health Research (1995) emphasises that risks must be taken in order to obtain more successful outcomes for children. Child protection can never be risk free. Interventions have to be seen *in the context of the individual case* together with an awareness of *the possible long-term outcomes*. They summarise the features associated with better protection of children. Among these are five features of effective practice:

Sensitive and informed professional/client relationships; an appropriate balance of power between the key parties; a wide perspective on child abuse; effective supervision and training of social workers; and a determination to enhance the quality of children's lives. (Department of Health, 1995, *Child Protection—Messages from Research*, p. 45)

They also noted that protection was best achieved by building on the strengths of the child's existing living situation rather than expecting miracles from short-term interventions. Respecting family rights can also contribute to the child's protection. Finally, and this is relevant from our perspective of breaking intergenerational patterns of maltreatment, the outcome from the abuse has to be balanced against the likely long-term outcome of interventions and the overall needs of the child.

CONCLUSIONS

In the last 30 years, research has, if anything, complicated rather than clarified the issues in protecting children and breaking intergenerational patterns of child maltreatment. From the early studies which highlighted pathological factors in families and children who were abused, research demonstrated extrafamilial factors which indicated circumstances where child maltreatment was more likely to happen. In the UK and elsewhere the tragedies of children who died led to a focus on careful identification of those at risk and 'child rescue' policies to effect better outcomes for such children. Such policies in both the US and the UK led to many children being brought up in state care. Research then demonstrated that for some children such 'rescue' policies did not necessarily promote the welfare of children. In fact some of these children may have been poorly prepared to parent their own children. Finally research is now suggesting that the welfare of *many* but *not all* children at risk will be better ensured by supporting them within their families. Careful assessment needs to be made of individual cases within the context of the situation in which they are living and the likely effects both short-term and long-term of interventions.

Mullen *et al.*'s (1996) study on the long-term impact of physical, emotional and sexual abuse of children in a self-report community study in Dunedin in New Zealand cautions against an exclusive focus on abuse which may obscure the unfolding of other damaging developmental influences. Such studies which look beyond abuse *per se* and explore the longitudinal developmental outcomes for children afflicted by a range of childhood adversities will do much to extend our knowledge. Such knowledge is needed if we are to break patterns of intergenerational child maltreatment.

SUMMARY: INTERVENTIONS IN THE INTRAFAMILIAL CYCLE

Aim: Providing 'Buffers' for Those at Risk

Identification

- Thresholds and context in identification
- The need for, yet controversies about, risk lists
- Screening parent–child relationships/ family problem checklists
- The use of check lists

The challenges of assessment

- Risk and protective factors

- Assessment in the intergenerational cycle
- The inseparable links between intrafamilial and extrafamilial factors
- The ecological framework
- The child who may never be safe within the family

Intervention

- Proven intervention programmes
- The developmental approach in intervention strategies
- Packages of care

Evaluation of outcomes

- Intervening to effect a *better quality of life* for children
- Monitoring change and outcomes
- The hope of creating a better world for children

IV

SOME ACHIEVEMENTS

11

ACHIEVEMENTS IN PRACTICE

In order for the goal of child maltreatment prevention to be achieved, ecologically sensitive, multifaceted, and continuous intervention programs must be utilised. Each well-intentioned intervention will not be successful, but through well-designed evaluations, the effectiveness of future efforts can be increased, and the hiatus that separates the intention and realisation of . . . aims can be diminished. (Kaufman & Zigler, 1992, pp. 287–288)

The above paragraph was the conclusion to a book by Willis, Holden and Rosenberg (1992), *Prevention of Child Maltreatment*. The emphasis on prevention is an appropriate introduction to this last chapter. As we have discussed, preventive strategies, within the ecological framework at all the levels, primary, secondary and tertiary, are central in our efforts to break cycles of child maltreatment.

The main focus of this final chapter is to document the achievements of different international bodies, nation states, communities and individuals that have, to a greater or lesser extent, impinged on the cycles of child maltreatment. Hopefully these will give encouragement to those who daily wrestle with the complexities of the task. In the final section of this chapter, a case-study based on a real family is outlined. This is to remind us that breaking cycles of maltreatment is about changing the lives of real children and real families. Figure 12 first summarises some of the strategies for intervention identified in the previous four chapters.

ACHIEVEMENTS IN THE SOCIO-POLITICAL CYCLE

At the international level, the first example may be well known, but the campaign it initiated to improve the overall health and welfare of mothers and children, and the plans set in place, represent a major milestone in breaking patterns of child maltreatment.

	Principles	
	Aim: **To promote the well-being of children in this generation and in future generations** • Children are best brought up in their own families • The child has rights to protection • Intervening to prevent child maltreatment at the different preventive levels • Partnership/participation with parents and child • Awareness of both risk and protective factors • Identification of both strengths and needs in child and family and community • Child maltreatment seen within its social context • View of child maltreatment beyond abuse • Measurement of outcomes • Intergenerational outcomes • Do no further harm	
Socio-political	**Cultural**	**Intrafamilial: Psychological and Biological**
Aim: **To create societies where 'permitting circumstances' for parenting are maximised** *International* • The campaigning role of UNICEF, ISPCAN, voluntary associations, e.g. ECPAT • Developing strategies to maximise the upward spiral • Specific international responsibilities • Monitoring supply and demand • Dissemination of information • Collection of data *National* • Policies that support the family • Recognition of family change • Legislative framework that supports families and protects children • Child Protection procedures and reporting systems • Policies to support children and families in need • Measuring outcomes *Local government level* • Training • Publishing guidelines • Disseminating research • Publishing indicators • Inspection of public facilities • Linking of health, education and social welfare services • Identifying areas of special need *Community level* • Universal support services • Specific programmes • Support centres, such as Family Centres • Quality day care	*Aim:* **To intervene within the EMIC and the ETIC perspective** *International* • Towards an international definition of child abuse • The development of an international data base • Disseminating information about child maltreatment • Limiting the export of violent entertainment *National* • Defining child abuse within an EMIC and ETIC perspective • Setting up ethnically sensitive services • Establishing frameworks of community consultation • Identification of levels of abuse in ethnic communities • Parental education and child development awareness • Building on the strengths of ethnic groups *Community* • Community participation and empowerment • Establishing community programmes • Learning to ask questions	*Aim:* **To provide 'buffers' for those at risk** *Identification* • Thresholds and context in identification • The need for, yet controversies about, risk lists • Screening parent-child relationships • The use of check lists *The challenges of assessment* • Risk and protective factors • Assessment in the intergenerational cycle • The inseparable links between intrafamilial and extrafamilial factors • The ecological framework • The child who may never be safe within the family *Intervention* • Proven intervention programmes • The developmental approach in intervention strategies *Evaluation of outcomes* • Intervening to effect a better quality of life for children • Monitoring change and outcomes • The opportunity of creating a better world for children

Figure 12: Intervention strategies in the cycles of child maltreatment

Outcomes from the World Summit for Children 1990

Following the 1990 World Summit for Children, most countries agreed to draw up national programmes of action (NPAs) for achieving basic social goals. Those goals include control of the major childhood diseases, a halving of child malnutrition, a one-third reduction in under-five death rates, a halving of maternal mortality rates, the provision of safe water for all communities, the universal availability of family planning information and services, and a basic education for all children. (UNICEF, 1993, p. 60)

Following the World Summit 139 countries signed the Declaration and by 1993 46 countries had national programmes of action in preparation, 34 had a national plan in draft form, and 54 had finalised their plans. In addition, all countries were urged to ratify the Convention on the Rights of the Child which laid down minimal standards for the survival, protection and development of children. By 1993, 120 nations had ratified the Convention.

As a follow-up to the initial commitment by the countries attending the World Summit, annual statistics are published by UNICEF which monitor children's well-being. These illustrate that significant progress towards meeting targets have been made in many countries (UNICEF, 1993).

The other arm in breaking patterns of child maltreatment has been the International Society for the Prevention of Child Abuse and Neglect (ISPCAN) founded by Henry Kempe.

The ISPCAN Example

The International Society was founded in 1977 to prevent cruelty to children in every nation—whether cruelty occurs in the form of abuse, neglect, or exploitation—and thus to enable the children of the world to develop physically, mentally, and socially in a healthy and normal manner. The Society welcomes those who wish to work toward the alleviation and ultimate prevention of such maltreatment. The Society aims to provide a forum for discussions for sharing of knowledge and experience through holding congresses at approximately two-year intervals. (Child Abuse and Neglect, June 1995)

The main purpose of the Society is to increase international collaboration. Their main strategies have been to raise the profile of harm caused to children by disseminating information and supporting professionals.

International congresses are held biannually. The tenth International Congress was held in 1994 in Malaysia. In addition linked Regional and National groups have staged their own Conferences bringing together large numbers of policy-makers, legislators, administrators and child welfare professionals to share information on research and strategies, and to create hope for change.

At the fourth European Conference on Child Abuse and Neglect which was held in Padova, Italy, in 1993, more than 600 delegates came together and 350 papers were presented. Papers on intergenerational child maltreatment were strongly featured:

> A number of conference papers emphasised the transfer for CAN from one generation to the next (i.e. that parents who were maltreated as children, maltreat their own children) . . . and the consequences of CAN on various phases of the child's development. (Dunovsky & Browne, 1994, p. 2)

Linked conferences and seminars have also been held in Cape Town in South Africa where a Resource Centre and Research Unit has been developed, and in French-speaking West Africa in April 1994. In Brazil the fourth Latin American Conference was held in May 1993, with training workshops and courses following in Santiago in Chile, and in Haiti and Paraguay. Magazines such as *Pronino* (Costa Rica) and *Derecho a la Infancia* (Chile) regularly update professionals.

The *Resource Book* has been prepared by Deborah Daro and her colleagues at the National Committee for Prevention of Child Abuse (NCPCA, Chicago, USA) and was published by ISPCAN with UNICEF in 1992. This book includes survey results, major milestones in addressing the child abuse problem worldwide; selected information from individual countries and bibliographies as well as selected information from individual countries. A second resource book is planned which will also have support from NCPCA and UNICEF. A further initiative to establish an international *data bank* is planned (ISPCAN, 1994).

In addition ISPCAN founded *Child Abuse and Neglect, The International Journal* as their official publication. Although this is a scientific subscription journal, a number of complimentary copies are sent to colleagues in developing countries. This journal is published monthly and:

> provides an international, multidisciplinary forum on all aspects of child abuse and neglect including sexual abuse, with special emphasis on prevention and treatment. The scope extends further to all those aspects of life that either favor or hinder optimal family interaction. While contributions will primarily be from the fields of psychology, psychiatry, social work, medicine, nursing, law, law enforcement, legislation, education, and anthropology, the journal aims to encourage the concerned lay individual and child-orientated advocate organisations to contribute. (*Child Abuse and Neglect*, June 1995, Preface)

Other journals such as the *Child Abuse Review*, from the British Association for the Study and Prevention of Child Abuse and Neglect, now publish papers with international relevance. This association was founded by the paediatricians Alfred White Franklin and Tina Cooper.

ACHIEVEMENTS AT NATIONAL AND REGIONAL LEVEL

Within the wider remit of improving the welfare of children, there have been a number of useful initiatives. Among these are efforts to improve the conditions for children in areas of armed conflict.

The Central American Accord for Human Development

Central America for decades was one of the world's most conflict-ridden regions. Civil wars, rebellions and cold war confrontations turned many of these small countries into battlefields. By the end of the 1980s, there were more than two million displaced persons—10% of the region's population. (UNDP, 1994, p. 52)

Since 1990, a concerted effort by national and international leaders has produced a remarkable change. Fourteen presidential summits have helped to silence the guns, defused tensions and promoted cooperation in human development. The *Esquipulas Declaration 1987* became the basis for an appeal to the international community to support peace and development throughout the region. The General Assembly resolution of May 1988 established the Special Plan for Economic Cooperation for Central America supported by two internationally supported programmes. These programmes, CIREFCA and PRODERE, have helped 210 000 refugees return to their homeland and 470 000 to benefit from credit and other programmes to rebuild their communities. (UNDP, 1994).

National policies, as we have seen, are a powerful force in promoting the well-being of children. The following outline demonstrates the benefits of policies to promote social integration.

Successes in Social Integration—Malaysia

Malaysia presents one of the world's most striking examples of positive policy action in favour of one disadvantaged ethnic group. By achieving a broad national consensus for this objective, it has steadily created a more cohesive and more prosperous society. (UNDP, 1994, p. 44)

Malaysia's population today is 61% Bumiputra (groups indigenous to the country), 30% Chinese and 8% Indian. In 1970 the Chinese and Indian populations owned 33% of corporate assets, foreign nationals owned approximately 61%, while the Bumiputras owned only 2%. Racial tensions prompted the formation of the New Economic Policy in 1971. Between 1970 and 1990 corporate assets owned by Bumiputra rose to 20.3% and the incidence of poverty fell dramatically from 49% of all households to 16%.

Breaking the Cycle of Teenage Pregnancy in Jamaica

> Teen pregnancy is a big problem in Jamaica—its impact compounded when young mothers drop out of school. Many go on to form a series of unstable partnerships, each resulting in another child, each with a different 'baby father'. And this pattern is likely to be repeated by their children. (Brown, 1994, p. 16)

The Women's Centre Foundation of Jamaica offers these young women a chance to break the cycle. Since 1978, the Foundation has changed the lives of more than 11 000 young Jamaicans whose average age is 14 years. Counselling services have also reduced the numbers of girls who need their services. In 1989 a quarter of all Jamaica's 55 726 births were to mothers under 20. In 1978, before the Foundation, the figure was one third. The Foundation now has seven centres in Jamaica which provide pregnancy testing, counselling for the girls, their families and their 'baby fathers'; skills training and more important academic programmes. Girls sit for exams while pregnant. 'Some can't even sit on the chair properly, they're writing sideways'. The Foundation reports that the message is getting through that they need not fall into the same trap as their mothers and older sisters. The academic results from those studying at the Foundation are above the national average (Brown, 1994).

Progress at the Local Level

One of the problems at the local level is identifying areas where there are high levels of need. With the use of modern technology maps of need of any given area can be developed. In the UK, Noble and Smith (1994) have been developing this idea further by using Geographical Information Systems linking census and available data to create comprehensive maps for informing strategic planning.

In a study in a local authority area in the UK, census data were used to create *composite* maps of need (Buchanan *et al.*, 1995). Census data in the UK are related to Enumeration Districts (EDs). Broadly speaking this relates to around 500 households. In Figure 13 individual maps were first created from census data for the relevant EDs for three categories of need: lone parents more than 10%; unemployed exceeded 20%; more than 25% of households owned by the local authority. The three maps were then superimposed. Under this system extreme levels of need come out as black, whereas lesser levels come out as grey. Figure 13, showing an industrial town in an English home county with a population of around 200 000 and an under-18 population of around 50 000 illustrates comparative levels of need.

This information was used to link referral data from social services (children and families) to see to what extent those coming for services related to the areas of need. The maps were also useful in demonstrating to locally elected politicians the need for resources.

BREAKING INTO THE CULTURAL CYCLE

ISPCAN has led the campaign against child maltreatment on the international front, but each country, as we have seen, has had to come to decisions within the wider *etic* framework of what is *emically* acceptable, possible and desirable within the limitations of their communities' resources. The following achievements come from countries with different levels of economic development, and illustrate strategies undertaken to combat child maltreatment within the context of cultural patterns and available resources.

Early Stages in Developing Strategies to Respond to Child Abuse and Neglect

The following example comes from Tanzania. Although Tanzania had one of the highest levels of primary school enrolment in sub-Saharan Africa in the late 1970s, they have been hard hit by the economic problems of the 1980s. Reduced state subsidies on food, education, health and the entire social service sector has increased financial pressure on households. Urban families have increasingly had to resort to survival strategies and children have increasingly had to be involved in contributing to the household economy (Mallya, 1993).

In Tanzania, Kitinya (1993) at a multi-disciplinary workshop outlined the situation in his country and their initial plans to combat child abuse and

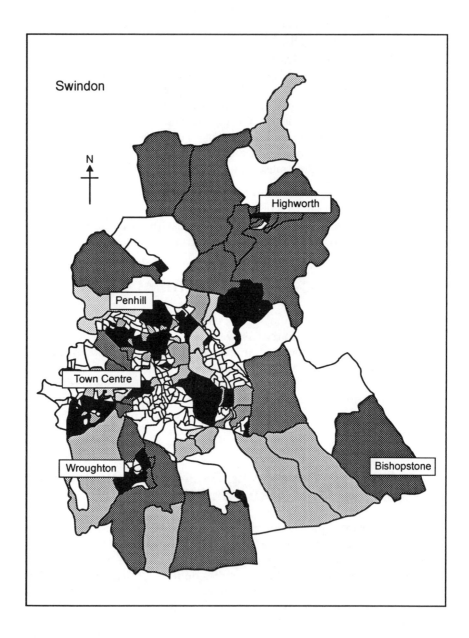

Figure 13: Swindon Area: composite census map: lone parents, unemployment, local authority households

neglect. He felt their first task was to *sensitise* the public about the problem of child abuse. Their second task was to *train* teachers, doctors and health care providers on how to identify, confirm and manage child abuse. It was felt that instruction about child abuse needed to be included in the training of various health cadres, social welfare officers and law enforcement officers. Although at that date there had been no systematic study of child abuse in Tanzania, house boys and girls were identified as a particularly vulnerable group (Kitinya, 1993).

Innovative Approaches in the Face of Overwhelming Poverty

In Buenos Aires in Argentina a different approach has been taken. Innovative solutions are sought to respond to child abuse in the face of overwhelming poverty. Of those living in poverty nearly half are located in Buenos Aires or the *villas miserias* (squatter settlements) surrounding the capital. Given this situation it was felt unrealistic to respond to individual cases presenting at hospitals or through reports. This suggested that hospital staff and multi-disciplinary teams went out from the hospitals and interacted with the community, notably through the extensive public education system. Such efforts have been effective in building trust with the communities and initiating preventive programmes. To date around 200 schools and 25 health centres have been involved. Garrahan concludes that this is a cost-effective and efficient way to increase social awareness and improve the number of children reported at risk (Garrahan, 1994).

Moving On to Develop Effective Procedures

The next two examples come from Japan (Kobayashi, 1994) and China (Meng, 1994). These examples come from abstracts published in the proceedings of the tenth International ISPCAN Congress in Malaysia. Not all those who submitted abstracts to the congress were, however, able to attend. In China, they are grappling with the sensitive issue of defining *the extent* of the problem, the *characteristics* of those who are abused and abusing, and eliciting evidence on *what action* is necessary. In China there is a national law prohibiting child abuse and in Shandong Province there are regulations to protect children. In Osaka in Japan they are moving beyond this to develop procedures, training and effective systems to combat child maltreatment.

In the Chinese example the figures given for abuse appear to relate to physical chastisement. In Shandong, interviewers using a standardised questionnaire sampled 1139 children under 18. Boys were more likely to be abused than girls and younger children more likely to be abused than older. Children were beaten on average 3.43 times per month. Two children suffered fractures as a result of their beating (0.2%), 18 children (2.2%) were beaten to 'blooding', 210 children (24.7%) were severely bruised and 512 (60.2%) were beaten to 'crying'. Fourteen children were felt to be suffering disease as a result of neglect. In keeping with research from other parts of both the developed and developing world, the study concluded: 'The findings of the research on the scope and nature of child abuse proved that child abuse and neglect in China may be a serious social and health problem to which the society needs to pay more attention' (Meng, 1994, p. 136). A related study by Liu (1994) of 572 rural and urban residents in Shandong Province found that 32% did not know there was a national law against child abuse in China and 62% did not know that there was a provincial regulation to protect the children in Shandong.

Japan already has data on child abuse, but these are mostly surveys from single agencies. As of 1994 there was no integrated child protection system (Kobayashi, 1994). The following study took place in the Osaka Prefecture and was part of a wider programme to develop child abuse awareness and professional practice through training, a staff handbook, a case conference system and a telephone hot line for the public. The specific study was focused on case identification, service delivery and outcomes for pre-school abused children known to health and welfare agencies. Overall 318 cases were identified: of these 51% related to physical abuse, 45% to neglect and 5% to emotional abuse. Ten children (3%) had died. Overall the characteristics of families reflected research elsewhere—poverty, social isolation, marital conflict, history of violence. A third of the children were born premature, and 40% had behavioural problems. Outcomes suggested that in 93% there was an overall improvement, in 28% reduced levels of abuse, and in 38% appropriate growth and development. Child behaviour problems and fear of parents remained. Only a third of parents were accepting of interventions and kept appointments. Only 16% spoke positively about their children. The conclusion was: 'Despite reports of general improvement, many serious problems remained. Agencies differed markedly in their response to cases. The results indicate a need for increased awareness about abuse and improved integration and development of child abuse services in Japan' (Kobayashi, 1994, p. 136). Such research reports are effective both in developing services and in influencing central and local government officials.

Child Protection Legislative and Procedural Systems in Advanced Economies

Systems developed in advanced economies have become extremely complex. Child protection responses in different nations are as much to do with historical and cultural constructions about children's rights and family rights and the historical development of legislative frameworks to protect children, as they are to do with the individual differences and social contexts of the children they seek to protect. Comparison of different systems, however, can offer useful insights.

In *Germany*, although the country is a signatory of the UN Convention on the Rights of the Child, it is reported that the concept of family rights is very strong (Ivory, 1994). Consequently, it is felt that judges may be reluctant to order the removal of a child from the family home against the wishes of the parents, even when the reasons for doing so may be compelling (Ivory, 1994).

Indirectly this forces local welfare systems to allocate more resources to preventive work. Germany's recent Children Act, the *Kinder und Jugendhilfegesetz* (Children and Youth Services Act) has been successful in persuading local authorities to allocate a greater share of resources to family support work. In Germany, money for social services is mostly raised regionally by the provinces or *Lander* so although the legislation emanates centrally, there is considerable opportunity for local interpretation. In Stuttgart, the legislation is probably interpreted more liberally than in other areas. Ivory notes that in the spick-and-span city centre, where street after street is brightly light and lined with expensive shops, there are few signs of poverty and deprivation (Ivory, 1994).

Despite the overt signs of prosperity there are families with problems. Such families have two options. They can either go for counselling with one of Struttgart's *Heilpedagogische Gruppen,* where they can call on the skills of a clinical psychologist and social workers, or after referral they may be visited by a family support worker. The city's *Jugendamt*, which is a division of the social services for children and families, unusually employs some of its own family support workers. Most family support workers, however, are employed by the vibrant voluntary sector such as church-run organisations, the Red Cross and Caritas. Family support workers offer an intensive service lasting up to two years. Each family receives between 6 and 15 hours of support each week. A list of ten basic standards is given to every family support worker. The emphasis is to help the family help themselves by identifying problems and building on strengths. Strategies include role-playing to illustrate intergenerational cycles of abuse and neglect. It is felt *Familienhilfe* has been very successful in reducing the number of children admitted into public care.

Social workers in Germany also have had greater freedom to develop preventive approaches because they are largely free from the fear and paranoia pervading UK social services following the high-profile child abuse inquiries. However, there is concern that the strong tradition on family rights may in some cases be at the expense of the rights of the child to protection (Ivory, 1994).

In *France*, since the Revolution of 1789, society is firmly involved in *Collectivism* principles. This can be compared to Anglo-Saxon traditions which emphasise the rights of the individual or *Individualism*. The adversarial legal culture in the UK, which is a reflection of this ideology, can even be seen in Child Protection case conferences (Cooper *et al.*, 1995). In France the concept of *collectivism* in child protection work leads to an emphasis on the family as opposed to individual functioning, on *social inclusion* with universal standards of behaviour. There is an emphasis on the integration of civil and state responsibilities. In child protection, the legal and social work functions are closely linked. It is not adversarial. Social workers have ready access to the Children's Judge or the *Inspecteur* who brings the parties together with the expectation that his or her questions will be answered in return for the opportunity of the family or child to state their case. Within the judiciary this has been called 'negotiated justice'.

Children's Judges are part of the judicial system, or deal with statutory cases, whereas the *Inspecteur* is part of the administrative system, which deals with non-statutory cases. The Children's Judge wields considerable power with respect to children, families and social workers. The Judge, however, does not dispense justice from a distance but is expected to be involved with the consequences of his/her decisions. 'In effect the judge is a kind of child protection case manager, combining a judicial, a therapeutic, a social and a moral function' (Cooper *et al.*, 1995, p. 15). The *Inspecteur* is employed by *Aide Sociale à L'Enfance* (ASE), the section of a local authority social services department responsible for child care work. He or she has a wide range of responsibilities, in particular, in relation to the allocation of resources. One of the most important responsibilities is the coordination of the multi-disciplinary child protection meeting *Commission de Prévention* and deciding when to refer from the administrative sphere to the judicial.

Formal administrative intervention in the French system is framed in terms of a package of support and *education* rather than child protection. Cannan, Berry and Lyons (1992) would suggest that this focus on *education* is deeply rooted in French collectivism ideology. The state should assume an active role in encouraging all citizens to use public services in order that they receive adequate education.

The generous allocation of supportive services available to families is a reflection of this principle. Family allowances are high and nursery school places are available for virtually all children over three years old. Although there is a shortage of French social workers, perhaps because they spent less time collecting evidence for legal procedures, they will generally see their clients more often and over a longer period than social workers in the English and Welsh system.

Social workers together with the *Inspecteur* and the Children's Judge are freer to take risks in order to keep the family together. The identification of risk is as acute as it is in England, but what is done about it appears to result in more preventive action rather than investigation and surveillance (Cooper *et al.*, 1994).

The French concept of *inclusion* is closely tied to *integration*. Schnapper (1992) notes the problem: 'Politics which aims at the integration of individuals cannot but be "colour blind": particular measures are seen as discriminatory' (Schnapper, 1992, p. 118).

Meeting the Needs of Discriminated Groups

In many societies, the needs of discriminated groups cannot be effectively ameliorated without policies which actively respond to 'difference'. The Australian response to their Non-English-speaking communities outlined earlier is a model of a large-scale initiative, but small initiatives undertaken 'against the odds' by single individuals with limited resources can herald the way for further work. The following project was initiated by Diósi in Hungary, who developed an ethnically sensitive fostering service for Gypsy children.

> Throughout the Czech Republic, Slovakia, Hungary and Romania, a large ethnic minority group, generally known as Gypsies, have for generations suffered from severe discrimination and social ostracism. Under Hitler, many Gypsies were sent, along with the Jewish population, to the concentration camps. Today, in many areas because their skin colour and hair is often darker than the rest of the population, they are easily identified and consequently the focus of intense prejudice. Since the fall of Communism and the subsequent economic difficulties, this appears to be getting worse. . . . In some areas, up to 90% of children in state care in Hungary, are of Gypsy origin. The tragedy is that these children have little chance of obtaining work on leaving care, and indeed . . . may not be offered any care at all. (Diósi, 1995, p. 38)

Diósi was aware that although fostering in Hungary had a long history, the service was generally not available for children of Gypsy origin as it was felt they 'lived outside society'. The large number of Gypsy children who were 'rescued' into state care under the Communist regime emerged from state care to enter adulthood having lost their roots, their identity and their self-respect. Unable to find work, many took to offending in order to survive. Diósi , who spoke many of the Gypsy dialects and who had an intimate knowledge of their culture, managed to recruit ten foster parents of Gypsy extract and persuaded the Ministry of Welfare to pay professional fees. In placing children with families Diósi matched the inherent cultural talents of a child, for instance a musical ability, with the talents of the foster families. From this small start, further projects to find Gypsy foster parents for Gypsy children are now being developed.

In the Czech Republic, fostering of Gypsy children has a longer history, but not necessarily with Gypsy families. Koluchová has led the way in demonstrating that children who may appear mentally disordered because of severe deprivation can be reparated following placement with carefully selected foster parents (Buchanan & Sluckin, 1995).

EXAMPLES OF STRATEGIES TO BREAK INTRAFAMILIAL PATTERNS

In Hawaii, a programme similar to that developed by Olds and Henderson (1989) to support new mothers who may be at risk is demonstrating positive outcomes.

Healthy Start Programme

This programme has demonstrated proven results in preventing abuse and neglect for infants at risk to age five. The programme is serving as a model for the Healthy Families America initiative in establishing universal perinatal home visiting services in the United States (Breakey, 1994; Fuddy, 1994).

Systematic needs/risk assessment with referral to a home visiting service is conducted at all the major hospitals within the state of Hawaii. Home visiting services in the families' community include parental mentoring, role-modelling of bonding and attachment, age-appropriate child development activities, developmental screening with referrals to appropriate services, linkage to a 'medical home', housing and public health services. Among these are nursing, child care, services for victims of domestic violence, and substance abuse services. Home visitors are para-professionals who are carefully selected, culturally 'competent' and supported by professional supervision.

Of the 1134 families at risk served as of July 1992, there was no abuse in 99% cases, no neglect in 98% of cases. Of the remaining 10 000 families not considered at risk there was no abuse or neglect in 99% of families. All mothers received family planning advice, and referrals were made where necessary for prenatal care in subsequent pregnancies. Among the factors used in screening, which were linked to a scoring system, were marital status, employment, housing, education, substance abuse, late presentation at prenatal services, abortion, psychiatric care, unsuccessful abortion, and family stress levels as measured by the Family Stress checklist.

The results compare to the Olds and Henderson study (1989) where only 4% of the nurse-visited high-risk group, compared to 19% of the high-risk non-visited comparison group, abused or neglected their children within the first two years. The Hawaii experience, however, further confirms that screening mothers at risk and linking this to supportive services over the early years has positive outcomes.

Screening Families with Children in Need at the Point of Referral to Social Services

In England and Wales, local providers are deliberating how they can move from a focus on child protection cases to more family support services. In a home county local authority in England with a population of more than half a million, of which 128 000 are under 18, there are around 8000 initial referrals to social services (children and families) per annum (Buchanan et al., 1995). An initial pilot study elicited the range of presenting problems that came to social workers at the 'front desk'. In this authority as in others in the UK, referrals can either be made directly by families—'self-referred'—or from other professionals in the field, schools, health visitors, neighbour reports, etc.—'referred'. The ratio of self-referred and referred is around 6:4.

From an initial pilot study a 'Needs Matrix' was developed. This was a method of classifying referrals to social services, at point of referral by type and level of need. The purpose was to encourage social workers at point of referral to look beyond child abuse and to be alert to the wider developmental needs of the child. There were seven categories for referrals ranging from overt child protection, to concerns about parent–child relationships, to offending behaviour, to self-harm, to supervision needs, to concerns about child development, and disability. Each category of referral was rated according to the severity of need. Clear examples indicated the types of cases which fell into each level. Generally speaking, the first and second category of severity would be eligible for services. Separate from the Matrix of Need were categories where the local authority had statutory responsibilities, such as to children they were looking after.

Linked to the Matrix of Need was an Additional Factor Analysis. This was a range of factors which indicated that although the actual severity of need might not suggest that services should be provided, families could jump the levels if they had additional factors. Among these factors were evidence of violence in the home, three or more children, illness in the family, a history of past abuse, other children who had been looked after, lone parenthood and reconstituted families, housing problems, lack of support networks, financial difficulties, education problems with children, current divorce or separation, recent death, alcohol or substance abuse. Army families and those from ethnic minorities were also given priority for services. Social workers had to categorise the type of need and its severity before applying the additional factor analysis.

Data from the Needs Matrix were then centralised, giving managers vital information about the types of needs, changing patterns, and the resource implications. The Matrix operated, therefore, both at the level of decision-making at point of referral and at the level of decision-making at the point of policy-making and resource allocation.

Child protection cases now constitute only 20% of all referrals. By far the largest grouping are those cases where there are concerns about the health and development of the child. These cases, if the need is sufficiently great, now have ready excess to services in their own right without having to compete with resources allocated to child protection. Half of these cases receive the services of a social worker.

RETURNING TO THE SKILLS OF THE SOCIAL WORKER AND THE INDIVIDUAL CASE

In the final analysis we return to the skills of the individual social worker in handling the individual case. The following case is based on a real life scenario (Figure 14). Necessary modifications have been made to highlight issues and to protect confidentiality. Although the case is based within the framework of English and Welsh procedures, it is hoped the issues grappled with will ring true to workers elsewhere, and stimulate a debate on how *the issues* presented might have been handled.

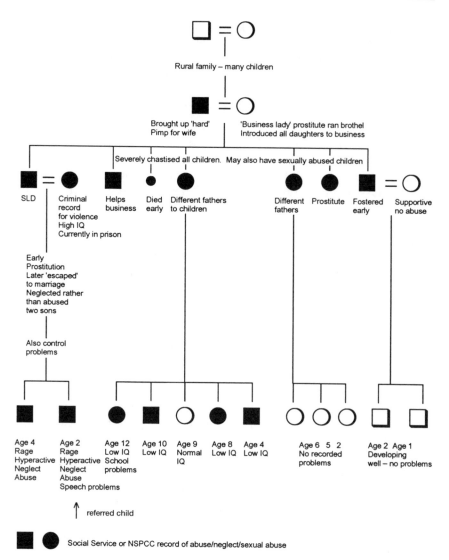

Figure 14: Four generations of maltreating families in the UK

REFERRAL

The second child, as identified in the family tree (Figure 14), was referred to the local social welfare services from his school with very severe bruising on the back of his legs and some older bruises. *Preliminary Investigation* was initiated under section 47 of the Children Act 1989 (England and

Wales). The new social worker picked up an already 'thick' file on the
family with numerous short-term social worker contacts. The children
were not, however, on the child protection register. Checks with local
Health Visitors and further checks with the school suggested long-
standing concerns about this mother's parenting with some minor injuries to the children, and non-attendances at hospital appointments. There
were references to other 'thick files' relating to other family members.

On an initial home visit to the family, the social worker was able to overcome the mother's reticence about 'having social workers around who
took away kids'. She did not want to lose her children. Mother agreed
that she was finding it difficult to control her two very overactive young
sons, particularly since her husband was in prison. 'They are getting their
own back at me—they do things to make me feel bad.' On viewing the
bruises and talking to the children, it was apparent that the bruises were
severe, with old as well as new ones. The children were anxious and
appeared frightened of their mother. Mother was shouting at them for
much of the initial interview. There were also old bruises on the older
child. The condition of the house suggested that the mother was finding it
very difficult to cope.

In many social service departments in England and Wales, such a case
would be formally processed through the child protection procedures
towards a Child Protection Conference. In this case, however, after the
social worker had *discussed the case with her supervisor*, it was decided *not*
to take the case to Child Protection Conference at this stage. The plan was
to monitor the case carefully, maintain links with the family, assess the
risk and protective factors, elicit strengths and needs, find out more about
the wider family situation, and develop a 'package' of care under section
17 of the Children Act 1989 services for children 'in need'. The children's
development was to be monitored using the Assessment and Action Records (Ward, 1995). Because the social worker was able to gain Mother's
cooperation, it was felt the children were not in immediate danger. It was
suggested that Mother should be persuaded to see her General Practitioner to have the children checked out.

ASSESSMENT

Crucially, *the social worker was given the time*, because of the long-standing
history of parenting problems, to make a comprehensive assessment even
although the child was not going to be 'conferenced'. She was also allowed to take *a degree of risk*. Mother went to see her GP and although he
expressed concern about the bruising, the care of children and the unmet

developmental needs, he was in *agreement not to conference* the child as long as the social worker kept in touch. He was aware that the Health Visitor visited regularly, and he met her weekly to discuss general issues about patients.

Assessment of the Wider Family and Early History

Using a genogram, the social worker was able to sketch out the basic details of the family. Mother was, however, 'vague' about various details. She was not sure why her brother had died early. She remembered him not waking up after her father was 'cross about his crying'. She remembered her youngest brother being 'removed' into social services care. She had not seen him for many years. She talked about her father 'who treated us all hard, just as he had been, because we were "bad" '. She spoke fondly about the relationships with her sisters, and wished she could get in touch with her brother who had been fostered. Her own mother would have nothing to do with her as she had walked out on the family when she married. School for her had been a distressing experience. She had been bullied because she was 'slow' and she felt her school friends' parents did not like her associating with them. She dropped out of school without taking exams at 14 and despite efforts from the Education Welfare Officer did not return.

She eventually talked about how her mother had dressed her up as a 14 year old for the 'business'. The pocket money she was given helped her buy 'nice things'. She had hated the work, even although all her sisters and mother were involved, and for a short time took drugs 'to block it all out'. She was grateful to her husband who she had 'met on the job' and for helping her 'get away' before it was too late. She had not taken drugs since.

She wanted to be a 'good' mother. She was more reticent about her relationship with her husband. She did not like the 'way he beat the children' even though she admitted that she did it. She mentioned she had received similar discipline as a child and 'it did not hurt me, so it probably won't hurt them, but sometimes he goes too far'. She also did not like the way her husband treated her when the boys misbehaved and the house was in a mess, but 'I depend on him and I miss him now he is away'.

Examination of the immediate and extended family files vividly demonstrated that Mother had painted a rather rosier picture about her early life than was evidenced by the records. Her grandfather had been known to the local NSPCC inspector himself as a child. All her brothers and sisters had repeatedly been reported for child abuse and neglect and numerous assessments had taken place with no change to the patterns. All her surviving brothers and sisters had spent short periods in care, as she had herself, but placements had broken down and they had returned home. Her younger brother had been grossly physically and possibly sexually abused and neglected before a Care Order was made on him age three. Long-term fostering had been successful. The placement had not broken down and he had achieved at school. He had been of average or above average ability and had gone on to be apprenticed as an electrician. His wife had come from a caring home and was supportive. Their two young children were apparently doing well.

Using the Assessment and Action Records (Ward, 1995) the social worker was able to make a start on identifying the children's needs.

Links with the Cycles of Child Maltreatment

The case illustrates many of the issues raised in this book. In the extra-familial cycle the *poverty* in Mother's own childhood, where her father had *only ever had short-term employment,* had been mitigated by the illegal income from the business, to which she was forced to contribute. Her father had *migrated* from a rural area, where farmers were no longer employing young men, into the town *in order to find work,* but perhaps also *to escape from his 'harsh' treatment* at home. History does not relate where his wife came from, but she may have already been in the 'business' when she met him. Initially, her income may have given him an easy way to earn a living. However, *with the stresses of the children,* the *uncertain income* and stresses of running an illegal 'business', *abusive patterns repeated.*

When his daughter, Mother in this case study, possibly because of *low ability dropped out of school,* she was offered an opportunity to increase the family income. Fortunately Mother *did not fall pregnant until she married* in her late 20s. Her younger sister had not been so fortunate and had her first child soon after she was 14. Although the cultural patterns in the urban setting generally, did not support their life style, there was a supportive *micro-culture* consisting of a number of families who earned their living from *prostitution and petty crime.* All the children of these families were known to the Social Services and many spent short periods *in care.*

One of *Mother's strengths* was that she wanted to escape. She wanted to be a *'good mother'* which suggests that she had *some awareness* that her own childhood had been problematic. It may be she had picked up these ideas at school, but because of her low ability *school had not been a completely compensating factor*. Her husband offered an escape, but *he brought with him additional problems*. His criminal behaviour was *violent*. When her husband was imprisoned, she was back to *living on benefits* and because she had tried to escape was *emotionally unsupported* by her parents. Lonely and *depressed*, with *poor self-esteem, she attribute*d her children's behaviour to 'getting at her'. This was *compounded by the developmental difficulties in her children*. The children would have been *'harder' to rear'*. Their behaviour in turn *was compounded by their social and family situation*. A strength, however, was that the children were *young enough* to benefit from intervention and this was helped by Mother's *wish 'to change things'*. Table 18 sums up the risk and protective factors in the ecological framework.

INTERVENTION

Table 19 outlines the initial 'package' which was negotiated with Mother and later included on a written agreement. Starred items were issues raised by Mother. Identified strengths were *available resources* within the family and community which could be mobilised to meet needs; things Mother *wanted* help with, areas of her life Mother *wanted to change*, skills Mother had which could *be built on* to meet needs. With older children it would have also been appropriate to involve them in the plan. In making the plan, the social worker had to be *open and honest* about her statutory role in promoting the welfare of the children and the potential powers inherent upon that role.

Outcome after Three Months

Mother was reunited with her younger brother and his wife who proved supportive. After initial difficulties, the children gradually learned to play together, and both families helped each other out with babysitting. Local volunteers had decorated the home and made the garden safer by clearing all the rubbish. Initially Mother attended the local Family Centre three days a week. Her children attended the crèche there and later the older boy attended the local nursery. Behavioural training helped Mother cope with the children's behaviour and gave her some understanding of her children's developmental needs. On-going speech therapy which was arranged on site at the Family Centre also helped to improve her son's behaviour. Regular reviews demonstrated the progress they were making

Table 18: Risk and protective factors in the current situation

INTRAFAMILIAL (Psychological and biological)		EXTRAFAMILIAL (Sociopolitical and cultural)	
Ontogenetic	Micro-system	Exo-system	Macro-system

Risk

In Mother	*In partner*		Economic recession
Extensive and severe intergenerational family history of maltreatment	History of violence and criminal behaviour	Husband will find it difficult to find work when he returns	Micro-culture acceptance of prostitution Micro-culture acceptance of harsh discipline
Low ability	History of violence to wife	High crime rate area	Micro-culture acceptance of crime
Poor parenting skills	History of violence to children		
Low self-esteem			
Attributes children's behaviour negatively			
Isolated to some degree from family			
Many stresses			
Admission of abuse to children			
In child			
Over-active behaviour			
Some developmental delay			
Poor speech			
Both brothers in nappies			

Protective factors

In Mother			
Positive response to social worker	Paradoxically husband's absence is protective	Good local family support facilities	Wider community unaccepting of severe discipline
Wish to 'change things'	Reasonable local authority housing	Available quality day care	Wider community unaccepting of high crime
Is aware that own parenting was problematic	Some emotional support from family		
Good money manager			
In child/children			
Child could be responsive to behavioural interventions and speech therapy			

Table 19: Using strengths to meet needs

NEEDS	STRENGTHS TO MEET NEEDS
Protection of children	See GP, weekly/fortnightly visits by social worker for 3 months SW liaison with Health Visitor
Welfare of children	Developmental assessment and speech therapy Attendance at local family centre and later *Day nursery for older child *Behavioural programmes for children at Family Centre Progress monitored by Assessment and action records
Improving mother's confidence and self-esteem	Attendance at family centre. Involvement in activities. *Use of Mother's money-managing skills to help other parents
*Help with garden and home	*Volunteers
*Contact with brother	*Social worker would try to find out where he was living

Family Centre worker would visit Mother and explain service. Attendance was expected to be three days a week. Social worker would visit fortnightly for three months. Mother could ring alternate weeks and speak to social worker from the Family Centre when the social worker was in the office (timetable was given when she would be available). Mother would ensure the children were up and ready to go to with her to Family Centre on the agreed days. Social worker would arrange transport to the hospital for assessments and speech therapy. Mother would work with the social worker to complete the Assessment and Action records. These would be repeated after three months. Thereafter she would complete them with the Family Centre worker.

*Interventions suggested by mother.

on Assessment and Action records. Mother found the positive feedback from these encouraging.

Mother took part in a Child Management Group at the Centre. She later chose to take part in fund raising at the centre and this considerably increased her self-esteem. She also was involved in a self-help group supporting other mothers living on benefit.

Setback a Year Later

When the husband returned from his prison sentence, however, there were considerable problems. He resented his wife's newfound confidence and Mother appeared at the Family Centre with considerable bruises. Husband was unable to find work and the family situation deteriorated. The social worker with whom Mother had worked changed jobs and Mother found it harder to trust the new worker. School reported that both children had *minor suspicious bruising,* but the decision was again taken not to take the case to Child Protection conference.

Two months later, Father moved on to another relationship. Mother became very depressed and potentially suicidal. Her sister-in-law, however, was supportive as was the Family Centre. About this time, Mother was given a small job at the Centre helping to cook dinners. This considerably improved her depression and brought in additional income.

Four Years Later

Four years after the initial social worker became involved, the situation remains sensitive with occasional calls for help to social services, but there is evidence that the children are progressing in school. Mother has entered into a new relationship which appears supportive and non-violent. It is, however, known that he has a record for petty theft. The reality is that in the course of bringing up these children there will be other crises and other serious concerns. The long-term outcomes will not be known until the next generation.

Mother's contact with the original social worker was fortnightly or more for the first three months. The case was then officially closed as Mother was being well supported by the Family Centre. Perhaps unusually Mother was still encouraged to make periodic calls to the known social worker. More often these calls were to report her achievements. When this social worker left, she was given the name of the next social worker who was briefed on her history. This social worker took the second referral when the children were reported by the school as having bruises.

THE CONFLICTS AND THE DILEMMAS

This case illustrates many of the conflicts and dilemmas raised in this book. The reality is, in the first place, that whether the condition of such a child is a matter of concern relates to the political priorities given to child protection, the extent of families in need in any given area, the sort of resources available to meet those needs and the threshold for state intervention in such cases.

Different countries also have different legal procedures. In many local authorities in England and Wales, as we have mentioned, this case would probably have been processed through formal child protection procedures. It could, however, be argued that with *this child* a limited focus on the abuse would not have resolved the long-term parenting concerns.

On the other hand, it could also be argued that as both children were reabused they were not protected. One wonders, however, whether legal procedures and possible separation from their family into public care would have better promoted their welfare in the long term. This question cannot be answered without a detailed local knowledge on the outcomes of children looked after in public care.

In such cases, there are few things that can be predicted for certain. Each case has to be considered in the light of the local situation and the procedures and the resources available to help such children. The challenge in breaking cycles of child maltreatment, is to respond to such cases in the best way we know how, within the context of what is possible.

12

CONCLUSION

The knowledge of man is as the waters, some descending from above, and some springing from beneath; the one informed by the light of nature, the other inspired by divine revelation (Book I.v.1)

If a man will begin with certainties, he will end in doubts; if he is content to begin with doubts, he will end in certainties (Book I.v.8)

They are ill discoverers that think there is no land, when they can see nothing but sea (Book II.vii.5)
(Francis Bacon, 1561–1621: *Advancement of Learning*, 1605 edn)

The case-study described in the last chapter is not unique. Around the world, there are many such families, many such histories. In Tanzania, China, Japan, France, Germany, the USA, Australia, South Africa, the Argentine, Malaysia, Hong Kong, for example, the evidence suggests that such families are not unusual. They may be more or less common according to differing socio-political and cultural structures but in essence they are the same. The extended patterns of child maltreatment permeate the generations and operate in all the cycles. Given the deeply entrenched needs, how do we break patterns of intergenerational child maltreatment?

Firstly, all of us who are involved in family and parenting policy, and all of us who make the day-to-day decisions that affect children's lives need *to know what is already known,* and this knowledge needs to be accessible and practical. The organisations described in the last chapter have played an important part in this process but disseminating an overview of findings from different disciplines, different countries, in a way that is meaningful to decision-makers at every level is an enduring challenge.

This book has sought to give a multi-national and multidisciplinary overview of some of the main mechanisms for intergenerational transmission and link these to possible interventions. The danger in such an overview, is that these will lead to simplistic solutions. Readers are cautioned that they will need to explore further. This short book can only flag up areas that require investigation.

Secondly, we need to know *what is not known*. Cicchetti (1989), in a review of perspectives from developmental psychopathology, summarises some of the areas where more knowledge is needed. Further links are needed between maltreatment research and studies of normal development in children. In effect studies of maltreating children are 'experiments in nature'; that is experiments where for one reason or other the normal coping skills of parents and children have broken down. Cicchetti (1989) indicates that further large-scale longitudinal research on the causes and consequences of intergenerational transmission which is linked to studies of normal child development is required. Also, rather than focusing on isolated areas of functioning, there is increasingly a need for multidisciplinary research, and for this to be integrated into a coherent framework. Parenting in cases of child maltreatment needs to be placed against a backcloth of how parents and children cope without resorting to maltreatment.

From this we will learn more about what makes 'resilient' children and the alternate pathways whereby children 'make it' in the face of extreme adversity. More knowledge is also needed about the role of persistent poverty, how the community context affects the dynamics of child maltreatment and how children and parents avoid maltreatment. There is also a need to know more about the role of fathers, father-figures and extended families. We would add that this knowledge must be related to the different cultural and political contexts in which children live.

In the final analysis, however, research can only assist in the decision-making process. The infinite variety of human experience dictates that knowledge will always be imperfect. Each family, each child, is unique.

When the world is a better and fairer place; when the conditions in which parents are 'permitted' to parent are maximised; when services are at hand to support them in their parenting task; when children are born healthy and enabled to keep healthy; when child welfare processes and procedures are at their most refined; there will still be the need for the clinician to exercise his/her judgement and skills based on an imperfect knowledge base, in order to work with the family and child to maximise his or her potential and to protect him/her from maltreatment so that he or she can in turn be a better parent.

Each well-intentioned intervention, at all the different levels, and in each of the different cycles, will not be successful, but by monitoring our interventions and sharing our successes and failures with the wider community, we may one day be able say that 'we are on the way' to breaking the cycles of child maltreatment.

REFERENCES

Abbott, M. (1992). 'Television violence: A proactive prevention campaign.' In G. Albee, L. Bond & T. Monsey (Eds) *Improving Children's Lives. Global Perspectives on Prevention.* Newbury Park, CA: Sage.

Aber, J. L. & Zigler, D. (1981). 'Developmental considerations in the definition of child maltreatment.' In R. Rizley & D. Cicchetti (Eds), *New Directions in Child Development: Developmental Perspectives in Child Maltreatment.* San Francisco: Jossey-Bass.

Ackerman, R. J. (1988). 'Complexities of alcohol and abusive families.' *Focus on Chemically Dependent Families,* **11**, 3, 15.

Adnopez, J., Nagler, S. & Sinanaglu, P. (1987). The family support service: Servicing families in crisis. Paper submitted for publication, in *American Journal of Orthopsychiatry* quoted in Kaufman, J. & Zigler, E., 'The prevention of child maltreatment: Programming, research and policy.' In D. Willis, E. Holden & M. Rosenberg, *Prevention of Child Maltreatment.* New York: John Wiley.

Agathonos-Georgopoulou, H. (1992). 'Cross-cultural perspectives in child abuse and neglect.' *Child Abuse Review,* **1**, 80–88.

Ainsworth, M. D. S. (1973). 'The development of infant–mother attachment.' In B. M. Caldwell & H. N. Riccinti (Eds), *Review of Child Development Research,* vol. 3. Chicago: University of Chicago Press.

Ainsworth, M. D. S., Blehar, M. C., Waters, E. & Wall, S. (1978). *Patterns of Attachment: A Psychological Study of the Strange Situation.* Hillsdale, NJ: Erlbaum.

Albee, G. (1980). 'Primary prevention and social problems.' In G. Gerbner, C. Ross, & E. Zigler (Eds) *Child Abuse: An Agenda for Action.* New York: Oxford University Press.

Albee, G. W. (1992). 'Saving children means social revolution.' In G. W. Albee, L. A. Bond & T. C. Monsey (Eds), *Improving Children's Lives. Global Perspectives on Prevention.* Newbury Park, CA: Sage.

Aldgate, J. (1989). *Using Written Agreements with Children and Families*: London: Family Rights Group.

Allerton, M. (1995). 'Self-regulation of television viewing among children.' *National Children's Bureau, Children UK,* vol. 5, p. 3.

Alperstein, G. & Arnstein, E. (1988). 'Homeless children. A challenge for pediatricians.' *Pediatric Clinics of North America,* **35**(6), 1413–1425.

Altemeier, W. A., O'Connor, S., Sherrod, K. B. & Tucker, B. A. (1986). 'Outcome of abuse during childhood among pregnant low income women.' *Child Abuse and Neglect,* 10, 319–330.

Altemeier, W., O'Connor, S., Vietze, P., Sandler, H. & Sherrod, K. (1982). 'Antecedents of child abuse.' *Journal of Pediatrics,* **100**, 823–829.

American Association for Protecting Children (1987). *Highlights of Official Child Neglect and Abuse Reporting 1986.* Denver, CO: American Humane Association.

Amphlett, S. (1991). *Parents against injustice, the parent's dilemma.* Paper given at Cumberland Lodge, 12–14 September, Bishop's Stortford, UK.

Androp, S. (1935). *Genetics and Mental Disorders*. New York: Eugenics and Research Association.

Aries, P. (1962). *Centuries of Childhood*. New York: Vintage Books.

Armstrong, K. A. (1981). 'A treatment and education program for parents and children who are at risk of neglect.' *Child Abuse and Neglect*, **5**, 2 167–175.

Armstrong, K. & Fraley, Y. (1985). 'What happens to families after they leave the program?' *Children Today*, May–June, 17–29.

Arnstein, S. (1969). 'A ladder of citizen participation.' *Journal of the American Institute of Planners*, **35**, 4, 216–224.

Audit Commission (1994). *Seen but Not Heard*. Audit Commission, London: HMSO.

Avison, W. R., Turner, R. J. & Noh, S. (1986). 'Screening evidence for problem parenting: Preliminary evidence on a promising instrument.' *Child Abuse and Neglect*, **10**, 157–170.

Ayalon, O. & Van Tassel, E. (1987). 'Living in dangerous environments.' In M. Brassard, R. Germain & S. Hart (Eds), *Psychological Maltreatment of Children and Youth* (pp.171–182). New York: Pergamon.

Azar, S. & Siegal, B. (1990). 'Behavioral treatment of child abuse: A developmental perspective.' *Behavior Modification*, **14**, 279–300.

Baker, B., Grant, J., Squires, J., Johnson, P. & Offermann, L. (1981). 'Parent aides as a preventive strategy.' *Child and Youth Services Review*, **3**, 115–125.

Bays, J. (1990). 'Substance abuse and child abuse: Impact of addiction on the child.' *Pediatric Clinics of North America*, **37**(4), 881–904.

Barn, R. (1990). 'Black children in local authority care: Admission patterns.' *New Community*, **16**, 229–246.

Barrowclough, C. & Fleming, I. (1986). *Goal Planning with Elderly People. Making plans to meet individual needs. A Manual of Instruction*. Manchester: Manchester University Press.

Barth, R. (1989). 'Evaluation of a task-centred child abuse prevention programme.' *Children and Youth Services Review*, **11**, 117–131.

Barth, R. P. (1994). 'Adoption of drug-exposed infants.' In R. Barth, J. D. Berrick & N. Gilbert, *Child Welfare Research*. New York: University of Columbia Press.

Barth, R. & Berry, M. (1994). 'Implications of research on the welfare of children under permanency planning.' In R. Barth, J. Berrick & N. Gilbert, *Child Welfare Research*. New York: Columbia University Press.

Barth, R. Berrick, J. & Gilbert, N. (1994). *Child Welfare Research*. New York: Columbia University Press.

Bebbington, A. & Miles, J. (1988). *Children entering care: a need indicator for in care services for children*. Discussion Paper 574/2 PSSRU, University of Kent at Canterbury, UK.

Belsey, M. & Royston, E. (1987). *Overview of the health of women and children* (World Health Organisation Report). Paper presented at the International Conference on Better Health for Women and Children Through Family Planning, Nairobi, Kenya.

Belsky, J. (1980). 'Child maltreatment. An ecological integration.' *American Psychologist*, **35**, 320–335.

Belsky, J. & Vondra, J. (1989). 'Lessons from child abuse: The determinants of parenting.' In D. Cicchetti & V. Carlson (Eds), *Child Maltreatment. Theory and Research on the Causes and Consequences of Child Abuse and Neglect*. New York: Cambridge University Press.

Belson, W. (1978). *Television Violence and the Adolescent*. Hampshire, UK: Saxon House.

Berger, P. & Luckmann, R. (1967). *The Social Construction of Reality*. Harmondsworth: Penguin Books.

Berridge, D. (1985). *Children's Homes*. Oxford: Basil Blackwell.

Berridge, D. & Cleaver, H. (1987). *Foster Home Breakdown*. Oxford: Basil Blackwell.

Berrueta-Clement, J.-R., Schweinhard L. J., Barnett, W. S., Epstein, A. S. & Weikart, D. P. (1984). *Changed Lives. The Effects of the Perry Pre-School Program Through Age 19*. Ypsilanti, Michigan High/Scope Educational Research Foundation.

Berry, J. (1969). 'On cross-cultural comparability.' *International Journal of Psychology* **4**, 119–28.

Berry, J. (1989). 'Imposed etic–emics–derived etics: The operationalisation of a compelling idea.' *International Journal of Psychology*, **24**, 721–735.

Besharov, D. (1985). 'Rights versus rights: The dilemma of child protection,' *Public Welfare*, **43**, 19–27.

Besharov, D. (1989) 'The children of Crack: Will we protect them?' *Public Welfare*, **47**, 7–11.

Besharov, D. (1990). *Recognising Child Abuse: A Guide for the Concerned*. New York: Free Press.

Besharov, D. (1993). 'Overreporting and underreporting are twin problems.' In R. Gelles & D. Loseke, *Current Controversies in Family Violence*. Newbury Park, CA: Sage.

Biller, H. & Solomon, R. (1986). *Child Maltreatment and Paternal Deprivation*. Lexington, MA: Lexington Books.

Bjurek, H., Gustafsson, B., Kjulin, K. & Karrby, G. (1994). *Efficiency and quality when providing social services—the example of public day care centres in Sweden*, Memorandum No 197. Goteborg: School of Economics and Commercial Law, Gothenburg University.

Bottomley, Rt Hon. Mrs (1994). In *Crime and the Family. Conference Report*. London: Family Policy Studies Centre.

Black, C. (1981). *It Will Never Happen to Me*. Denver, CO: MAC.

Blaxter, M. (1982). *The Health of the Children: A Review of Research on the Place of Health in Cycles of Disadvantage*. SSRC/DHSS Studies in Deprivation and Disadvantage, No. 3. London: Heinemann Educational Books.

Blaxter, M. & Paterson, E. (1981). *Mothers and Daughters: A Three-generational Study of Health Attitudes and Behaviour*. SSRC/DHSS Studies in Deprivation and Disadvantage, No. 5. London: Heinemann Educational Books.

Block, J. H., Block, J. & Gjerde, P. F. (1986). 'The personality of children prior to divorce: A prospective study.' *Child Development*, **57**, 827–840.

Bolton, F. G., Charlton, J. K., Gal, D. S., Laner, R. H. & Shunway, S. M. (1985). 'Preventive screening for adolescent mothers and infants: Critical variables in assessing risk for child maltreatment.' *Journal of Primary Prevention*, **5**, 169–185.

Bourne, P. G., Rose, R. M. & Mason, J. W. (1967). 'Urinary 17-OHCS levels: Data on seven helicopter ambulance medics in combat.' *Archives of General Psychiatry*, **17**, 104–110.

Bowlby, J. (1953). *Child Care and the Growth of Love*. London: Pelican Penguin Books.

Bowlby, J. (1979). *The Making and Breaking of Affectional Bonds*. London: Tavistock.

Bowlby, J. (1984). *Attachment and Loss*, Vol 1, *Attachment*. London: Pelican Penguin Books.

Bradshaw, J. (1990). *Child Poverty and Deprivation in the UK*. London, National Children's Bureau.

Bradshaw, J. & Millar, J. (1991). *Lone Parent Families in the UK*. London: HMSO.

Brams, J. S. & Courcy, D. L. (1985). 'Primary prevention of failure to thrive'. In D. Drotar (Ed.), *New Directions for Failure to Thrive: Implications for Research and practice*. p312–336. New York: Plenum.

Breakey, G. F. (1994). *Prevention of child abuse and neglect through maternal child health systems*. Proceedings of the tenth International Congress on Child Abuse and Neglect, Kuala Lumpur, Abstracts: p.181.

Breger, E. (1987). *Recovery Program. Child Victims of Armed Conflict*. United Arab Emirates University Press, PO Box 17666, Al-Ain, UAE.

Bretherton, I. (1985). 'Attachment theory: Retrospect and prospect.' In I. Bretherton & E. Waters (Eds), *Growing Points of Attachment Theory and Research*. Monographs of the Society for Research in Child Development, vol. 50 (1 and 2), pp.3–35. Serial 209.

Broberg, A. & Hwang, P. (1991). 'Day care for young children in Sweden. In Melhuish, E. & Moss, P. (Eds), *Day Care for Young Children*. London: Routledge.

Bronfenbrenner, U. (1977). 'Toward an experimental ecology of human development.' *American Psychologist*, **56**, 197–198.

Bronfenbrenner, U. (1979). *The Ecology of Human Development: Experiments by Nature and Design*. Cambridge, MA: Harvard University Press.

Brown, G. W., Brolchain, N. I., Harris, M. & Harris, T. (1975). 'Social class and psychiatric disturbance among women in an urban population.' *Sociology*, **9**, 225–254.

Brown, G. W. & Harris, T.O. (1978). *Social Origins of Depression*. London:Tavistock.

Brown, M. & Madge, N. (1982:).*Despite the Welfare State*.A report on the SSRC/ DHSS Programme of Research into Transmitted Deprivation. SSRC/DHSS Studies in Deprivation and Disadvantage. London: Heinemann Educational Books.

Brown, S.F.(1994). 'Breaking the cycle of teenage pregnancy.' *Children First (UNICEF)*, issue 25, 16.

Browne, K. & Saqi, S. (1987). 'Parent–child interaction in child abusing families: possible causes and consequences.' Chapter 5 in P. Maher (Ed.), *Child Abuse: An Educational Perspective*. Oxford: Basil Blackwell.

Browne, K. & Saqi, S. (1988). 'Approaches to screening for child abuse and neglect.' In K. Browne, C. Davies & P. Stratton, *Early Prediction and Prevention of Child Abuse*. Chichester: John Wiley.

Browne, K. & Stevenson, J. (1983). *A checklist for completion by health visitors to identify child 'at risk' for child abuse*. Report to the Surrey County Area Review Committee on Child Abuse.

Brubaker, T. (1993) (Ed.), *Family Relations. Challenges for the Future*. Newbury Park, CA: Sage.

Brubaker, T. & Kimberly, J. (1993). Challenges to the American family. In T. Brubaker (Ed.), *Family Relations. Challenges for the Future*. Newbury Park, CA: Sage.

Bruce-Chwatt, L. (1976). 'Female circumcision and politics.' *World Medicine*, **1**, 44–47.

Bruce-Chwatt, L. (1985). 'History, slavery and ill-health.' *British Medical Journal*, **291**, 1179–1180.

Buchanan, A. (1992). *Children Who Soil. Assessment and Treatment*. Chichester: John Wiley.

Buchanan, A. (Ed.) (1994). *Partnership in Practice. The Children Act 1989*. Avebury, UK.

Buchanan, A. (1995). 'The Dolphin Project: The impact of the Children Act, 1989.' In C. Cloke & M. Davies (Eds), *Participation and Empowerment in Child Protection*. London: Pitman.

Buchanan, A., Barlow, J., Croucher, M., Hendron, J., Seal, H. & Smith, T. (1995). *Seen and Heard. Wiltshire Family Services Study*. London: Barnardos.

Buchanan, A. & Oliver, J. (1977). 'Abuse and neglect as a cause of mental retardation.' *British Journal of Psychiatry*, **131**, 458–467.

Buchanan, A. & Sluckin, A. (1995). 'Gypsy children in post-communist Eastern Europe.' *Children & Society*, **8**, 4, 333–343.

Buchanan, A. Wheal, A., Walder, D., Macdonald, S. & Coker, R. (1993). *Answering Back. Report by young people being looked after on the Children Act 1989*. University of Southampton: CEDR.

Burgess, R. (1979). 'Child abuse: A social interactional analysis.' In B. Lahey & A. Kazdin (Eds), *Advances in Clinical Child Psychology*, vol. 2 pp. 142–171. New York: Plenum.

Burghes, L. (1993). *One Parent Families: Policy Options for the 1990s*. London: Family Policy Studies Centre, Joseph Rowntree Foundation.

Butler Sloss, E. (1988). Report of the Inquiry into Child Abuse in Cleveland 1987, Cmd 412. London: HMSO.

Cadoret, R. J. (1982). 'Genotype–environmental interaction in antisocial behaviour.' *Psychological Medicine*, **12**, 235–239.

Cadoret, R. J. (1985). 'Genes, environment and their interaction in the development of psychopathology.' In T. Sakai & T. Tsuboi (Eds), *Genetic Aspects of Human Behaviour* (pp. 165–175). Tokyo: Igaku-Shoin.

Caffey, J. (1946). 'Multiple fractures in the long bones of infants suffering from chronic subdural hematoma.' *American Journal of Roentgenology Radium Therapy & Nuclear Medicine*, **56**, 163–173.

Cairns, E. (1987). *Caught in the Crossfire: Children and the Northern Ireland Conflict*. New York: Appletree Press, Belfast and Syracuse University Press.

Cairns, E. (1989). 'Society as child abuser: Northern Ireland.' In W. Stainton Rogers, D. Hervey & E. Ash (Eds) *Child Abuse and Neglect Facing the Challenge*. Batsford, UK: Open University.

Calvert, G. (1994). *Preventing Child Abuse. Australia's Strategy*. Proceedings of the tenth International Congress on Child Abuse and Neglect, Kuala Lumpur ISPCAN.

Cannan, C., Berry, L. & Lyons, K. (1992). *Social Work and Europe*. London: Macmillan.

Cantwell, D. P. (1975). 'Genetic studies of hyperactive children: Psychiatric illness in biological and adopting parents.' In R. Fieve, D. Rosenthal & H. Brill (Eds), *Genetic Research in Psychiatry*. Baltimore, MD: Johns Hopkins University Press.

Caplan, F. (1964). *Principles of Preventive Psychiatry*. London: Tavistock.

Caprara, G. V. & Rutter, M. (1995). 'Individual development and social change.' In M. Rutter & D. Smith (Eds), *Psychosocial Disorders in Young People*. Chichester: John Wiley.

Caprara, G. V. & Van Heck, G. (Eds) (1992). *Modern Personality Psychology*. London: Harvester Wheatsheaf.

Carlson, V., Cicchetti, D., Barnett, D. & Braunwald, G. (1989). 'Finding order in disorganisation: Lessons from research on maltreated infants' attachments to their caregivers.' In D. Cicchetti & V. Carlson, *Child Maltreatment*. Cambridge: Cambridge University Press.

Carr, A. (1977). *Some preliminary findings on the association between child maltreatment and juvenile misconduct in eight New York counties*. Report to the Administration for Children, Youth and Families, National Center of Child Abuse and Neglect.

Carter, J. (1974). 'Problems of professional belief'. In J. Carter (Ed.), *The Maltreated Child*. London: Priory Press.

Carter, J. (1977). 'Is child abuse a crime?' In A. W. Franklin, *The Challenge of Child Abuse*. London: Academic Press; New York: Grune & Stratton.

Cartwright, T. (1973). 'Problems, solutions and strategies. A contribution to theory and practice in planning.' *Journal of the American Institute of Planners*, **39**, 179–187.

Casanova, G. M ., Dominic, J., McCann, T. R. & Milner, J. S. (1992). 'Physiological responses to non-child-related stressors in mothers at risk for child abuse.' *Child Abuse and Neglect*, **16**, 31–44.

Caspi, A., Elder, G., & Herbener, E. (1990). 'Childhood personality and the prediction of life-course patterns'. In L. Robins & M. Rutter (Eds), *Straight and Devious Pathways to Adulthood*. Cambridge: Cambridge University Press.

Cassell, E. J. (1986). 'Ideas in conflict: The rise and fall (and fall and rise) of new views of disease.' *Daedelus*, **115**, 19–41.

Cassidy, M. (1987). 'World-view conflict and toddler malnutrition: Change agent dilemmas.' In N. Scheper-Hughes (Ed.), *Child Survival*. Dordrecht: D. Reidel.

Chamberlin, R .W. (1994). 'Primary prevention: The missing piece in child development legislation.' In R. J. Simeonsson (Ed.), *Risk, Resilience and Prevention*. Baltimore, MD: Brookes Publishing.

Chang, H. (1993). 'Serving ethnically diverse communities.' *Education and Urban Society*, **25**,(2), 212–221.

Chasnoff, I. J. (1989). 'Drug use and women. Establishing a standard of care.' *Annual of New York Academy of Science*, **562**, 208.

Cherlin, A. J., Furstenberg Jr, F. F., Chase-Lansdale, P. L., Kiernan, K. E., Robins, P. K., Morrison, D. R. & Teitler, J. O. (1991). 'Longitudinal studies of effects of divorce on children in Great Britain and the United States.' *Science*, **252**, 1386–1389.

Chess, S. & Thomas, A. (1990). 'Continuities and discontinuities in temperament.' In L. Robins & M. Rutter (Eds), *Straight and Devious Pathways to Adulthood*. Cambridge: Cambridge University Press.

Chesser, E. (1951). *Cruelty to Children*. London: Victor Gollancz.

Child Abuse Prevention and Treatment Act 1974, USA.

Cheung, F., Chau, B. & Larn, M. (1986). *Caretaking forms and styles in urban Hong Kong—a pilot study on three-year old children*. A monograph published by the Centre for Hong Kong Studies, Institute of Social Studies, The Chinese University of Hong Kong.

Cheung, S. I. & Buchanan, A. (forthcoming). High Malaise Scores in adulthood amongst children and young people who have been in care. University of Oxford.

Cicchetti, D. (1989). 'How research on child maltreatment has informed the study of child development: Perspectives from developmental psychopathology.' In D. Cicchetti & V. Carlson (Eds), *Child Maltreatment*. Cambridge: Cambridge University Press.

Cicchetti, D. (1992). 'A historical perspective on the discipline of developmental psychopathology.' In J. Rolf, A. Masten, D. Cicchetti, K. Nuechterlein & S. Weintraub (Eds), *Risk and Protective Factors in the Development of Psychopathology*. Cambridge: Cambridge University Press.

Cicchetti, D. & Aber, L. A. (1980). 'Abused children—abusive parents: An overstated case?' *Harvard Educational Review*, **50**, 244–255.

Cicchetti, D. & Olsen, K. (1990). 'The developmental psychopathology of child maltreatment.' In M. Lewis & S. M. Miller (Eds), *Handbook of Developmental Psychopathology* (pp. 261–280). New York: Plenum.

Cicchetti, D. & Rizley, R. (1981). 'Developmental perspectives on the etiology of intergenerational transmission, and sequelae of child maltreatment.' *New Directions for Child Development*, **11**, 31–55.

Clark, K.B. (1992). 'Infecting our children with hostility.' In G. W. Albee, L. A. Bond & T. V. Cook Monsey, *Improving Children's Lives*. Newbury Park, CA: Sage.

Clarke-Stewart, K. A. (1987). 'In search of consistencies in child care research.' In D. A. Phillips (Ed.), *Quality in Child Care: What Does Research Tell Us?* NAEYC.

Clayden, G. S. (1988). 'Reflex anal dilation associated with severe chronic constipation in children.' *Archives of Disease in Childhood*, **63**, 832–836.

Cleaver, H. & Freeman, P. (1995). *Parental Perspectives in Cases of Suspected Child Abuse*. London: HMSO.

Cliffe, D. (1990). *An End to Residential Care? The Warwickshire Experiment*. London: National Children's Bureau.

Cloke, C. & Davies, M. (1995). *Participation and Empowerment in Child Protection*. London: Pitman Publishing.

Cockett, C. & Tripp, J. (1994). *Family Breakdown and its Impact on Children*. Exeter University, UK.

Coffield, F., Robinson, P. & Sarsby, J. (1980). *A Cycle of Deprivation? A Case Study of Four Families*. SSRC/DHSS Studies in Deprivation and Disadvantage, No 2. London: Heinemann Educational Books.

Cohen, B. (1990). *Caring for Children*: report for the European Commission's Childcare Network on Childcare Services and Policy in the UK. Scottish and Child Family Alliance. London: Family Policy Studies Centre.

Cohn, A. (1981). *An approach to preventing child abuse*. Chicago: National Committee for Prevention of Child Abuse.

Cohn, A. (1982a). *An approach to preventing child abuse*. US National Commission for Prevention of Child Abuse.

Cohn, A. (1982b). 'Stopping abuse before it occurs: Different solutions for different population groups.' *Child Abuse and Neglect*, **6**, 473–483.

Cohn, A. (1992). Foreword: 'Child abuse prevention.' In D. Willis, E. Holden & M. Rosenberg, *Prevention of Child Maltreatment*. New York: John Wiley.

Commission for Racial Equality (1988). *Learning in Terror*. London: CRE.

Comstock, G. (1976). 'The role of social and behavioral science in policymaking for television.' *Journal of Social Issues*, **32**, 157–178.

Conger, R. D., Burgess, R. L. & Barrett, C. (1979). 'Child abuse related to life change and perceptions of illness: Some preliminary findings.' *Family Coordinator*, **28**, 73–78.

Conger, R., Lahey, B. & Smith, S. (1981). *An intervention program for child abuse. Modifying maternal depression and behaviour*. Paper presented to Family Violence Research Conference, University of New Hampshire, Durham NH, quoted in D. Gough (1993), *Child Abuse Interventions*. London: HMSO.

Coninger, C. R. & Gottesman, I. (1987). 'Genetic and environmental factors in antisocial behavior disorders.' In S. A. Mednick, T. E. Moffitt & S. A. Stack (Eds), *Causes of Crime: New Biological Approaches* (pp. 92–109). Cambridge: Cambridge University Press.

Connor, M. (1987). *Treatment programs for abused children*. NCPCA Working Paper. No. 37. Chicago: National Committee for Prevention of Child Abuse.

Cooper, A., Hetherington, R., Baistow, K., Pitts, J. & Spriggs, A. (1995). *Positive Child Protection*: Lyme Regis, Dorset, UK: Russell House Publishing.

Cousin, J., Cousin, G., McGrath, S. & Fine, R. (1993). *System Abuse of Children: The Orkney Case*. London: NSPCC Library.

Coussins, J. & Coote, A. (1981). *The Family in the Firing Line*. London: Child Poverty Action Group.

Cox, A. D., Puckering, C., Pound, A., Mills, M. & Owen, A. L. (1990). *Newpin: the evaluation of a home visiting and befriending scheme in South London*. Report to the Department of Health, London.

Creighton, S. J. (1988). 'The incidence of child abuse and neglect.' In K. Browne, C. Davies & P. Stratton (Eds), *Early Prediction and Prevention of Child Abuse.* Chichester: John Wiley.

Crittenden, P. M. (1984). 'Sibling interaction: Evidence of generational effect in maltreating children.' *Child Abuse and Neglect,* **8**, 433–438.

Crittenden, P. M. (1985). *Children's strategies for coping with adverse home environments: abuse and neglect.* Paper presented at the meeting of the Society for Research in Child Development, Toronto, Canada, 25–28 April.

Crittenden, P. M. & Ainsworth, M. D. S. (1989). 'Child maltreatment and attachment theory.' In D. Cicchetti & V. Carlson (Eds), *Child Maltreatment. Theory and Research on the Causes and Consequences of Child Abuse and Neglect.* Cambridge: Cambridge University Press.

Crittenden, P. M. & Bonvillian, J. D. (1984). 'The relationship between maternal risk status and maternal sensitivity. *American Journal of Orthopsychiatry,* **54**, 250–262.

Crockenberg, S. (1987). 'Predictors and correlates of anger toward and punitive control of toddlers by adolescent mothers.' *Child Development,* **58**, 964–975.

Crowe, H. P. & Zeskind, P. S. (1992). 'Psychophysiological and perceptual responses to infant cries varying in pitch: Comparison of adults with low and high scores on the Child Abuse Potential Inventory.' *Child Abuse and Neglect,* **16**, 19–29.

Culbertson, J. L. & Schellenbach, C. J. (1992). In D. J. Willis, E. W. Holden & M. Rosenberg (Eds), *Prevention of Child Maltreatment.* New York: John Wiley.

Curtis, J. M. (1986). 'Factors in sexual abuse of children.' *Psychological Reports,* **58**, 591–597.

Daly, M. & Wilson, M. I. (1982). 'Whom are newborn babies said to resemble?' *Ethology & Sociobiology,* **3**(2) 69–78.

Daly, M. & Wilson M. I. (1985). 'Child abuse and other risks of not living with both parents.' *Ethology and Sociobiology,* **6**(4), 197–210.

Daly, M. & Wilson, M. I. (1994). 'Some differential attributes of lethal assaults on small children by stepfathers versus genetic fathers.' *Ethology and Sociobiology,* **15**(4), 207–217.

Daro, D. (1992). *The Resource Book.* National Committee for the Prevention of Child Abuse, ISPCAN & UNICEF.

Davenport, C. (1911). *Medicine and Society in America* (reprint). New York: Arno Press.

Dawkins, R. (1976). *The Selfish Gene.* New York: Oxford University Press.

De'Ath, E. & Pugh, G. (Eds) (1985–6). *Partnership Papers.* London: National Children's Bureau.

De Mause, L. (Ed.) (1974). *The History of Childhood.* New York: Psychohistory Press.

De Mause, L. (1984). *Reagan's America.* New York: Creative Roots.

Denzin, N. (1977). *Childhood Socialisation,* San Francisco: Jossey-Bass.

Department of Health (1991a). *Child Abuse: a Study of Inquiry Reports.* London: HMSO.

Department of Health (1991b). *Patterns and Outcomes in Child Placement.* London: HMSO.

Department of Health (1992). LAC(92)18: *Children's Services Plans.* London: HMSO.

Department of Health (1994a). *Looking After Children Project. Assessment and Action Records.* London: HMSO.

Department of Health (1994b). *The Children Act Report 1993.* London: HMSO.

Department of Health (1995). *Child Protection—Messages from Research.* London: HMSO.

Department of Health and Social Security (1974). *The Family in Society: Dimensions of Parenthood.* London: HMSO.

Department of Health and Social Security (1982). *Child Abuse: A Study of Inquiry Reports 1973–1981.* London: HMSO.

Department of Health and Social Security (1985). *Social Work Decisions in Child Care, Recent Research Findings and their Implications.* London: HMSO.

Dingwall, R. (1994). 'The dilemmas of family policy in liberal states.' In M. Maclean & J. Kurczewski, *Families, Politics and the Law.* Oxford: Clarendon Press.

Dingwall, R., Eekelaar, J. & Murray, T. (1983). *The Protection of Children. State Intervention and Family Life.* Oxford: Basil Blackwell.

Dinnage, R. (1978). 'Throwaways.' *New York Review of Books,* **25** (11), 37–39.

Diósi, A. (1995). 'Learning from each other—professional Gypsy foster parents in Hungary.' *Adoption and Fostering,* **4**, 38–42.

Divale, W. T. & Harris, M. (1976). 'Population, warfare and the male supremist complex,' *American Anthropologist,* **78**, 531–538.

Dobash, R. E. & Dobash, R. P. (1979). *Violence Against Wives. A Case Against Patriarchy.* New York: Free Press.

Dobash, R. E. & Dobash, R. P. (1992). *Women, Violence and Social Change.* New York: Routledge.

Doherty, D. (1990). *Public Opinion and Broadcasting Standards* vol. 1. *Violence in Television Fiction.* London: John Libbey.

Donald, I. (1979). 'Prematurity.' In I. Donald (Ed.), *Practical Obstetric Problems* (5th edn, pp. 939–977). London: Lloyd-Luke.

Dorris, M. (1992). 'Fetal alcohol syndrome. A parent's perspective.' In G. W. Albee, L. A. Bond & T. V. Cook Monsey (Eds), *Improving Children's Lives. Global Perspectives on Prevention.* Newbury Park, CA: Sage.

Drotar, D, (1992). 'Prevention of neglect and nonorganic failure to thrive.' In D. Willis, W. Holden & M. Rosenberg (Eds), *Prevention of Child Maltreatment.* New York: John Wiley.

Dugdale, R. (1877, 1910). 'The Jukes.' In R. Wade (Ed.), *The Rise of Urban America. A Record and Study of Relations of Crime, Pauperism, Disease and Heredity.* New York: Arno Press.

Dunn, J. (1986). 'Commentary: Issues for future research.' In R. Plomin & J. Dunn (Eds), *The Study of Temperament: Changes, Continuities, and Challenges* (pp. 163–171). Hillsdale, NJ: Lawrence Erlbaum.

Dunovsky, J. & Browne, K. (1994) 'ISPCAN holds fourth European Conference on Child Abuse and Neglect.' *The Link, The Official Newsletter of the International Society for Prevention of Child Abuse and Neglect* (ISPCAN), **3**, 2, 2.

Dunst, C. J. & Trivette, C. M. (1988). 'A family system model of early intervention with handicapped and developmentally at risk children.' In D. R. Powell (Ed.), *Parent Education as Early Childhood Intervention* (pp. 131–179). Norwood, NJ: Ablex.

Duquette, D. (1982). 'Protecting individual liberties in the context of screening for child abuse.' In R. Starr Jr (Ed.), *Child Abuse Prediction: Policy Implications* (pp. 191–204). Cambridge, MA: Ballinger.

Durning, A. (1992). 'Life on the brink.' In G. Albee, L. Bond & T. Cook Monsey (Eds), *Improving Children's Lives.* Newbury Park, CA: Sage.

Dytrych, Z. (1992). 'Children born of unwanted pregnancies.' In G. Albee, L. Bond & T. Cook Monsey (Eds), *Improving Children's Lives.* Newbury Park, CA: Sage.

Edmondson, R. (1994). 'Drug use and pregnancy.' In R. J. Simeonsson (Ed.), *Risk, Resilience, and Prevention.* Baltimore, MD: Paul H. Brookes.

Edna McConnell Clark Foundation (1985). *Keeping Families Together. The Case for Family Preservation*: New York, EMcCF.

Eekelaar, J. (1986). 'The emergence of children's rights.' *Oxford Journal of Legal Studies*, **6**, 161.

Eekelaar, J. (1992). 'The importance of thinking that children have rights.' *International Journal of Law and the Family*, **6**, 221–234.

Egan, K. (1983). 'Stress management and child management with abusive parents.' *Journal of Clinical Child Psychology*, **12**, 292–299.

Egeland, B. (1993). 'A history of abuse is a major risk factor for abusing the next generations.' In R. J. Gelles & D. R. Loseke (Eds), *Current Controversies on Family Violence*. Newbury Park, CA: Sage.

Egeland, B. & Erickson, M. F. (1993). 'Attachment theory and findings: Implications for prevention and interventions.' In S. Kramer & H. Parens (Eds), *Prevention in Mental Health: Now, Tomorrow, Ever?* Northvale, NJ: Jason Aronson.

Egeland, B. & Jacobvitz, D. (1984). *Intergenerational continuity of parental abuse: causes and consequences*. Paper presented at the Conference on Biosocial Perspectives on Abuse and Neglect, York ME.

Egeland, B., Jacobvitz, D. & Sroufe, L. A. (1988). 'Breaking the cycle of abuse.' *Child Development*, **59**, 1080–1088.

Egeland, B. & Sroufe, L. A. (1981). 'Attachment and early maltreatment.' *Child Development*, **52**, 44–52.

Egeland, B., Sroufe, L. & Erickson, M. (1983). 'The developmental consequences of different patterns of maltreatment.' *Child Abuse and Neglect*, **7**, 459–469.

Elder, J. (1991). 'Lives and social change.' In W. R. Heinz (Ed.), *Theoretical Advances in Life Course Research*. Series title: Status Passages and the Life Course. Weinheim: Deutscher Studien Verlag.

Elder, G. H. & Caspi, A. (1990). 'Studying lives in a changing society. Sociological and personological explorations' (Henry A. Murray Lecture Series). In A. I. Rabin, R. A. Zucher & S. Frank (Eds), *Studying Persons and Lives* (pp. 201–247). New York: Springer Verlag.

Elliott, F.A. (1988). 'Neurological factors.' In V. B. Van Hasselt, A. Morrison, S. Bellack & M. Hersen (Eds), *Handbook of Family Violence*. New York: Plenum.

El-Mouelhy, M. (1992). 'The impact of women's health and status on children's health and lives in the developing world.' In G. Albee, L. Bond & T. Cook Monsey (Eds), *Improving Children's Lives*. Newbury Park, CA: Sage .

Emery, R. E. (1982). 'Interparental conflict and the child of discord and divorce.' *Psychological Bulletin*, **92**, 310–330.

Endler, N. S. & Parker, J. S. (1992). 'Interactionism revisited. Reflections on the continuing crisis in the personality area.' *European Journal of Personality*, **6**, 177–198.

EPOCH-WORLDWIDE (1992). *End Physical Punishment for Children Worldwide*. European Seminar, London, Radda Barnen and EPOCH-WORLDWIDE.

Erikson, E. H. (1968). *Identity, Youth and Crisis*. New York: Norton.

Erikson, M. F., Egeland, B. & Pianta, R. (1989).'The effects of maltreatment on the development of young children.' In D. Cicchetti & V. Carlson (Eds), *Child Maltreatment*. New York: Cambridge University Press.

Eron, L. & Huesmann, L. (1987). 'Television as a source of maltreatment of children.' *School Psychology Review*, **16**, 195–202.

Eskay, R. & Linnoila, M. (1991). 'Potential biochemical markers for the predisposition toward alcoholism.' In M. Glanter (Ed.), *Recent Developments in Alcoholism*: vol. 9, *Children of Alcoholics*, (pp. 41–49). New York: Plenum.

Essen, J. & Wedge, P. (1983) *Continuities in Childhood Disadvantage*. SSRC/DHSS Studies in Deprivation and Disadvantage, No. 6. London: Heinemann Educational Books.

Fagan, J. & Wexler, S. (1987). 'Family origins of violent delinquents.' *Criminology*, **25**, 643–669.

Fahlberg, V. (1991). *A Child's Journey through Placement*. London: BAAF. First published in USA by Perspectives Press, Indianapolis.

Family Rights Group (1991). *The Children Act 1989—an FRG Briefing Pack*, London: Family Rights Group.

Fanshel, D. & Shinn, E. (1978). *Children in Foster Care: A longitudinal investigation*. New York: Columbia University Press.

Farmer, G. & Blanchard, J. (1994). 'Partnerships at a resource centre for children who have special needs.' In A. Buchanan (Ed.), *Partnership in Practice: The Children Act 1989*. Avebury, UK.

Farmer, E. & Owen, M. (1995). *Child Protection Practice: Private Risks and Public Remedies*. London: HMSO.

Farquhar, S. E. (1989). 'Assessing New Zealand child care quality using the early childhood environment rating scale.' *Early Child Development and Care*, **47**, 93–105.

Farrell, G. (1992). 'Multiple victimisation: Its extent and significance.' *International Journal of Victimology*, **2**, 2, 85–102.

Farrington, D. P. (1987). 'Stepping stones to adult criminal careers.' In D. Olweus, J. Block & M. Yarrow (Eds), *Development of Antisocial and Prosocial Behavior* (pp. 359–384). New York: Academic Press.

Farrington, D. & West, D. (1981). 'The Cambridge Study in delinquent development.' In S. Mednick & A. Baert (Eds), *Prospective Longitudinal Research*. Oxford: Oxford University Press.

Faupel, A. (1994). 'Partnership and children with special needs in education.' In A. Buchanan (Ed.), *Partnership in Practice: The Children Act 1989*. Avebury, UK.

Feig, L. (1990). *Drug Exposed Infants and Children. Service Needs and Policy Questions*. Washington, DC: US DHHS.

Feldman, M., Towns, F., Betel, J., Case, L., Rincover, A. & Rubino, C. A. (1986). 'Parent Education Project II: Increasing stimulating interactions of developmentally handicapped mothers.' *Journal of Applied Behavior Analysis*, **19**, 23–27.

Fergusson, D. M., Horwood, L. J. & Lynskey, M. T. (1993). 'Early dentine lead levels and subsequent cognitive and behavioural development.' *Journal of Child Psychology and Psychiatry*, **34**, 2, 215–227.

Feshbach, N. (1974). 'The development and regulation of aggression. Some research gaps and a proposed cognitive analysis.' In J. De Wit and W. Hartup (Eds), *Determinants and Origins of Aggressive Behaviour*. Paris: Mouton.

Feshbach, N. (1989). 'The construct of empathy and the phenomenon of physical maltreatment of children.' In D. Cicchetti & V. Carlson, *Child Maltreatment*. Cambridge: Cambridge University Press.

Feshbach, N. D. & Caskey, N. (1985). 'A new scale for measuring parent empathy and partner empathy: factorial structure, correlates and clinical discrimination.' Cited in Feshbach, N.D. (1989). 'Empathy and physical abuse.' In D. Cicchetti & V. Carlson (Eds), *Child Maltreatment. Theory and Research on the Causes and Consequences of Child Abuse and Neglect*, (pp. 349–373). New York: Cambridge University Press.

Finkelhor, D. (1990). 'Is child abuse over-reported? The data rebut arguments for less intervention.' *Public Welfare*, **48**, 23–29.

Finkelhor, D. (1992). *Young people's concern about being bullied*. Paper to NSPCC Research and Policy Forum, Cardiff, December 1992.

Finkelhor, D. (1993). 'The main problem is still underreporting, not overreporting.' In R. Gelles & D. Loseke, *Current Controversies on Family Violence*. Newbury Park, CA: Sage.

Finkelhor, D. & Korbin, J. (1988). 'Child abuse as an international issue.' *Child Abuse and Neglect*, **12**, 3–23.

Fletcher, B. (1993). *Not Just a Name. The Views of Young People in Foster and Residential Care*. London: British Association of Adoption and Fostering.

Flynn, K. (1995). *Linking the Assessment and Action Records with standardised tests of outcome*. Paper to the International Seminar, 18–19 July: Looking after Children: Good Parenting, Good Outcomes. London.

Folstein, S., Franz, M. L., Jensen, B. A, Chase, G. A. & Folstein, M. F. (1983). 'Conduct disorder and affective disorder among the offspring of patients with Huntington's disease.' *Psychological Medicine*, **13**, 45–52.

Foster, G. (1965). 'Peasant society and the image of unlimited good.' *American Anthropologist*, **67** (2), 283–315.

Freud, A. & Burlingham, D. (1943). *War and Children*. New York: New York Medical Books.

Freud, A. & Dann, S. (1951). 'An experiment in group upbringing.' *Psychoanalytic Study of the Child*, **6**, 127–168.

Friedrich, W. & Wheeler, K. (1982). 'The abusing parent revisited: A decade of psychological research.' *Journal of Nervous and Mental Disease*, **170**, 577–587.

Frodi, A. M. & Lamb M. E. (1980). 'Child abusers' responses to infant smiles and cries.' *Child Development*, **51**, 238–241.

Fuddy, L. (1994). *Steps for Identification: the Hawaiian Experience*. Proceedings of the tenth International Congress on Child Abuse and Neglect, Kuala Lumpur, Abstracts: p. 171.

Fuller, R. & Myers, R. (1941). 'The natural history of a social problem.' *American Sociological Review*, **6**, 6, June, 320.

Galston, R. (1975). Preventing the abuse of little children: The parents' center project for the study and prevention of child abuse.' *American Journal of Orthopsychiatry*, **45**, 372–381.

Garbarino, J. (1976). 'A preliminary study of some ecological correlates of child abuse: The impact of socioeconomic stress on the mother.' *Child Development*, **47**, 178–185.

Garbarino, J. (1977). 'The human ecology of child maltreatment: A conceptual model for research.' *Journal of Marriage and the Family*, **39**, 721–736.

Garbarino, J. (1993). 'Preventing adolescent maltreatment.' In D. Willis, E. W. Holden & M. Rosenberg, *Prevention of Child Maltreatment*. New York: John Wiley.

Garbarino, J., Guttman, E. & Seeley, J. W. (1986). *The Psychologically Battered Child*. San Francisco: Jossey-Bass.

Garmezy, N. & Rutter, M. (Eds), *Stress, Coping and Development in Children*. New York: McGraw-Hill.

Garrahan, A. P. D. (1994). *Child Abuse in a Third World Country: a Problem that needs Innovative Solutions*. The tenth International Congress on Child Abuse and Neglect, Kuala Lumpur, Abstracts: p. 261.

Gelles, R. J. (1973). 'Child abuse as psychopathology: A sociological critique and reformation.' *American Journal of Orthopsychiatry*, **43**, 611–621.

Gelles, R. J. (1974). *The Violent Home*. Newbury Park, CA: Sage.

Gelles, R. J. (1979). *Family Violence*. Newbury Park, CA: Sage.

Gelles, R. (1982). 'Problems in defining and labelling child abuse.' In R. Starr Jr (Ed.), *Child Abuse Prediction: Policy implications* (pp. 1–30). Cambridge, MA: Ballinger.

Gelles, R. (1983). 'An exchange/social theory.' In D. Finkelhor, R. Gelles, G. Hotaling & M. Straus (Eds), *The Dark Side of Families. Current Family Violence Research* (pp. 151–165). Newbury Park, CA: Sage.

Gelles, R. (1993). 'Through a sociological lens: Social structure and family violence.' In R. Gelles & D. Loseke, *Current Controversies on Family Violence*. Newbury Park, CA: Sage.

Gelles, R. J. & Cornell, C. P. (1985, 1990). *Intimate Violence in Families*, 2nd edn. Newbury Park, CA: Sage.

Gelles, R. & Edfeldt, A. (1986). 'Violence towards children in the United States and Sweden.' *Child Abuse and Neglect*, **10**, 501–510.

Gelles, R. J. & Loseke, D. R. (Eds) (1993). *Current Controversies on Family Violence*, Newbury Park, CA: Sage.

Gelles, R. J. & Straus, M. A. (1979). 'Determinants of violence in the family: Toward a theoretical integration.' In W. Burr, R. Hill, F. Nye & I. Reiss (Eds), *Contemporary Theories about the Family*. New York: Free Press.

Gelles, R. J. & Straus, M. A. (1988). *Intimate Violence*. New York: Simon & Schuster.

Gibbons, J., Conroy, S. & Bell, C. (1995). *Operating the Child Protection System*. London: HMSO.

Gibbons, J., Gallagher, B., Bell, C. & Gordon, D. (1995). *Development after Physical Abuse in Early Childhood: A Follow-up Study of Children on Child Protection Registers*. London: HMSO.

Gibbons, J. & Thorpe, S. (1989). 'Can voluntary support projects help vulnerable families? The work of Home Start.' *British Journal of Social Work*, **19**, 3, 189–201.

Gibbons, J., Thorpe, S. & Wilkinson, P. (1990). *Family Support and Prevention*. London: HMSO.

Gil, D. (1970). *Violence against Children: Physical Child Abuse in the United States*. Cambridge, MA: Harvard University Press.

Gil, D. (1979). *Child Abuse and Violence*. New York: AMS Press.

Gil, D. (1981). 'The United States versus child abuse.' In L. H. Pelton (Ed.), *The Social Context of Child Abuse and Neglect* (p. 295). New York: Human Sciences Press.

Gillick v. West Norfolk and Wisbech Area Health Authority 1986 AC, 112.

Ginsburg, N. (1993). 'Sweden: The social-democratic case.' In A. Cochrane & J. Clarke, *Comparing Welfare States*. London: Open University and Sage Publications.

Giovannoni, J. & Becarra, R. (1979). *Defining Child Abuse*. New York: Free Press.

Goddard, H. (1912). *The Kallikak Family*. New York: Macmillan.

Goddard, H. (1914) (reprinted 1972). *Feeble-mindedness: Its Causes and Consequences*. Hallandale, FL: New World Book Co.

Goldsmith, T. H. (1991). *The Biological Roots of Human Nature. Forging Links between Evolution and Behaviour*. Oxford: Oxford University Press.

Gomes-Schwartz, B. (1994). 'Nature of sexual abuse.' In B. Gomes Schwartz (Ed.), *Sexually Exploited Children Service and Research Response*. Office of Juvenile Justice and Delinquency, US Department of Justice.

Goode, W. (1971). 'Force and violence in the family.' *Journal of Marriage and the Family*, **33**, 624–636.

Goodman, R. & Stevenson, J. (1989). 'A twin study of hyperactivity – II. The aetiological role of genes, family relationships and perinatal adversity.' *Journal of Child Psychology and Psychiatry*, **30**, 691–709.

Goodwin, J. (1994). 'Partnership and a family link scheme for families with special needs.' In A. Buchanan (Ed.), *Partnership in Practice: The Children Act 1989*, Avebury.

Gough, D. (1993). *Child abuse interventions—a review of the research literature*. London: HMSO.

Graham, P. & Stevenson, J. (1985). 'A twin study of genetic influence on behavioral deviance.' *Journal of the American Academy of Child and Adolescent Psychiatry*, **24**, 33–41.

Grant, J. (1987). 'Getting it right: Health and maternity care in multi-racial Britain.' *Medicine in Society*, **13**, 2, 21–25.

Granzberg, G. (1973). 'Twin infanticide: A cross-cultural test of a materialistic explanation.' *Ethos*, **4**, 405–412.

Gray, E. (1983). *Final Report, collaborative research of community and minority group action to prevent child abuse and neglect*, vol 1 to 3, National Committee for Prevention of Child Abuse, Chicago. (Summaries of this research in D. Gough (1993), *Child Abuse Interventions. A Review of Research Literature*. London: HMSO.)

Gray, E. & Cosgrove, J. (1985). 'Ethnocentric perception of childrearing practices in protective services.' *Child Abuse and Neglect*, **9**, 389–396.

Grossman, H. J. (Ed.) (1983). *Classification of Mental Retardation*. Washington, DC: American Association of Mental Deficiency.

Gulbenkian Foundation (1993). *One scandal too many . . . the case for comprehensive protection for children in all settings*. UK, Calouste Gulbenkian Foundation.

Gurry, G.-L. (1993). 'A brighter future for ASEAN children.' *Child Abuse Review*, **2**, 119–126.

Gusfield, J. (1981). *The Culture of Public Problems: Drinking, Driving and the Symbolic Order*. Chicago: University of Chicago Press.

Haeuser, A. (1992). 'Let's stop physical punishment of children. How Sweden's success can be applied to the United States.' In *Ending Physical Punishment of European Children*. London: Radda Barnen & EPOCH WORLDWIDE.

Haines, H. (1983). *Violence on Television*. Auckland: Mental Health Foundation of New Zealand.

Halpern, R. & Weiss, H. (1988). *What is known about the effectiveness of family orientated early childhood intervention programs*. Unpublished paper from Harvard Family Research Project, Harvard University School of Education.

Hampton, R. L., Gullotta, T. P., Adams, G. R., Potter, E. H., & Weissberg, R. P. (1993). *Family Violence. Prevention and Treatment*. Newbury Park, CA: Sage.

Hanmer, J. & Maynard, M. (1987). *Women, violence and social control*. Atlantic Highlands, NJ: Humanities.

Hardiker, P., Exton, K., Barker, M. (1991). *Policies and Practices in Preventive Child Care*. Aldershot, UK: Avebury.

Hargrave, A. (1993). *Broadcasting Standards Council—Public Opinion and Broadcasting Standards*, vol. 4: *Violence on Factual Television*, London: John Libbey.

Harlow, H. F. (1961). 'The development of affectional patterns in infant mothers.' In B. M. Foss (Ed.), *Determinants of Infant Behaviour* (vol. 1). New York: John Wiley.

Harlow, H. F. & Suomi, S. J. (1971). 'Social recovery by isolation-reared monkeys.' *Proceedings of the National Academy of Science*, **68**, 1534–1538.

Harms, T. & Clifford, R. M. (1980). *Early Childhood Environment Rating Scale*. Teachers' College, Columbia University, New York and London.

Harrington, D. & Dubowitz, H. (1993). 'What can be done to prevent child maltreatment.' In R. L. Hampton, T. P. Gullotta, G. R. Adams, E. H. Potter & R. Weissberg (Eds), *Family Violence. Prevention and Treatment*. Newbury Park, CA: Sage.

Hayes, H. R. & Emshoff, J. G. (1993). 'Substance abuse and family violence.' In R. Hampton, R. Gullotta, G. Adams, E. Potter, R. Weissberg (Eds). *Family Violence. Prevention and Treatment*. Newbury Park, CA: Sage.

Headland, T. N., Pike, K. L. & Harris, M. (Eds) (1990). *Emic and Etic. The Insider and Outsider*. Newbury Park, CA: Sage.

Helfer, R. (1984). 'The epidemiology of child abuse and neglect.' *Pediatric Annuals*, **13**, 747–751.

Hennessy, J. W. & Levine, S. (1979). 'Stress, arousal and the pituitary-adrenal system: A psychoendocrine hypothesis.' In J. M. Srague & A. N. Epstein (Eds), *Progress in Psychobiology and Physiological Psychology* (pp. 134–178). New York: Academic Press.

Herbert, M. (1981). *Behavioural Treatment of Problem Children. A Practice Manual,* London: Academic Press; New York: Grune & Stratton.

Herrenkohl, E. C., Herrenkohl, R. C. & Toedtler, L. J. (1983). 'Perspectives on the intergenerational transmission of abuse.' In D. Finkelhor, R. J. Gelles, G. T. Hotaling & M. Straus (Eds), *The Dark Side of Families: Current Family Violence Research.* Newbury Park, CA: Sage.

Hertzberger, S. (1983). 'Social cognition and the transmission of abuse.' In D. Finkelhor, R. Gelles, G. Hotaling & M. Straus (Eds), *The Dark Side of Families. Current Family Violence Research,* Newbury Park, CA: Sage.

Hess, L. E. (1995). 'Changing family patterns in Western Europe: Opportunity and risk factors for adolescent development.' In M. Rutter & D. Smith, *Psychosocial Disorders in Young People. Time Trends and Their Causes.* Chichester: John Wiley.

Hiew, C. C. (1992). 'Endangered children in Thailand: Third World families affected by socioeconomic changes.' In G. Albee, L. Bond. & T. Cook Monsey (Eds), *Improving Children's Lives.* Newbury Park, CA: Sage.

Holloway, S. D. & Reichhart-Erikson, M. (1988). 'The relationship of day care quality to children's free-play behaviour and social problem-solving skills.' *Early Childhood Research Quarterly,* **3**, 39–52.

Holman, B. (1988). *Putting Children First: Prevention in Child Care,* Children's Society, London: Macmillan.

Holman, B. (1992). *Family Centres.* National Children's Bureau Highlight No. 111. London: National Children's Bureau.

Holzman, P. S. (1992). 'Schizophrenia: A new model for its transmission and its variations.' In J. Rolf, A. Masten, D. Cicchetti, K. Nuechterlein & S. Weintraub (Eds), *Risk and Protective Factors in the Development of Psychopathology.* Cambridge: Cambridge University Press.

Howing, P., Kohn, S., Gaudin, J., Kurtz, D. & Wodarski, J. (1992). 'Current research issues in child welfare.' *Social Work Research and Abstracts,* **28** (1), 5–12.

Howlett, A., Lunan, S. & Symons, R. (1985). *Aberdeen mother and child groups.* Save the Children Project 1981–1984. Unpublished report quoted in D. Gough (1993), *Child Abuse Interventions.* London: HMSO.

Hudson, B. & Macdonald, G. M. (1986). *Behavioural Social Work: An Introduction.* London: Macmillan.

Hughes, D. M. (1987). 'When cultural rights conflict with the "Best Interests of the Child".' In N. Scheper-Hughes (Ed.), *Child Survival.* Dordrecht: D. Reidel Publishing.

Hunt, J. M. (1961). *Intelligence and Experience.* New York: Ronald.

Hunter, R. S. & Kilstrom, N. (1979). 'Breaking the cycle in abusive families.' *American Journal of Psychiatry,* **136**, 1320–1322.

Huntington, G. S., Lima, L. & Zipper, I. N. (1994). 'Child abuse: A prevention agenda.' In R. J. Simeonsson (Ed.), *Risk, Resilience & Prevention.* Baltimore, MD: Brookes Publishing.

Hutchison, E. (1994). 'Defining child abuse and neglect.' In R. Barth, J. Berrick & N. Gilbert (Eds), *Child Welfare Research Review.* New York: Columbia University Press.

Hutchinson, R. (1994). 'Partnership and the Children Act 1989. The local authority's powers and duties.' In A. Buchanan (Ed.), *Partnership in Practice.* Aldershot: Avebury.

Hynd, G. W. & Hooper, S. R. (1992). *Neurological Basis of Childhood Psychopathology.* Newbury Park, CA: Sage.

van Ijzendoorn, M. H., Juffer, F. & Duyvesteyn, M. G. C. (1995). 'Breaking the intergenerational cycle of insecure attachment: A review of the effects of attachment based interventions on maternal sensitivity and infant security.' *Journal of Child Psychology and Psychiatry,* **36** (2), 225–248.

Ikeda, T. (1982). 'A short introduction to child abuse in Japan.' *Child Abuse and Neglect,* **5,** 487–490.

Illich, I. (1973). *Deschooling Society.* Harmondsworth: Penguin Books.

International Coalition Against Violent Entertainment 8 June (1990). *Mass media watchdog group protests introduction of violent entertainment into the Eastern Block.* Press Release.

ISPCAN (1994). 'Resource Book update.' *The Link, The Official Newsletter of the International Society for Prevention of Child Abuse and Neglect* 3, 2, 3.

Ivory, M. (1994). 'Small is beautiful. Policy Europe.' *Community Care,* 1–7 December, 26–27.

Jackson, S. (1993). 'Under fives: Thirty years of no progress.' *Children & Society,* **7** (1), 82–94.

Jaffe, P., Wolfe, D. & Wilson, S. (1990). *Children of battered women. Issues in Child Development and Intervention Planning.* Newbury Park, CA: Sage.

Jellinger, J. (1972). 'Neuropathological features of unclassified mental retardation.' In J. B. Cavanagh (Ed.), *The Brain in Unclassified Mental Retardation.* (pp. 283–321). Baltimore, MD: Williams & Wilkins.

Jenkins, J. M. & Smith, M. A. (1990). 'Factors protecting children living in disharmonious homes. Maternal reports.' *Journal of the American Academy of Child and Adolescent Psychiatry,* **29,** 60–69.

Johnston, C. (1976). *The art of the crisis line: A training manual for volunteers in child abuse prevention.* Oakland, CA: Parent-Stress Service.

Jones, D. P. H. (1987). 'The untreatable family.' *Child Abuse and Neglect,* **11,** 409–420.

Kahan, B. (1993). 'Children living away from home.' *Children and Society,* **7** (1), 95–108.

Kahn, A. & Kamerman, S. (1980). 'Child abuse: A comparative perspective.' In G. Gerbner, C. Ross, & E. Zigler (Eds), *Child Abuse: An Agenda for Action* (pp. 118–24). New York: Oxford University Press.

Kalmuss, D. (1984). 'The intergenerational transmission of marital aggression.' *Journal of Marriage and the Family,* **46,** 11–19.

Kamerman, S. & Kahn, A. (1989). 'Family policy: Has the United States learned from Europe?' *Policy Studies Review,* **8** (3), 581–589.

Kaplan, B. (1967). 'Mediations on genesis.' *Human Development,* **10,** 65–87.

Karrby, G. & Giota, J. (1994). 'Dimensions of quality in Swedish day care centers—An analysis of the early childhood environment Rating Scale.' *Early Child Development and Care,* **104,** 1–22.

Kaufman, J. & Zigler, E. (1987). 'Do abused children become abusive parents?' *American Journal of Orthopsychiatry* **57** (2), 186–192.

Kaufman, J. & Zigler, E. (1989). 'The intergenerational transmission of child abuse.' In D. Cicchetti & V. Carlson (Eds), *Child Maltreatment.* Cambridge: Cambridge University Press.

Kaufman, J. & Zigler, E. (1992). 'The prevention of child maltreatment: Programming, research and policy.' In J. Willis, E. Holden & M. Rosenberg (Eds), *Prevention of Child Maltreatment. Developmental and Ecological Perspectives.* New York: John Wiley.

Kaufman, J. & Zigler, E. (1993). 'The intergenerational transmission of abuse is overstated.' In R. J. Gelles & D. R. Loseke (Eds), *Current Controversies on Family Violence*. Newbury Park, CA: Sage.

Kaufman, K., Johnson, C., Cohn, D. & McCleery, J. (1992). 'Child maltreatment prevention in the health care and social service system.' In J. Willis, E. Holden & M. Rosenberg (Eds), *Prevention of Child Maltreatment. Developmental and Ecological Perspectives*. New York: John Wiley.

Kempe, C., Silverman, F., Steele, B., Droegemueller, W. & Silver, H, (1962). 'The Battered Child Syndrome.' *Journal of the American Medical Association*, **181**, 17–24.

Kempe, R. & Kempe, C. (1978). *Child Abuse*. Cambridge, MA: Harvard University Press.

Kenyatta, J. (1938). *Facing Mount Kenya*. London: Secker & Warburg.

Kirkwood, A. (1993). *The Leicestershire Inquiry 1992*. UK, Leicestershire County Council.

Kitinya, J. (1993). 'Child abuse.' *Childright, the Newsletter of ANPPCAN Tanzania Chapter*, **2**, p. 9.

Kitzinger, J. (1989). 'Feminist self-help.' In W. Stainton Roger, D. Hevey & E. Ash, *Child Abuse and Neglect. Facing the Challenge*. Batsford, UK: Open University.

Klingman, A. (1978). 'Children in stress: Anticipatory guidance in the framework of the educational system.' *Personnel and Guidance Journal*, **57**, 22–26.

Knutson, J. F. (1978). 'Child abuse as an area of aggression research.' *Journal of Pediatric Psychology*, **3**, 20–27.

Kobayashi, M, (1994). *Identification and management of child abuse cases in Osaka Prefecture, Japan*. The tenth International Congress on Child Abuse and Neglect, Kuala Lumpur, Abstracts: p. 153.

Kokkevi, A. & Agathonos, H. (1987). 'Intelligence and personality profile of battering parents in Greece: A comparative study.' *Child Abuse and Neglect*, **11**, 93–99.

Kolvin, I., Miller, F. J. W., Scott, D. M., Gatzanis, S. R. M. & Fleeting, M. (1990). *Continuities of Deprivation? The Newcastle 1000 Family Study*. Aldershot: Avebury.

Korbin, J. (1980). 'The cultural context of child abuse and neglect.' *Child Abuse and Neglect*, **4**, 3–13.

Korbin, J. (1981). *Child Abuse and Neglect: Cross-cultural Perspectives*. Berkeley, CA: University of California Press.

Korbin, J. (1987). 'Child maltreatment in cross-cultural perspective: Vulnerable children and circumstances.' In R. Gelles & J. Lancaster (Eds), *Child Abuse and Neglect*. New York: Aldine de Gruyter.

Korbin, J. (1991). 'Cross-cultural perspectives and research directions for the 21st century.' *Child Abuse and Neglect*, **15**, (Supp. 1), 67–77.

Kramer, M. (1992). 'Barriers to primary prevention.' In G. Albee, L. Bond & T. Cook Monsey (Eds), *Improving Children's Lives*. Newbury Park, CA: Sage.

Kufeldt, K. (1995). *What are the benefits for organisations in assessing outcomes?* Paper to the International Seminar 18–19 July, Looking after Children: Good Parenting, good outcomes. London.

La Fontaine, J. (1991). *Bullying: The Child's View*. Calouste Gulbenkian Foundation; also through Turnabout Distribution Ltd, 27 Horsell Road, London N5 1XL.

Lahey, B., Conger, R., Atkeson, B. & Treiber, F. (1984). 'Parenting behavior and emotional status of physically abusive mothers.' *Journal of Consulting and Clinical Psychology*, **52**, 1062–1071.

Langer, W. (1974). 'Infanticide: An historical survey.' *History of Childhood Quarterly: Journal of Psychohistory*, **1**, 353–365.

Larrance, D. T. & Twentyman, C. T. (1983). 'Maternal attributions and child abuse.' *Journal of Abnormal Psychology*, **92**, 544–547.

Lau, L. (1995). 'Defining child abuse in Hong Kong.' *Child Abuse Review*, **4**, 38–45.

Lau, S.-K., Lee, M.-K., Wan, P.-S. & Wong, S.-L. (1992). *Indicators of Social Development, Hong Kong 1990*. Hong Kong Institute of Asia-Pacific Studies, The Chinese University of Hong Kong.

Lauderdale, M., Valiunas, A. & Anderson, R. (1980). 'Race, ethnicity and child maltreatment. An empirical analysis.' *Child Abuse and Neglect*, **4**, 163–169.

Leach, P. (1993). 'Should parents hit their children?' *The Psychologist*, **6**, 216–220.

Lerner, J. V. & Vicary, J. R. (1984). 'Difficult temperament and drug use: Analyses from the New York longitudinal study.' *Journal of Drug Addiction*, **14**, 1–8.

Levine, M., Ewing, C. P. & Levine, D. I. (1987). 'The use of law for prevention in the public interest.' In L. Jason, R. Selner, R. Hess & J. Moritsuga (Eds), *Communities: Contributions from Allied Disciplines. Series in Human Services*, **5**, 239–276.

Lewis, D., Mallouh, C. & Webb, V. (1989). 'Child abuse, delinquency and violent criminality.' In D. Cicchetti & V. Carlson, *Child Maltreatment*. New York: Cambridge University Press.

Lewis, D., Shanok, S., Pincus, J. & Glaser, G. (1979). 'Violent juvenile delinquents: Psychiatric, neurological, psychological and abuse factors.' *Journal of the American Academy of Child Psychiatry*, **18**, 307–319.

Levinson, D. (1989). *Family Violence in Cross-cultural Perspective*. Newbury Park, CA: Sage.

Levinson, D. & Malone, M. (1980). *Toward Explaining Human Culture*. New Haven, CT: HRAF.

Levy, A. & Kahan, B. (1991). *The Pindown Experience and the Protection of Children*, UK, Staffordshire County Council.

Levy, S. R., Perhats, C., Nash-Johnson, M. and Welter, J. F. (1992). 'Reducing the risks in pregnant teens who are very young and those with mild mental retardation.' *Mental Retardation*, **30**, 4, 195–203.

Lewis, C. (1991). 'Fighting to end horrors of female circumcisions.' *Hospital Doctor*, 21 March, 12.

Lieber, L. (1983). 'The self-help approach: Parents Anonymous.' *Journal of Clinical Child Psychology*, **12**, 288–291.

Liu, X. Z. (1994). *Recognition and attitudes of general public towards child abuse: a sampling survey in People's Republic of China*. The Tenth International Congress on Child Abuse and Neglect, Kuala Lumpur, Abstracts: p.8.

Loadman, W. & Vaughn, M. (1986). 'Child abuse prevention: Implementation and evaluation considerations for the special education professional.' *Maladjustment and Therapeutic Education*, **2**, 20–28.

Loeber, R. & Stouthamer-Loeber, M. (1986). 'Family factors as correlates and predictors of juvenile conduct problems and delinquency.' In M. Tonry & N. Morris (Eds), *Crime and Justice: An Annual Review of Research*, vol. VII 7, 29, 149. Chicago: University of Chicago Press.

Loehlin, J. C. (1992). *Genes and Environment in Personality Development*. Newbury Park, CA: Sage.

Loseke, D. R. & Gelles, R. J. (1993). 'Examining and evaluating controversies on family violence.' In R. J. Gelles & D. R. Loseke (Eds), *Current Controversies on Family Violence*. Newbury Park, CA: Sage.

Lutzker, J., Welsch, D. & Rice, J. M. (1984). 'A review of project 12-Ways: An ecobehavioral approach to the treatment and prevention of child abuse and neglect.' *Advances in Behavior Research and Therapy*, **6**, 63–73.

Lynch, M. (1975). 'Ill health and child abuse.' *Lancet*, **2**, 317–319.

Lynch, M. (1976). 'Child abuse—the critical path.' *Journal of Maternal and Child Health*, July, 25–9.

Lynch, M., Lindsay, J. & Ounsted, C. (1975). 'Tranquillisers causing aggression.' *British Medical Journal* 1, 266.

Lynch, M. (1985). 'Child abuse before Kempe: An historical literature review.' *Child Abuse and Neglect*, **9**, 7–12.

Lynch, M. & Roberts, J. (1978). 'Predisposing factors within the family.' In J. Carver (Ed.), *Child Abuse: A Study Text*: Milton Keynes: Oxford University Press.

Lynch, M. & Roberts, J. (1982). *Consequences of Child Abuse*. London: Academic Press.

Lynch, M., Roberts, J. & Gordon, M. (1976). 'Early warning of child abuse.' *Developmental Medicine and Child Neurology*, **18**, 759–766.

McCauley, R. (1977). *Child Behaviour Problems*. London: Macmillan.

McGraw, S. & Sturmey, P. (1994). 'Assessing parents with learning disabilities: The parental skills model.' *Child Abuse Review*, **3**, 36–51.

McGuffin, P. & Gottesman, I. I. (1985). 'Genetic Influences on normal and abnormal development.' In M. Rutter & L. Hersov (Eds), *Child and Adolescent Psychiatry. Modern Approaches* (2nd edn, pp. 17–33). Oxford: Blackwell Scientific.

McGuffin, P. & Katz, R. (1986). 'Nature, nurture and affective disorder.' In J. F. W. Deakin (Ed.), *The Biology of Depression* (pp. 26–52). London: The Royal College of Psychiatrists/Gaskell Press.

McLaughlin, E. (1993). 'Ireland: Catholic corporatism.' In A. Cochrane & J. Clarke, *Comparing Welfare States*. London: Open University and Sage Publications.

Macaskill, C. (1985). *Against the Odds. Adopting Mentally Handicapped Children*. London: BAAF.

Mackay, Rt Hon. Lord of Clashfern (1995). *Looking to the Future. Mediation and the Ground for Divorce. CM 2799*. Government Proposals. London: HMSO.

Maclean, M. & Kurczewski, J. (1994). *Families, Politics and The Law*. Oxford: Clarendon Press.

Madge, N. (1983). *Families at Risk*. SSRC/DHSS Studies in Deprivation and Disadvantage, No.8. London: Heinemann Educational Books.

Magnusson, D. (1988). *Individual Development from an Interactional Perspective. A Longitudinal Study*. Hillsdale, NJ: Lawrence Erlbaum.

Magnusson, D. (1990). 'Personality research-challenges for the future.' *European Journal of Personality* **4**, 1–17.

Main, M. & Goldwyn, R. (1984.) 'Predicting rejection of her infant from mother's representation of her own experience: Implications for the abused-abusing intergenerational cycle.' *Child Abuse and Neglect*, **8**, 203–217.

Main, M. & Hesse, P. (1990). 'Lack of resolution in mourning in adulthood and its relationship to infant disorganisation: Some speculations regarding causal mechanisms.' In M. Greenberg, D. Cicchetti & M. Cummings (Eds), *Attachment During the Preschool Years*. Chicago: University of Chicago Press.

Majlajlic, D. (1993). *Child Welfare in Croatia*. Paper to the Conference of the International Federation of Social Workers (IFSW) , Debrecen, Hungary.

Malamud, N. (1964). 'Neuropathology.' In H. A. Stevens & R. Heber (Eds), *Mental Retardation* (pp. 429–452). Chicago: University of Chicago Press.

Mallucio, A. & Fein, E. (1983). 'Permanency planning: A redefinition.' *Child Welfare*, **62** (3), 195–201.

Mallya, W. J. (1993). 'Child labour in Tanzania.' *Childright, The Newsletter of ANPP-CAN Tanzania Chapter*, No. 3, 3–6.

Mama, A. (1989). *The Hidden Struggle: Statutory and Voluntary Sector Responses to Violence against Black Women in the Home*. Runnymede Trust, UK.

Margolin, G. (1981). 'The reciprocal relationships between marital and child problems.' In J. P. Vincent (Ed.), *Advances in Family Intervention, Assessment and Theory*. vol. 2. Greenwich, CT: JAI Press.

Martin, D. (1976). *Battered Wives*. New York: Pocket Books.

Matsuura, M., Okubo,Y., Kojima, T., Takahashi, R., Wang Y.-F., Shen Y.-C & Lee, C. K. (1993). 'A cross-national prevalence study of children with emotional and behavioural problems—a WHO collaborative study in the Western Pacific Region.' *Journal of Child Psychology and Psychiatry*, **34** (3), 307–315.

Mattox, W. R. (1991). 'The parent trap.' *Policy Review*, **55**, 6–13.

Maughan, B. & Pickles, A. (1990). 'Adopted and illegitimate children growing up.' In L. Robins & M. Rutter (Eds), *Straight and Devious Pathways from Childhood to Adulthood*. Cambridge: Cambridge University Press.

Mejiuni, C. O. (1991). 'Educating adults against socioculturally induced abuse and neglect of children in Nigeria.' *Child Abuse and Neglect*, **15**, 139–145.

Meng, Q. (1994). *Frequency and intensity of child abuse and neglect in Shandong, China. Findings from a sampling study*. The tenth International Congress on Child Abuse and Neglect, Kuala Lumpur, Abstracts: page 136.

Meyer-Lindenberg, J. (1991). 'The Holocaust and German psychiatry.' *British Journal of Psychiatry*, **159**, 7–12.

Miller, B. (1987). 'Female infanticide and child neglect in rural North India.' In N. Scheper-Hughes (Ed.), *Child Survival*. Dordrecht: Reidel Publishing.

Miller, K., Fein, E., Howe, G. W., Gaudio, C. P. & Bishop, G. V. (1984). 'Time-limited, goal-focused, parent aide service.' *Social Casework*, **65**, (8) 472–477.

Milner, J. S. (1986). *The Child Abuse Potential Inventory: Manual* (2nd edn). Webster, NV: Psytec Corporation.

Milner, J. (1988). 'An ego-strength scale for the Child Abuse Potential Inventory.' *Journal of Family Violence*, **3**, 151–162.

Minturn, L. (1982). 'Changes in the differential treatment of Rajput girls and boys.' *Behavior Science Research*, **17** (1–2), 70–90.

Minturn, L. & Lambert, W. (1964). *Mothers of Six Cultures. Antecedents of child rearing*. Chichester: John Wiley.

Moore, M., Meredith, P. & Goldberg, A. (1977). 'A retrospective analysis of blood-lead in mentally retarded children.' *The Lancet*, **2**, April, **1** (No. 8014), 717–719.

Moorehead, C. (1989). *Betrayal. Child Exploitation in Today's World*. London: Barrie & Jenkins.

Morely, R. & Mullender, A. (1994). *Preventing domestic violence to women*. Home Office Police Research Group Paper 48.

Morrison, J. & Stewart, M. (1973). 'The psychiatric status of the legal families of adopted hyperactive children.' *Archives of General Psychiatry*, **28**, 888–891.

Morrison, G. M., Furlong, M. J. & Smith, G. (1994). 'Factors associated with the experience of school violence among general education, leadership class, opportunity class and special day class pupils.' 17th Annual Conference of Teacher Educators for Children with Behavior Disorders, Tempe, Arizona. *Education and Treatment of Children*, **17** (3), 356–369.

Mortimore, J. & Blackstone, T. (1982). *Disadvantage and Education*. SSRC/DHSS Studies in Deprivation and Disadvantage. London: Heinemann Educational Books.

Mountjoy, P. (1974). 'Some early attempts to modify penile erection in horse and human.' *Psychological Record*, **24**, 291–308.

Mtezuka, M. (1989). 'Toward a better understanding of child sexual abuse among Asian communities.' *Practice*, **3 & 4**, 248–260.

Mullen, P. E., Martin, L. J., Anderson, J. C., Romans, S. E., & Herbison, G. P. (1996). 'The long-term impact of the physical, emotional and sexual abuse of children. A community study.' *Child Abuse and Neglect*, **20** (1), 7–21.

Munir, A. (1993). 'Child protection: Principles and applications.' *Child Abuse Review*, **2**, 119–126.

Murie, A. (1982) *Housing Inequality and Deprivation*. SSRC/DHSS Studies in Deprivation and Disadvantage. London: Heinemann Educational Books.

Murphy, S., Orkow, B. & Nicola, R. (1985). 'Prenatal prediction of child abuse and neglect. A prospective study.' *Child Abuse and Neglect*, **9**, 225–235.

Nagi, S. Z. (1977). *Child Maltreatment in the United States*. New York: Columbia University Press.

National Children's Bureau (1992). *Children Now*. London: The Children's Society/National Children's Bureau.

National Conference of State Legislatures (1989). *Family Policy. Recommendations for State Action*. Denver: National Conference of State Legislatures.

National Research Council (1993). *Understanding Child Abuse and Neglect*. Washington, DC: National Academy Press.

National Resource Center on Family Based Services (1986). *Annotated Directory of Selected Family-Based Service Programs*. School of Social Work, University of Iowa.

Needleman, H. (1979). 'Deficits in psychological and classroom performance of children with elevated dentine lead levels.' *New England Journal of Medicine*, **300**, 689–695.

Nelson, B. (1984). *Making an Issue of Child Abuse: Political Agenda Setting for Social Problems*. Chicago: University of Chicago Press.

Nelson, K. E., Landsman, M. J. & Deutelbaum, W. (1990). 'Three models of family-centred placement prevention services.' *Child Welfare*, **LXIX** (1), 3–21.

Newberger, C. M. (1977). 'Parental conceptions of children and child-rearing. A structural developmental analysis.' Unpublished doctoral dissertation, Harvard University, Cambridge, MA.

Newberger, C. M. (1980). 'The cognitive structure of parenthood. The development of a descriptive measure.' In R. Selman & R. Yando (Eds), *New Directions of Child Development: Clinical Developmental Research*. San Francisco: Jossey-Bass.

Newberger, C. M. & Cook, S. J. (1986). 'Becoming the parent: the development of conceptions of parenthood during childhood and adolescence.' Unpublished manuscript, Boston, MA, quoted in Newberger & White (1989).

Newberger, C. M. & White, K. M. (1989). 'Cognitive foundations for parental care.' In D. Cicchetti & V. Carlson (Eds), *Child Maltreatment*. Cambridge: University of Cambridge Press.

Newberger, E. (1985). 'The helping hand strikes again. Unintended consequences of child abuse reporting.' In E. Newberger & R. Bourne (Eds), *Unhappy Families*. Littleton, MA: PSG Publishing.

New South Wales Child Protection Council (1995). *Child Protection in Non-English-Speaking Background Communities. Culture—No Excuse*. NSW Child Protection Council, Level 4, Remington Centre, 169–183 Liverpool Street, Sydney, NSW 2000, Australia.

Newell, P. (1989). *Children are People too*. London: Bedford Square Press.

Newell, P. (1991). *The UN Convention & Children's Rights in the UK*. London: National Children's Bureau/Calouste Gulbenkian Foundation.

Newell, P. (1992). Introduction, in Radda Barnen Organisation, *Ending Physical Punishment of European Children*. London: Epoch Worldwide.

Newson, J. & Newson, E. (1965). *Patterns of Infant Care in an Urban Community*: Harmondsworth: Penguin Books.

Newth, S. J., & Corbett, J. (1993). 'Behaviour and emotional problems in three-year-old children of Asian parentage.' *Journal of Child Psychology and Psychiatry*, **34** (3), 333–352.

Nicol, A. R., Smith, J., Kay, B., Hall, D., Barlow, J. & Williams, B. (1988). 'A focused casework approach to the treatment of child abuse. A controlled comparison.' Unpublished report quoted in D. Gough (1993), *Child Abuse Interventions*. London: HMSO.

Noble, M. & Smith, T. (1994). 'Children in need: Using geographical information systems to inform strategic planning for social service provision.' *Children and Society*, **8** (4), 360–376.

Nunno, M. & Rindfleisch, N. (1991). 'The abuse of children in out-of-home care.' *Children and Society*, **5** (4), 295–305.

Obikeze, D. S. (1984). 'Perspectives on child abuse in Nigeria.' *International Child Welfare Review*, **63**, 25–32.

O'Brian, C. & Lau, L. (1995). 'Defining child abuse in Hong Kong.' *Child Abuse Review*, **4**, 28–46.

O'Connor, S., Vietze, P., Sherrod, K., Sandler, H. & Altemeier, W. I. (1980). 'Reduced incidence of parenting inadequacy following rooming in.' *Pediatrics*, **66**, 176–162.

O'Grady, R. (1994a). *The Rape of the Innocent*. Published by End Child Prostitution in Asian Tourism (ECPAT) Thailand, in association with Pace Publishing, Auckland, New Zealand.

O'Grady, R. (1994). 'Ending the prostitution of Asian children.' Paper to the tenth International Congress on Child Abuse and Neglect, ISPCAN.

Olds, D. L. & Henderson, R. (1989). 'The prevention of maltreatment.' In D. Cicchetti & V. Carlson (Eds), *Child Maltreatment*. Cambridge: Cambridge University Press.

O'Leary, D. (1993). 'Through a psychological lens: Personality traits, personality disorders and levels of violence.' In R. Gelles & D. Loseke (Eds), *Current Controversies on Family Violence*. Newbury Park, CA: Sage.

O'Leary, K. & Emery, R. (1983). 'Marital discord and child behaviour problems.' In M. Levine and P. Satz (Eds), *Developmental Variations and Dysfunction*. New York: Academic Press.

Oliver, J. E. (1993). 'Intergenerational child abuse. Rates, research and clinical implications.' *American Journal of Psychiatry*, **150** (9), 1315–1325.

Oliver, J. E. & Buchanan, A. (1979). 'Generations of maltreated children and multiagency care in one kindred.' *British Journal of Psychiatry*, **135**, 289–303.

Oliver, J. E. & Cox, J. (1973). 'The family kindred of ill-used children. The burden on the community.' *British Journal of Psychiatry*, **123** (572), 81–90.

Oliver, J. E., Cox, J. M., Taylor, A. & Baldwin, J. (1974). *Severely ill-treated young children in North East Wiltshire*. Oxford Regional Linkage Study. Oxford University Unit of Clinical Epidemiology, ORLS Research Report 4, Oxford RHA.

Oliver, J. E. & Dewhurst, K. E. (1969). 'Six generations of ill-used children in a Huntington's pedigree.' *Postgraduate Medical Journal*, **45**, 757–760.

Oliver, J. E. & Taylor, A. (1971). 'Five generations of ill-treated children in one family pedigree.' *British Journal of Psychiatry*, **119** (552), 473–480.

Open University (1992). 'The pre-school child.' Milton Keynes, UK: Open University.

O'Toole, R., Turbett, T. P. & Nalepka, C. (1983). 'Theories, professional knowledge and diagnosis of child abuse.' In D. Finkelhor, R. Gelles, G. Hotaling & M. Straus (Eds) *The Dark Side of Families: Current Violence Research*. Newbury Park, CA: Sage.

Ounsted, C., Oppenheimer, R. & Lindsay, J. (1974). 'Aspects of bonding failure: The psychopathology and psychotherapeutic treatment of battered children.' *Developmental Medicine and Child Neurology*, **16**, 447.

Packman, J., Randall, J. & Jacques, N. (1986). *Who Needs Care? Social Work Decisions about Children.* Oxford: Basil Blackwell.

Pagelow, M. (1981). *Women-battering: Victims and their Experiences.* Newbury Park, CA: Sage.

Pancoast, A. S. (1980). 'Finding and enlisting neighbors to support families.' In J. Garbarino & S. Stocking (Eds), *Protecting Children from Abuse and Neglect.* San Francisco: Jossey-Bass.

Parton, N. (1985). *The Politics of Child Abuse.* London and Basingstoke: Macmillan.

Pecora, P. J., Whittaker, J. K. & Maluccio, A. N. (1992). *The Child Welfare Challenge: Policy, Practice and Research.* New York: Aldine de Gruyter.

Perlez, J. (1990) In AIDS-stricken Uganda area, the orphans struggle to survive. *New York Times,* 10 June, p. 41. Cited in Kramer, M. (1992). 'Barriers to primary prevention.' In G. W. Albee, L. Bond, & T. Cook Monsey (Eds), *Improving Children's Lives. Global Perspectives on Prevention.* Newbury Park, CA: Sage.

Petrie, C. & Garner, J. (1990). 'Is violence preventable?' In D. J. Besharov (Ed.), *Family Violence: Research and Public Policy Issues.* (pp. 164–184). Washington, DC: AEI Press.

Phillips, D., McCartney, K. & Scarr, S. (1987). 'Child-care quality and children's social development.' *Developmental Psychology,* **23** (4), 537–543.

Pianta, R., Egeland, B. & Erickson, M. (1989). 'The antecedent of maltreatment: Results of the Mother–Child Interaction Research Project.' In D. Cicchetti & V. Carlson (Eds), *Child Maltreatment.* Cambridge: University of Cambridge Press.

Pizzey, E. (1974). *Scream Quietly or the Neighbours Will Hear.* Harmondsworth: Penguin Books.

Plomin, R. (1992). Series Editor Preface, in T. D. Wachs, *The Nature of Nurture.* Newbury Park, CA: Sage.

Plomin, R. (1994a). *Genetics and Experience. The Interplay between Nature and Nurture.* Newbury Park, CA: Sage.

Plomin, R. (1994b). 'The Emmanuel Miller Memorial Lecture 1993: Genetic research and identification of environmental influences.' *Journal of Child Psychology and Psychiatry,* **35** (5), 817–835.

Powell, D. (1987). 'Methodological and conceptual issues in research.' In S. Kagan, D. Powell, B. Weissbound & E. Sigler (Eds), *America's Family Support Programs: Perspectives and Prospects.* New Haven, CT: Yale University Press.

Powell, D. F. (1993). 'Supporting parent–child relationships in the early years. Lessons learned and yet to be learned.' In R. H. Brubaker (Ed.), *Family Relations—Challenges for the Future.* Newbury Park, CA: Sage.

Power, C. (1992). 'A review of child health in the 1958 birth cohort: National Child Development Study.' *Paediatric and Perinatal Epidemiology,* **6**, 81–110.

Power, C., Manor, O. & Fox, A. (1991). *Health and Class: The Early Years.* London: Chapman & Hall.

Pugh, G., Aplin, G., De'Ath, E. & Moxon, M. (1987). *Partnership in Action. Working with Parents in Preschool Centre.* London: National Children's Bureau.

Pugh, G. & De'Ath, E. (1985). *The Needs of Parents.* London: Macmillan.

Pyle, J. (1990). 'Export lead development and the under employment of women: the impact of discriminatory development policy in the Republic of Ireland.' In K. Ward (Ed.), *Women Workers and Global Restructuring.* Cornell University, Ithaca, NY: ILR Press.

Quinton, D. & Rutter, M. (1984). 'Parents with children in care: Current circumstances, and parenting.' *Journal of Child Psychology and Psychiatry,* **25**, 231–250.

Quinton, D., Rutter, M. & Liddle, C. (1984). 'Institutional rearing, parenting difficulties and marital support.' *Psychological Medicine,* **14**, 107–124.

Rabb, J. & Rindfleisch, N. (1985). 'A study to define and assess severity of institutional abuse/neglect.' *Child Abuse and Neglect,* **9**, 285–294.

Radbill, S. (1968). 'A history of child abuse and infanticide.' In R. Helfer & C. Kempe (Eds), *The Battered Child.* Chicago: University of Chicago Press.

Radio Times (1991). Anonymous letter . . . 'I deeply resent . . .' London: *Radio Times.*

Radulian, V. (1992). *Aspects of the Situation of the Romanian Children in 1992.* Keynote address at the second assembly of the world alliance of Christian Children's Fund in Bucharest, 11 May 1992.

Reder, P., Duncan, S. & Geray, M. (1993). 'A new look at child abuse tragedies.' *Child Abuse Review,* **2**, 89–100.

Reid, A. (1984). 'Cultural difference and child abuse intervention with undocumented Spanish-speaking families in Los Angeles.' *Child Abuse and Neglect,* **8**, 109–112.

Reid. J., Taplin, P. & Lorber, R. (1981). 'A social interactional approach to the treatment of abusive families.' In R. Stuart (Ed.), *Violent Behaviour: Social Learning Approaches to Prediction, Management and Treatment.* New York: Brunner/Mazel.

Reppucci, N. D. & Aber, M. S. (1992). 'Child maltreatment prevention and the legal system.' In D. J. Willis, E. W. Holden & M. Rosenberg (Eds), *Prevention of Child Maltreatment.* New York: John Wiley.

Resnick, G. (1985). 'Enhancing parental competencies for high-risk mothers: An evaluation of prevention efforts.' *Child Abuse and Neglect,* **9** (4), 479–489.

Richards, M. (1974). 'First steps in becoming social.' In *The Integration of a Child into the Social World.* Cambridge: Cambridge University Press.

Richman, N. (1976). 'Depression in mothers of pre-school children.' *Journal of Child Psychology and Psychiatry,* **17**, 75–78.

Richman, N. (1977). 'Behavioural problems in preschool children: family and social factors.' *British Journal of Psychiatry,* **131**, 523–527.

Richman, N. (1993). 'Children in situations of political violence.' *Journal of Child Psychology and Psychiatry,* **34** (8), 1286–1302.

Ricks, M. (1985). 'The social inheritance of parenting: Attachment across generations.' In I. Bretherton and E. Walters (Eds), *New directions for attachment research.* Monograph of the Society for Research in Child Development.

Rindfleisch, N. & Hicho, D. (1987). 'Institutional child protection: Issues in program development and implementation.' *Child Welfare,* **66**, 329–342.

Rivers, I. & Smith, P. K. (1994). 'Types of bullying and their correlates.' *Aggressive Behaviour,* **20** (5), 259–368.

Roberts, J. (1988). 'Why are some families more vulnerable to child abuse?' In K. Browne, C. Davies & P. Stratton (Eds), *Early Prediction and Prevention of Child Abuse.* Chichester: John Wiley.

Robin, M. (1982). 'Historical introduction. Sheltering arms: The roots of child protection.' In E. Newberger (Ed.), *Child Abuse.* Boston: Little Brown.

Robins, L. & Rutter, M. (1990). Introduction, in L. Robins & M. Rutter (Eds), *Straight and Devious Pathways from Childhood to Adulthood.* Cambridge: Cambridge University Press.

Rohner, R. & Rohner, E. (1980). 'Antecedents and consequences of parental rejection: A theory of emotional abuse.' *Child Abuse and Neglect,* **4**, 189–198.

Rosenbaum, M. (1993) *Children and the Environment.* London: National Children's Bureau.

Rosenberg, M. S. & Sonkin, D. J. (1992). 'The prevention of child maltreatment in school-age children.' In D. J. Willis, E. W. Holden, & M. Rosenberg (Eds), *The Prevention of Child Maltreatment.* New York: John Wiley.

Rosenstein, P. J. (1978). 'Family outreach: A program for the prevention of child abuse and neglect.' *Child Welfare*, **57** (8), 519–525.

Rosenthal, M. & Louis, J. (1981). 'The law's evolving role in child abuse and neglect.' In L. Pelton (Ed.), *The Social Context of Child Abuse and Neglect* (pp. 55–89). New York: Human Sciences Press.

Ross, C. & Zigler, E. (1980). 'An agenda for action.' In G. Gerbner, C. Ross & E. Zigler (Eds), *Child Abuse: An Agenda for Action* (pp. 293–304). New York: Oxford University Press.

Roth, H. J. (1985). 'Relationships between attendance at a Parents-Anonymous adult program and children's behaviour at the Parents-Anonymous child care program.' *Children and Youth Services Review*, **7** (19), 39–43.

Rowe, J. (1988). *Child Care Outcomes: A Research and Demonstration Project*. London: British Agencies for Adoption and Fostering.

Rowe, J. & Lambert, L. (1973). *Children Who Wait*. London: Association of British Adoption Agencies.

Rush, F. (1981). *The Best Kept Secret*. Englewood Cliffs, NJ: Prentice-Hall.

Rutter, M. (1971). 'Parent–child separation: Psychological effects on children.' *Journal of Child Psychology and Psychiatry*, **12**, 233–260.

Rutter, M. (1979). 'Protective factors in children's responses to stress and disadvantages.' In M. W. Kent & J. E. Rolf (Eds), *Primary Prevention of Psychopathology III: Social Competence in Children* (pp. 49–74). Hanover, NH: University Press of New England.

Rutter, M. (1980). *Changing Youth in a Changing Society*. London: Nuffield University Trust.

Rutter, M. (1981). *Maternal Deprivation Reassessed*. Harmondsworth: Penguin Books.

Rutter, M. (1984). 'Continuities and discontinuities in socio-emotional development: Empirical and conceptual perspectives.' In R. Emde & R. Harmon (Eds), *Continuities and Discontinuities in Development*. New York: Plenum.

Rutter, M. (1989). 'Intergenerational continuities and discontinuities in serious parenting difficulties.' In D. Cicchetti & V. Carlson (Eds), *Child Maltreatment*. Cambridge: Cambridge University Press.

Rutter, M. (1995). 'Causal concepts and their testing.' In M. Rutter & D. Smith (Eds), *Psychosocial Disorders in Young People. Time Trends and their Causes*. Chichester: John Wiley.

Rutter, M., Bolton, P., Harrington, R., Le Couteur, A., Macdonald, H. & Simonoff, E. (1990). 'Genetic Factors in Child Psychiatric Disorders I: A review of research strategies.' *Journal of Child Psychology and Psychiatry*, **31**(1), 3–37.

Rutter, M. & Giller, H. (1983). *Juvenile Delinquency: Trends and Perspectives*. Harmondsworth: Penguin Books.

Rutter, M., Graham, P., Chadwick, O. F. D. & Yule, W. (1976). 'Adolescent turmoil: Fact or fiction?' *Journal of Child Psychology and Psychiatry*, **17**, 35–36.

Rutter, M., Graham, P. & Yule, W. (1970). *A Neuropsychiatric Study in Childhood* (Clinics in Developmental Medicine, Nos 35–36). London: Spastics International Medical Publications/Heinemann Medical Books.

Rutter, M., Macdonald, H., Le Couteur, A., Harrington, R., Bolton, P. & Bailey, A. (1990). 'Genetic factors in child psychiatric disorders II: Empirical findings.' *Journal of Child Psychology and Psychiatry*, **31** (1), 39–83.

Rutter, M. & Madge, N. (1976). *Cycles of Disadvantage. A Review of Research*. SSRC/ DHSS Studies in Deprivation and Disadvantage, No. 1. London: Heinemann Educational Books.

Rutter, M. & Quinton, D. (1984). 'Long-term follow-up of women institutionalised in childhood. Factors promoting good function in adult life.' *British Journal of Developmental Psychology*, **2**, 191–204.

Rutter, M., Quinton, D. & Liddle, C. (1983). 'Parenting in two generations: Looking backwards and looking forwards.' In N. Madge (Ed.), *Families at Risk*. SSRC/DHSS Studies in Deprivation and Disadvantage, No. 8. London: Heinemann Educational Books.

Rutter, M. & Rutter, M. (1993). *Developing Minds: Challenge and Continuity Across the Lifespan*. Harmondsworth: Penguin Books; New York: Basic Books.

Rutter, M. & Smith, D. (Eds) (1995). *Psychosocial Disorders in Young People. Time Trends and their Causes*. Chichester: John Wiley.

Rutter, M., Tizard, J., Yule, W., Graham P. & Whitmore, K. (Eds) (1976). 'Research report. Isle of Wight studies 1964–74.' *Psychological Medicine*, **6**, 313–332.

Ryklief, F. (1994). *Parent Education and Support in South Africa*. Proceedings of the tenth International Congress on Child Abuse and Neglect, Kuala Lumpur, Malaysia.

Rzepnicki, T., Schuerman, J. R., Littel, J. H., Chak, A. & Lopez, M. (1994). 'An experimental study of family preservation services: Early findings from a parent survey.' In R. Barth, J. D. Berrick & N. Gilbert. *Child Welfare Research*. New York: University of Columbia Press.

Safer, D. J. (1973). 'A familial factor in minimal brain dysfunction.' *Behaviour Genetics*, **3**, 175–186.

Sameroff, A. & Chandler, M. (1975). 'Reproductive risk and the continuum of caretaking causality.' In F. Horowitz (Ed.), *Review of Child Development Research* (Vol. 4). Chicago, IL: University of Chicago Press.

Sameroff, A. J., & Seifer, R. (1992). 'Early contributors to developmental risk.' In J. Rolf, A. Masten, D. Cicchetti, K. Nuechterlein & S. Weintraub (Eds), *Risk and Protective Factors in the Development of Psychopathology*. Cambridge: Cambridge University Press.

Scaife, J. & Frith, J. (1988). 'A behaviour management and life stress course for a group of mothers incorporating training for health visitors.' *Child Care, Health and Development*, **14**, 25–50.

Scarr, S. (1981). *IQ, Race, Social Class, and Individual Differences. New Studies on Old Issues*. Hillsdale, NY: Lawrence Erlbaum.

Scarr, S. & McCartney, K. (1983). 'How people make their own environments: A theory of genotype-environmental effects.' *Child Development*, **54**, 424–435.

Schellenbach, C. & Guerney, L. (1987). Identification of adolescent abuse and future intervention prospects.' *Journal of Adolescence*, **10**, 1–12.

Scheper-Hughes, N. (1987). 'The cultural politics of child survival.' In N. Scheper-Hughes (Ed.), *Child Survival*. Dordrecht: D. Reidel.

Scheper-Hughes, N. & Stein, H. (1987). 'Child abuse and the unconscious in American popular culture.' In N. Scheper-Hughes (Ed.), *Child Survival*. Dordrecht: D. Reidel.

Schiff, M. & Lewontin, R. (1986). *Education and Class: the Relevance of IQ Genetic Studies*. Oxford: Clarendon Press.

Schinke, S. P., Schilling, R. F. & Barth, R. P. (1986). 'Stress-management intervention to prevent family violence.' *Journal of Family Violence*, **1** (1), 13–26.

Schmitt, B. & Kempe, C. (1975). 'Neglect and abuse of children.' In V. Vaughan and R. McKay (Eds), *Nelson Textbook of Pediatrics*. Philadelphia: W.B. Saunders.

Schnapper, D. (1992). *L'Europe des Immigrés*. Paris: Editions François Bourin.

Schneider-Rosen, K., Brauwald, K. G., Carlson, V. & Cicchetti, D. (1985). 'Current perspectives in attachment theory: Illustrations from the study of maltreated infants.' In I. Bretherton & E. Waters (Eds), *Monographs of the Society for Research in Child Development*, **55**, 648–658.

Schultz, L. G. (1988). 'One hundred cases of wrongfully charged child sexual abuse: A survey and recommendations.' Unpublished manuscript, West Virginia University, School of Social Work, Morgantown.

Schwebel, M. (1992). 'Making a dangerous world more tolerable for children. Implications of research on reactions to nuclear war, threat, war and disaster.' In G. Albee, L. Bond & T. Cook Monsey (Eds), *Improving Children's Lives. Global Perspectives on Prevention*. Newbury Park CA: Sage.

Schweinhart, L. J. & Weikart, D. (1993). *A Summary of Significant Benefits: The High/Scope Perry Pre-School Study through Age 27*. Ypsilanti, MI: High/Scope Press.

Sedlak, A. (1991). *Study Findings,: Study of National Incidence and Prevalence of Child Abuse and Neglect 1988*. Washington, DC: US Department of Health and Human Services.

Seligman, M. (1975). *Helplessness: On Depression, Development and Death*. San Francisco: Freeman.

Senate Office of Research (1990). *California's Drug Exposed Babies. Undiscovered, Unreported, Undeserved*. Sacramento: SOR.

Sharland, E., Seal, H., Croucher, M., Aldgate, J. & Jones, D. (1993). *Professional Intervention in Child Sexual Abuse*. Report to the Department of Health, Department of Applied Social Studies and Research, University of Oxford (Studies in Child Protection: to be published shortly by HMSO).

Sharpe, P. (1994). 'A study of some home and school factors which influence the social behaviour of some preschoolers in Singapore.' *Early Child Development and Care*, **104**, 23–33.

Shay, S. (1980). 'Community council for child abuse prevention.' In R. Helfer & C. H. Kempe (Eds), *The Battered Child*. Chicago: University of Chicago Press.

Sheppard, M. (1994). 'Maternal depression in child care: A review and bibliography.' *British Journal of Social Work*, **24** (3), 287–310.

Sherbini, F., Hamman, H., Omran, A., Torky, M. & Fahmy, S. (1981). 'Egypt.' In A. R. Omran, C. C. Standley, G. Ochoa, A. Gil, H. Hamman, F. Sherbini, B. Raza, T. Khan & F. Boustani (Eds), *Family Formation Patterns and Health:* Further Studies (pp. 153–164). Geneva: World Health Organisation.

Sheridan, M. J. (1995). 'A proposed intergenerational model of substance abuse, family functioning and abuse/neglect.' *Child Abuse and Neglect*, **19** (5), 519–530.

Simeonsson, R. (1994). 'Implications.' In R. Simeonsson (Ed.), *Risk, Resilience and Prevention*. Baltimore, MD: Brookes Publishing.

Simeonsson, R. & Thomas, D. (1994). 'Promoting children's well-being, priorities and principles.' In R. Simeonsson (Ed.), *Risk, Resilience and Prevention*. Baltimore, MD: Brookes Publishing.

Singapore Children's Society (1994). 'Singapore's Family Values.' *Newsletter of Singapore Children's Society*, Issue 2, p. 1.

Singhanetra-Renard, A., Chaparnond, P., Tiyayon, P. & Prabudhanitisarn, N. (1988). *Economics and the dynamics of recruitment for international contract labor*. Chiangmai University, Faculty of Social Sciences Abstracts.

Sirivardana, S. (1992). *Five stories. The Poor are Rich*. Janasaviya Commissioner's Department, 17A Barnes Place, Colombo 7, Sri Lanka.

Slater, E. (1936). 'German eugenics in practice.' *Eugenics Review*, **27**, 285–295.

Sluckin, A. (1981). 'Behavioural social work with encopretic children, their families and the school.' *Child Care, Health and Development*, **7**, 67–80.

Sluckin, W., Herbert, M. & Sluckin, A. (1983). *Maternal Bonding*. Oxford: Blackwell.

Smalley, C. (1994). 'Partnership and child health.' In A. Buchanan (Ed.). *Partnership in Practice: The Children Act 1989*. Aldershot: Avebury.

Smallwood, G. (1994). *Violence, child abuse and neglect amongst indigenous Australians since colonisation*. C. Henry Kempe Memorial Lecture, tenth International Congress on Child Abuse and Neglect, Kuala Lumpur, Malaysia.

Smith, D. J. & Rutter, M. (1995). 'Time trends in psychosocial disorders of youth.' In M. Rutter & D. J. Smith (Eds), *Psychosocial Disorders in Young People*. Chichester: John Wiley.

Smith, J. & Rachman, S. (1984). 'Non-accidental injury to children. II—A controlled evaluation of a behaviour management programme.' *Behaviour Research and Therapy*, **22** (4), 349–366.

Smith, P. B. & Bond Harris, M. (1993). *Social Psychology Across Cultures. Analysis and Perspectives*. London: Harvester Wheatsheaf.

Smith, S. & Hanson, R. (1974). '134 battered children: a medical and psychological study.' *British Medical Journal*, **3**, 666–670.

Smith, T. (1995). *Family Centres and Bringing Up Young Children*. London: HMSO.

Social Science Research Council (SSRC) and Department of Health and Social Security (DHSS) (1976–1983). *Studies in Deprivation and Disadvantage*. London: Heinemann Educational Books.

Sonuga-Barke, E. (1994). 'Annotation: On dysfunction and function in psychological theories of childhood disorder.' *Journal of Child Psychology and Psychiatry*, **35** (5), 801–815.

Spakes, P. (1985). 'The supreme court, family policy and alternative family lifestyles: The clash of interests.' *Lifestyles: A Journal of Changing Patterns*, **7** (3), 170–186.

Spearly, L. J. & Lauderdale, M. (1983). 'Community characteristics and ethnicity in the prediction of child maltreatment rates.' *Child Abuse and Neglect*, **7**, 91–105.

Sroufe, L. A. (1983). 'Infant-caregiver attachment and patterns of adaption in preschool. The roots of maladaptation and competence.' In M. Permutter (Ed.), *Minnesota Symposium on Child Development*, **16**, 41–83. Hillsdale, NJ: Erlbaum.

Sroufe, L. A. (1988). 'The role of infant-caregiver attachment in development.' In J. Belsky and T. Nezworski (Eds), *Clinical Implications of Attachment*. Hillsdale, NJ: Erlbaum.

Stacey, M., Dearden, R., Pill, R. & Robinson, D. (1970). *Hospital, children and their families: The report of a pilot study*. London: Routledge.

Stainton Rogers, R. (1989). 'The social construction of childhood.' In W. Stainton Rogers, D. Hevey & E. Ash (Eds), *Child Abuse and Neglect*. Batsford: Open University

Stark, W. (1992). 'Empowerment and social change: Health promotion with the Healthy Cities Project of WHO.' In G. Albee, L. Bond & T. C. Monsey (Eds), *Improving Children's Lives. Global Perspectives on Prevention*. Newbury Park, CA: Sage.

Stark, E. & Flitcraft, A. (1985). 'Women-battering, child abuse and social heredity: What is the relationship?' *Sociological Review Monograph*, **31**, 147–171.

Starr, R. H. (1987). 'Clinical judgement of abuse proneness based on parent–child interactions.' *Child Abuse and Neglect*, **11**, 87–92.

Starr, R. (1988). 'Physical abuse of children.' In V. Van Hasselt, R. Morrison, A. Bellack & M. Hersen (Eds), *Handbook of Family Violence*. New York: Plenum.

Statham, J. & Brophy, J. (1992). 'Using the Early Childhood Development Rating Scale in Playgroups.' *Educational Research*, **34** (2), 141–148.

Steele, B. F. & Pollock, C. B. (1968). 'A psychiatric study of parents who abuse infants and small children.' In R. E. Helfer & C. H. Kempe (Eds), *The Battered Child*. Chicago: University of Chicago Press.

Stein, T. J. (1984). 'The Child Abuse Prevention and Treatment Act.' *Social Services Review*, **58**, 302–314.

Steinhausen, H.-C., Willms, J. & Spohr, H.-L. (1994). 'Correlates of psychopathology and intelligence in children with Fetal Alcohol Syndrome.' *Journal of Child Psychology and Psychiatry*, **35**, 323–331.

Stevenson, J. (1987). *A feasible intervention in families with parenting difficulties: A primary preventive perspective on child abuse*. Paper presented at Conference on

Early Prediction and Prevention of Child Abuse and Neglect, Society for Reproductive and Infant Psychology, Leicester, UK, March 1987.

Straus, M. A. (1979). 'Family patterns and child abuse in a nationally representative sample.' *Child Abuse and Neglect*, **3**, 213–225.

Straus, M. (1980). 'Wife beating: How common and why?' In M. Straus & G. Hotaling (Eds), *The Social Causes of Husband–Wife Violence*. University of Minnesota Press.

Straus, M. A. (1983). 'Ordinary violence, child abuse and wife-beating. What do they have in common?' In D. Finkelhor, R. Gelles, G. Hotaling & M. Straus (Eds), *The Dark Side of Families: Current Family Violence Research*. Newbury Park, CA: Sage.

Straus, M. A., Gelles, R. J. & Steinmetz, S. K. (1988). (First published in 1980) *Behind Closed Doors: Violence in the American Family*. Newbury Park, CA: Sage.

Straus, M. & Hotaling, G. (Eds) (1980). *The Social Causes of Husband–Wife Violence*. University of Minnesota Press.

Sverne, T. (1992). 'The Swedish ban on physical punishment.' In *Ending Physical Punishment of European Children*. London: Radda Barnen/Epoch Worldwide.

Swarup, N. & Hayden, C. (1994). 'Partnership with black and minority ethnic communities.' In A. Buchanan (Ed.), *Partnership in Practice. The Children Act 1989*. Aldershot, Avebury.

Szasz, T. (1970). *Ideology and Insanity*. Harmondsworth: Penguin Books.

Szykula, S. & Fleischman, M. (1985). 'Reducing out-of-home placements of abused children—two controlled field studies.' *Child Abuse and Neglect*, **9** (2), 277–283.

Talbott, G. D. (1991). 'Alcoholism and other drug addictions. A primary disease entity.' 1991 update. *Journal of the Medical Association of Georgia*, June, 337–342.

Tatara, T. (1989). 'Characteristics of children in foster care.' *Newsletter of the Division of Child, Youth, and Family Services*, **12** (3), 3–16, 17.

Tatara, T. (1994). 'The recent rise in the US child substitute care population.' In R. Barth, H. Berrick & N. Gilbert (Eds), *Child Welfare Research*. New York: Columbia University Press.

Tarter, R. E., Alterman, A. E. & Edwards, K. L. (1985). 'Vulnerability to alcoholism in men: A behavior-genetic perspective.' *Journal of Studies in Alcoholism*, **46**, 329–356.

Telleen, S., Herzog, A. & Kilbrane, T. (1989). 'Impact of family support programs on mother's social support and parenting stress.' *American Journal of Orthopsychiatry*, **59** (3), 410–419.

Thanki, V. (1994). 'Ethnic diversity and child protection.' *Children and Society*, **8** (3), 232–244.

Thomas, A., Chess, S. & Birch, H. G. (1968). *Temperament and Behavior Disorders in Children*. New York: Brunner/Mazel.

Thorburn, J., Lewis, A. & Shemmings, D. (1995). *Paternalism or Partnership? Family Involvement in the Child Protection Process*. London: HMSO.

Thorburn, J., Murdoch, A. & O'Brien, A. (1986). *Permanence in Child Care*. Oxford: Basil Blackwell.

Tiernari, P., Lahti, I., Sorri, A., Naarala, M., Moring, J., Kaleva, M., Wahlberg, K.-E. & Wynne, L. (1990). 'Adopted-away offspring of schizophrenics and controls: The Finnish adoptive family study of schizophrenia.' In L. Robins & M. Rutter (Eds), *Straight and Devious Pathways from Childhood to Adulthood*. Cambridge: Cambridge University Press.

Time Magazine (1994). 'Battle fatigue. Scant hope emerges from this year's AIDS meeting.' *Time Magazine* 22 August, p. 40.

Titmuss, R. (1974). *Social Policy, An Introduction*. London: Allen & Unwin.

Trevor-Roper, H. (1985). 'Seas of unreason. Review of "Todliche Wissenschaft Die Aussonderung von Juden, Zigeunern und Geisteskranken 1933–1945" by Muller-Hill, B.' *Nature*, **313**, 407–408.

Trickett, P. K. & Susman, E. J. (1989). 'Perceived similarities and disagreements about childrearing practices in abusive and nonabusive families.' In D. Cicchetti & V. Carlson (Eds), *Child Maltreatment*. Cambridge: University of Cambridge Press.

Turbett, J. & O'Toole, R. (1980). *Physician's Recognition of Child Abuse.* Paper presented at the annual meeting of the American Sociological Association, New York.

Tyler, F. B., Tyler, S. L., Tommasello, A., Connolly, M. R. (1992). 'Huckleberry Finn and street youth everywhere: An approach to primary prevention.' In G. Albee, L. Bond, & T. Cook Monsey (Eds), *Improving Children's Lives, Global Perspectives on Prevention*. Newbury Park, CA: Sage.

Ulbrich, P. & Huber, J. (1981). Observing parental violence: Distribution and effects.' *Journal of Marriage and the Family*, **43**, 623–631.

UNICEF (1989). *Report on the State of the World Children*. New York: Oxford University Press.

UNICEF (1990). *Children and Development in the 1990s. A UNICEF sourcebook.* New York.

UNICEF (1991). *The Girl Child—An Investment in the Future*. New York: UNICEF.

UNICEF (1993). *The State of the Worlds' Children 1993*. New York: UNICEF/Oxford University Press.

UNICEF (1994a). *The State of the World's Children 1994*. New York: UNICEF/Oxford University Press.

UNICEF (1994b). 'Carpeting child labour.' *Children First*, issue 27, Winter 1994. London: UNICEF.

United Nations (1987). *Report of the Expert Group Meeting on Violence in the Family with Special Emphasis on Women*. New York: United Nations.

United Nations (1989). *The UN Convention on the Rights of the Child*. New York: United Nations.

United Nations Development Programme (1994). *Human Development Report*, UNDP. New York: Oxford University Press.

US Bureau of the Census (1989). *Poverty in the United States 1987* (Current Population Reports, Series P-60 No 433). Washington, DC: Government Printing Office.

Utting, D., Bright, J. & Henricson, C. (1994). *Crime and the Family. Improving Childrearing and Preventing Delinquency*. London: Family Policy Studies Centre.

Van der Eyken, W. (1982). *Home Start: A Four Year Evaluation*. Home Start Consultancy, Leicester, UK.

Van Oost, P. (1995). *Aggregate information and comparison groups*. Paper to the International Seminar, 18–19 July, Looking after Children: Good Parenting, Good Outcomes. London.

Vernon, J. & Fruin, D. (1986). *In Care: A Study of Social Work Decision-making*, London: National Children's Bureau.

Wachs, T. D. (1992). *The Nature of Nurture*. Newbury Park, CA: Sage.

Wachs, T. D. & Gandour, M. J. (1983). 'Temperament, environment and six month cognitive-intellectual development.' *International Journal of Behavioral Development*, **6**, 135–152.

Walker, E., Downey, G. & Berman, A. (1989). 'The effects of parental psychopathology and maltreatment on child behaviour.' *Child Development*, **60**, 15–24.

Walker, L. (1984). *The Battered Woman Syndrome*. New York, Springer.

Walton, D. (1995). 'Repeat victimisation. Vista.' *Perspectives on Probation*, **1** (1), 30–35.

Walton, J. (1994). 'Partnership in a locally based children's home.' In A. Buchanan (Ed.), *Partnership in Practice: The Children Act 1989*. Aldershot: Avebury.

Ward, H. (Ed.) (1995). *Looking After Children: Research into Practice. The Second Report to the Department of Health on Assessing Outcomes in Child Care*. London: HMSO.

Warner, N. (1992). *Choosing with Care. The report of the Committee of Inquiry into the Selection, Development and Management of Staff in Children's Homes*. London: HMSO.

Weissman, M. M., Merikangas, K. R., John, K., Wickramaratne, P. J., Kidd, K. K., Prusoff, B. A., Leckman, J. F. & Pauls D. L. (1986). 'Understanding clinical heterogeneity of major depression using family data.' *Archives of General Psychiatry*, **43**, 430–434.

Wells, K. & Biegal, D. E. (Eds), (1991). *Family Preservation Services: Research and Evaluation*. Newbury Park, CA: Sage.

Wheal, A. & Buchanan, A. (1994). *Handbook for Carers of Young People Being Looked After*. London: Longmans Reference/Pitman Publishing.

White Franklin, A. (1977). *The Challenge of Child Abuse*. London: Academic Press; New York: Grune & Stratton.

Whiteman, M., Fanshel, D. & Grundy, J. F. (1987). 'Cognitive behavioural interventions aimed at anger of parents at risk of child abuse.' *Social Work*, Nov/Dec, 469–474.

Whiting, B. B. & Edwards, C. P. (1988). *Children of Different Worlds*. Cambridge, MA: Harvard University Press.

Whittaker, L. K., Kinney, J., Tracy, E. M. & Booth, C. (1990). *Reaching High Risk Families. Intensive Family Preservation in Human Services*. New York: Aldine de Gruyter.

Whyte, M. (1978). 'Cross-cultural codes in dealing with relative status of women.' *Ethnology*, **2**, 211–237.

Widom, C. S. (1989). 'The cycle of violence.' *Science*, **244**, 160–166.

Wiener, C. (1981). *The Politics of Alcoholism: Building an Arena Around a Social Problem*. New Brunswick, NJ: Transaction Books.

Wilcox, R., Smith, D., Moore, J., Hewitt, A., Allan, G., Walker, H., Ropatam, M., Monu, L. & Featherstone, T. (1991). *Family Decision Making—Family Group Conferences—Practitioners' Views*. New Zealand: Practitioners Publishing. Also available from Family Rights Group, London.

Wild, M. (1975). 'State intervention on behalf of neglected children: A search for realistic standards.' *Stanford Law Review*, **7**, 985–1040.

Williams, G. & McCreadie, J. (1992). *Ty Mawr Community Home Inquiry*. Gwent County Council, Wales.

Willis, D., Holden, E. & Rosenberg, M. (1992). 'Child maltreatment prevention: Introduction and historical overview.' In D. Willis, E. Holden & M. Rosenberg (Eds), *Prevention of Child Maltreatment*. New York: John Wiley.

Wisendale, S. (1990). 'Approaches to family policy in state government.' *Family Relations*, **39**, 136–140.

Wisendale, S. K. (1993). 'State and Federal initiatives in family policy.' In T. Brubaker (Ed.), *Family Relations. Challenges for the Future*. Newbury Park, CA: Sage.

Wolfe, D. (1987). *Child Abuse: Implications for Child Development and Psychopathology*. Newbury Park, CA: Sage.

Wolfe, D. A., Edwards, B., Manion, I. & Koverola, C. (1988). 'Early intervention for parents at risk of child abuse and neglect: As preliminary investigation.' *Journal of Consulting and Clinical Psychology*, **56** (1), 40–47.

Wolfe, D.A., Fairbank, J. A., Kelly, J. A. & Bradlyn, A. S. (1983). 'Child abusive parents' psychological responses to stress and non-stressful behavior in children.' *Behavioral Assessment*, **5**, 363–371.

Wolfe & Harlon (1984). As cited in J. Kaufman & E. Zigler, 'The prevention of child maltreatment: Programming, research and policy.' In D. Willis, E. Holden & M. Rosenberg (Eds), *Prevention of Child Maltreatment* (1992), p. 274. New York: John Wiley.

Wolfgang, M. & Ferracuti, F. (1967). *The Subculture of Violence. Toward an Integrated Theory of Criminology.* London: Tavistock.

World Health Organisation (1987). *Evaluation of the Strategy for Health for All by Year 2000. Seventh Report on the World Health Situation—Global Review.* WHO.

Wulczyn, F. (1994). 'Status at birth and infant foster care placement in New York City.' In R. Barth, J. Berrick & N. Gilbert (Eds), *Child Welfare Research Review.* New York: Columbia University Press.

Wulczyn, F. & Goerge, R. (1992). 'Foster care in Illinois. The challenge of change.' *Social Service Review*, **66**, 278–294.

Yllo, K. A. (1993) 'Through a Feminist lens. Social structure and violence.' In R. Gelles & D. R. Loseke, *Current Controversies in Family Violence.* Newbury Park, CA: Sage.

Zeanah, C. H. & Anders, T. F. (1987). 'Subjectivity in parent–infant relationships: A discussion of internal working models.' *Infant Mental Health Journal*, **8**, 237–250.

Zeanah, C. H. & Zeanah, P. D. (1989). 'Intergenerational transmission of maltreatment: Insights from attachment theory and research.' *Psychiatry*, **52**, 177–196.

Zigler, E. (1977). 'Controlling child abuse in America: An effort doomed to failure.' In *Proceedings of the First National Conference on Child Abuse and Neglect*, p. 30. Washington, DC: Department of Health, Education and Welfare.

Zigler, E. (1990). 'Controlling child abuse: Do we have the knowledge and/or the will?' In G. Gerbner, C. Ross, & E. Zigler (Eds), *Child Abuse: An Agenda for Action.* New York: Oxford University Press.

INDEX

VOCAL (victims of child abuse laws),
58
Vocational interests, heritability, 119
Volunteers and parent aides, 214
Vondra, J., 207
Vulnerable children, 74, 91
Vulnerable parents, 91

Wachs, D., 117,119
Walder, D., 25
Walker, E., 121
Walker, H., 189
Walker, L., 99
Wall,S., 101
Walton, J., 146
Wang, Y.-F., 123, 160
War, consequences of, 48, 49
War situations, children in, 157
Ward, H., 150, 204, 244
Warner Inquiry, 59
Washington DC, 107
  street children, 52
Waters, E., 101
Watershed in television viewing, 186
Wedge, P., 18
Weikart, D., 142, 167
Weiss, H., 171
Weissberg, R., 13
Weissman, M., 121
Welfare state, unwinding of, 153
Wells, K., 215
Welsch, D., 211
Welter, J., 121
Wexler, S., 98
Wheal, A., 147
Wheeler, K., 25
White Franklin, A., 163, 229
White, K., 103, 207
Whiteman, M., 216
Whiting, B., 10, 63, 67
Whitmore, K., 122
Whittaker, J., 165

Whittaker, L., 215
Whyte, M., 69
Wickramaratne, P., 121
Widom, C., 4. 15, 33, 34
Wiener, C., 144
Wilcox, R., 189
Wild, M., 8
Williams, B., 216
Williams, G., 59
Williams report on residential care, 59
Willis, D., 54., 142
Wilson, S., 18, 56, 98
Wilson, M., 124
Wiltshire, 212
Wisendale, S., 58, 161, 162
Wolfe, D., 18, 26, 56, 98, 120, 216
Wolfe and Harlon, 211
Women's Centre Foundation of
  Jamaica, 230
Women,
  position of, 22
  role of, 55
World Health Organisation, 53, 114,
  115, 176, 182
World health profile, 115
World Summit for Children 1990, 158,
  227
Wulczyn, F., 59, 142, 169

Yllo, K., 22
Yugoslavia, former, rape of girls,
  157
Yule, W., 122, 213

Zeanah, C., 25, 31, 100, 207
Zeanah, D., 25, 31, 100, 207
Zeskind, P., 26, 120
Zigler, E., 15, 17, 18, 19, 27, 28, 29, 31,
  32, 33, 34, 43, 44, 54, 94, 147, 148,
  149, 197, 199, 202, 205, 206, 207,
  210, 211, 212, 225
Zipper, I., 142